I0887388

WRITING RESEARCH, PEDAGOGY, AND POLICY

Elizabeth Wardle, Series Editor

A SHARED HISTORY

Writing in the High School, College, and University, 1856–1886

Amy J. Lueck

Southern Illinois University Press
Carbondale

Southern Illinois University Press
www.siupress.com

Portions of chapter 2 previously appeared in "'A Maturity of Thought Very Rare in Young Girls': Women's Public Engagement in Nineteenth-Century High School Commencement Essays," *Rhetoric Review* 34, no. 2 (2015), and are reprinted by permission of the publisher (Taylor & Francis Ltd, http://www.tandfonline.com). Select portions throughout the book also appear in some form in "'High School Girls': Women's Higher Education at the Louisville Female High School," *Ohio Valley History* 17, no. 3 (2017), and "'Higher' School: Nineteenth-Century High Schools and the Secondary-College Divide," *Composition Studies* 46, no. 2 (2018).

Printed in the United States of America

22 21 20 19 4 3 2 1

Publication of books in the Writing Research, Pedagogy, and Policy series is supported by the Roger and Joyce Howe Center for Writing Excellence at Miami University.

Cover illustration: Artist's rendering of original Male High School building. COURTESY OF JEFFERSON COUNTY PUBLIC SCHOOLS.

Library of Congress Cataloging-in-Publication Data
Names: Lueck, Amy J., 1983– author.
Title: A shared history : writing in the high school, college, and university, 1856–1886 / Amy J. Lueck.
Description: Carbondale : Southern Illinois University Press, [2020] | Series: Writing research, pedagogy, and policy | Includes bibliographical references and index.
Identifiers: LCCN 2019016749 | ISBN 9780809337422 (paperback : alk. paper) | ISBN 9780809337439 (e-book) Subjects: LCSH: English language—Rhetoric—Study and teaching—United States—History—19th century.
Classification: LCC PE1405.U6 L84 2019 | DDC 808/.042071073—dc23
LC record available at https://lccn.loc.gov/2019016749

Printed on recycled paper ♲

For Dave (x2)

CONTENTS

List of Illustrations and Table ix
Preface xi
Acknowledgments xix

Introduction: High Schools, Higher Learning, and Our Histories 1
Inventing the High School 7
Disciplinary Boundaries and Beginnings 11
Why Louisville? 14

Part One. Establishing the First "Higher Schools" in Louisville

1. The Idea(l) of the High School 27
Public and Private Goods 29
Growing Out of and Serving the Common Schools 33
Establishing the High Schools 38
2. A Polished, Practical, or Profound Education: Collegiate Curricula in the First Ten Years 45
Rhetoric and Writing at Male High School 47
Rhetoric and Writing at Female High School 58
3. Practical Rhetoric and Progressive Pedagogies in the High Schools 73
The New Education and William N. Hailmann 80
Circulating the New Education 84
Beyond Treatises and Speeches 88
The Ambiguous Legacy of the New Education 92
Interchapter: The Civil War Years 94

Part Two. Higher Learning in Transformation

4. The "Absurd Effort": The University Idea and the Changing High School 101
   - A "University of Public Schools" 104
   - Changing the High Schools, Changing Writing Instruction 107
   - Women's Higher Schooling 119
   - Composition across the Public Schools 125
5. "Just on the Border of the Intellectual World": Central Colored High School 128
   - Legislating Learning 133
   - The "A" Grade 137
   - High School Beginnings, Again 142
   - "Incapable of Teaching High-School Classes" 148
6. Inventing the High School, Inventing Composition 154
   - "They Have Tightened the Screws on the Secondary Schools" 162
   - Composing First-Year Writing in the College 166

Conclusion: Blurring the Boundaries 170
- Dual Enrollment 172
- Translanguaging Higher Learning 175
- What College-Level Writers *Do* 178
- A History for the Present 181

Notes 187

Bibliography 215

Index 237

ILLUSTRATIONS AND TABLE

1.1. Male High School building 39
2.1. Freshman examination questions in rhetoric and composition at Male High School 52
Table. Comparison of Male High School and Kentucky University, 1865–66 110
4.1. Course requirements for Male High School and University of Public Schools 116
4.2. Female High School building 120
4.3. Graded course of instruction for Female High School 122
5.1. Central Colored High School building 137
5.2. Course of study for "A" grade of Central Colored School 140
5.3. Principal J. M. Maxwell, Central Colored School 148
6.1. Enrollment and graduation trends for Louisville High Schools, 1857–95 156

PREFACE

The project of this book began not so much with a research question as with a discomfort. I was researching the history of high schools in Louisville in a graduate course with Carol Mattingly and was finding that the primary documents about their teaching and learning gave fascinating insights into the history of writing. The language the schools used to describe themselves and their work challenged many of my expectations about what a high school is and what it is for. But I kept returning over and over again to the question of what these old high schools had to do with college writing and our discipline. My gut told me they mattered. My training at University of Pittsburgh under the direction of Jean Ferguson Carr, who introduced me to school textbooks as an area of study, told me they mattered. Carol herself must have told me they mattered. But my emerging sense of the discipline and its priorities told me that actually they *didn't* matter. That is, my emerging sense of disciplinary identity and disciplinary history firmly reinforced the divide between college-level and K–12 English instruction, and I had the vague sense that I shouldn't be researching high schools from the field of rhetoric and composition.

This point was driven home for me in the review of an article that grew out of this research, in which reviewers came back with smart and well-intentioned advice that held strong to the distinction between high schools and colleges in the nineteenth century. Not that I couldn't write about these high schools, but that I needed to be clear that they were, at the end of the day, distinct from colleges. I discovered then that my sense that our discipline thinks of itself and college as clearly separated from high schooling was not entirely imagined. The idea that high schools and their histories may have overlapped with colleges is just not part of our shared cultural assumptions; my argument was going to be a hard sell.

Though the immediate effect of this feedback was rejection of the article, this was also a clarifying moment for me as an author and historiographer, enabling me to make a distinction that was crucial to my argument and without which I could not move forward: that, of course, not *all* high schools did or *could* overlap with colleges. Though there is a history of such imbrication, the permeability of these boundaries has been broadly determined by gender, race, and class. Yes, it is important and surprising to note (as I do) that white men's high schools often functioned as comparable and equivalent to colleges, even going so far as to adopt state charters to grant college degrees. It is equally important to note that schools for women and African Americans did not—that *these* high schools were consistently differentiated from colleges. Even when they were not *pedagogically* distinct, these latter schools remained *politically* different from colleges. The clarification of this political versus pedagogical distinction between high schools and colleges came from this review process. It was a crucial insight for which I cannot give proper credit, due to the nature of blind peer review, but I want to acknowledge it here. It is also a useful distinction for thinking about the high school–college divide in the present day, inviting us to ask: Which students continue to cross this boundary with most ease, to blur the line between high school and college through AP credits, concurrent enrollment programs, and so forth, and on what pedagogical and political grounds?

Using Louisville as a historical case study, this book documents the story of just three of many nineteenth-century American high schools that invite this question, where students practiced advanced writing and rhetorical skills: Male High School, Female (later Girls) High School, and Central (Colored) High School.[1] In their curricula, their student populations, their status and function in the community, and even their degrees conferred, these schools challenge the inviolability of the high school–college divide. This is particularly true of the period of history discussed here. I have chosen to focus on the thirty years from 1856 to 1886 because that period captures the establishment of all three of the first high schools in Louisville and is also a period of general transformation and high aspirations for high schools across the country, as more urban centers developed these schools outside of Boston and Philadelphia but before they became widespread and increasingly regulated.[2] This is a period of particular fluidity in institutional morphology.

At the same time, this emphasis on periodization obscures a more important point, which I pursue at length in the closing chapters: that this period of blurring the high school–college divide was not historically anomalous, that this phenomenon is not isolable to this time in history. Instead, confusion and contestation over the high school–college divide have persisted uninterrupted into the present. Thus, current challenges to the ostensible high school–college divide—via dual credit and concurrent enrollment programs, in particular—are not new but instead are part of a long legacy of interaction and negotiation between students, teachers, and administrators in colleges, high schools, and other institutions providing higher learning.

I use the terms "higher learning" and "higher schooling" throughout the text in an attempt to break from the baggage of more familiar terms like "higher education," "high school," and "college" and to gesture toward this more diffuse field of interaction. Readers from rhetoric and composition will be interested in and perhaps even surprised by the long history of interanimation and local negotiation between institutions of "higher schooling" traced here. Educational historians, on the other hand, may find the existence of this overlap to be common knowledge. Having long studied "multipurpose colleges," academies, and other institutions that fit uneasily in present academic hierarchies, they may be unsurprised to find this to be the case in Louisville. This latter group, however, will be rewarded by the close attention to the story of an understudied city, in an ill-defined geographical region, during an oft-dismissed period of the century for educational history. Thus, this work fills a gap in that literature by providing a history of these gender- and race-segregated high schools in this border state, complementing work on high schools across the Eastern Seaboard and in various landmark sites of educational history such as Illinois, St. Louis, and others.[3] Readers in both groups will be interested in the ways I theorize our approach to institutional differences (and attendant questions of disciplinarity) in the closing chapter. There, I offer a reconsideration of institutional morphology that foregrounds difference and fluidity in our conception of institutional morphology and subsequent pedagogy and policy responses, applying this perspective to the contemporary moment of educational reform represented by accelerated learning models (such as dual credit and concurrent enrollment). Ultimately, I argue that dual credit and concurrent enrollment programs invite us to interrogate the political (not merely pedagogical or administrative) relationship between high school and college writing and to insist that students in all institutional contexts be invited to engage the full scope of rhetorical experiences and habits of mind that have come to characterize "college-level writing." These conclusions grow out of the long tradition of rich, complex, "college-level" writing in the high schools, of which this book seeks to represent an example.

These conclusions also grow out of a specific set of materials and methods that are worth introducing at the outset, particularly for those interested in archival research methods. Barbara L'Eplattenier has called archival researchers to more directly discuss their methods and, indeed, I find it is salient to my argument about the relative devaluation of the high school to discuss the archival materials with which I was able to work.[4] First of all, it may not be surprising that none of the schools discussed here have their own institutional archives, like most colleges would have. Two of these schools are still in operation (Male and Central) and the third has been merged with an existing school (Female, which merged with and became subsumed into DuPont Manual High School in 1950), but I was unsuccessful in connecting with their alumnae associations to identify archival holdings they might have as a school or organization.[5] Instead, their documents are scattered across the holdings of various institutions that have an interest in them: the Jefferson County Public Schools system, the Filson Historical Society, the University of Louisville, and the Louisville Free Public Library. The Filson Historical Society and the University of Louisville are the only two with holdings that would properly be called archival, including some original school roster books, grading records, and some limited student work. I was told that the majority of records on these schools was destroyed in the Great Flood of the Ohio River in 1937. According to the Filson Historical Society, 60 percent of the city flooded in that event, and two-thirds of the residents had to be evacuated. Though it is not possible to know what exactly was lost in that flood, we know it would have been substantial. The bulk of surviving archival materials on Male High School can be found in the Filson Historical Society collection, comprising thirty-one volumes (1856–1923). Female High School is represented by thirty-five volumes (1867–1913) at the Filson Historical Society and a single box of materials at the University of Louisville (1903–1988; 1.6 linear feet). Both schools also appear occasionally among personal collections and scrapbooks, with materials from the twentieth century being generally much more available.

Particularly scant, though, are traces of the work of students at Central High School, the historically African American high school discussed here. That school's records are almost wholly unpreserved by the local archives and historical societies, and the school is mentioned only briefly in the school-board minutes and annual reports. Compared to even the modest holdings described above, the Central High School collection held at the Filson Historical Society is comprised of just 3 items, with historical coverage from 1906 to 1932. A search in the online card catalogue there returns 96 hits for Male High School, but just 29 for Female High School (although it gives 110 for Girls High School, which was what the school was renamed in 1903),[6] and a mere 21 hits for Central High School (with an additional 4 for Colored High School).

But while we have limited archival records of these schools—including little information about their curricula and almost nothing in the way of student writing from the nineteenth century—we have one rich source from which to obtain glimpses into student writing and rhetoric: published reports.[7] One source of these reports are the local newspapers. In particular, Louisville's *Courier-Journal* reported regularly on high school events, specifically commencement ceremonies. From these reports, we can ascertain rich information about the schools and their students, including what kinds of topics students were writing about over the years, a sense of their approach to those topics, and assessments of their performance. I draw heavily on this public record to construct the story here.

In addition, the annual school-board reports to the superintendent provide hundreds of pages of details on the rationales, pedagogical philosophies, institutional challenges, and day-to-day operations of the city's public schools, including the high schools. The changing status of the high school is also reflected in the changing nature of school-board reports over the course of the century: from rich qualitative descriptions and philosophical reflections, they become tables of data with little interpretive framing as the high school becomes more stabilized and bureaucratic by the turn of the century. Though these reports become increasingly bureaucratic, quantified, and terse as the century draws to a close and the transformations to higher learning outlined in this book are well underway, the reports at midcentury include lengthy commentary not only from the superintendent and high school principals but also, on rare occasions, from individual teachers and students themselves. For better or worse, these reports and the city newspapers are essentially the only sources of student writing I was able to locate from the nineteenth century (though much more is available after the turn of the century, particularly by way of school yearbooks).[8] The district offices hold microfilm of these annual school-board reports and the minutes from school-board meetings; I tracked down others from places like the University of Kentucky and the University of Chicago, and the public library holds several of these rare volumes right on the shelf.

In addition, some of the faculty associated with these schools published their own work in various venues. The addresses of Central High School's principal J. M. Maxwell to the state's Education Association, of which he was president, give insights into the pedagogies and values of the high school. The books and magazines published by science professor and educational theorist William N. Hailmann provide similar insights, which I draw on extensively in the fourth chapter of this volume. And the work of the famous educational critic Abraham Flexner, who attended and taught at Male High School, offers insights into the schools' transformation in the last quarter of the century. Thus, the vast majority of primary sources used here are not manuscript materials but published items—newspaper articles and published reports—and, thus, this history is composed not from rich institutional archives but from fragments of memory serendipitously preserved, largely in public records.

The history of "higher schooling" I piece together from these fragments is an effort to highlight intersections, crossing-over, and change. It is composed from my location in the field of rhetoric and composition, motivated by my desire to connect to and understand these schools that provoked and challenged my conception of institutional morphology and the history of rhetoric and composition instruction. I consider this a feminist history, as its primary purpose is to recover and reevaluate a little-known rhetorical history and attend to the role of gender and race in shaping student experience and historical remembrance.

Of course, these same materials could be used to support any number of other histories and lines of argument. Indeed, many others have told the history of high schools—even of Louisville's schools—to other ends, and those stories should be put in conversation with this one to provide a richer and more complex understanding of our rhetorical and material past. I attempt to do so here, but also know there is much more that could be done. In the end, I hope this volume will provide readers with insights into nineteenth-century schooling that transcend the specific Louisville context, and that readers will use this angle of vision to illuminate and reconsider other contexts and practices. In order to facilitate readers in making their own interpretations and conclusions, I have quoted primary sources whenever possible and have included images of the published reports as visuals to immerse the reader in the original language, to capture the texture of the authors' own terminology and compositional style, and to show how they conveyed their understandings of terms and ideas through both text and page layout. In these ways, I hope I have left enough breadcrumbs for others to follow in order to extend and complicate this work in the future.

and I attempt to do so [illegible], but also hope that [illegible] more than could be done in this [illegible]. [illegible] this volume will provide readers with insight into [illegible] that [illegible] and the specific tools [illegible] context, and that readers will use this angle of vision to [illegible] and reconsider other contexts and practices. In order to facilitate readers in [illegible] their own interpretations and conclusions, I have quoted primary sources whenever possible and have included images of the published pamphlets as appendixes to immerse the reader in the original language, to capture the essence of the authors' own terminology and compositional style, and to show how they [illegible] their [illegible] and ideas through both text and [illegible]. Through these essays I hope I have set an example, or at times [illegible] for others to follow in order to extend and complicate this work in the future.

ACKNOWLEDGMENTS

I am indebted to many, many people who guided this project along its long process of becoming. First, my thanks go to Jean Ferguson Carr and Carol Mattingly, whose courses provided the foundations for my archival research methodology. In a similar vein, I am deeply thankful to the many archivists and librarians who helped me to locate these dispersed archival materials at the Filson Historical Society, the Jefferson County Public Schools archives, the Louisville Free Public Library, and elsewhere.

I also owe a great deal of gratitude to the people who helped me interpret and write about these materials, especially my dissertation directors, Karen Kopelson and Susan Ryan, and dissertation committee members, Bruce Horner, Mary P. Sheridan, and Jessica Enoch. The traces of each of these mentors is everywhere in this work, and I have been proud of and grateful for that influence every step of the way. Special thanks to Karen for helping me to "get a grip" at several key points in this process, and Jess for continuing to pave the way for the kind of work I hope to do in the future. Particular thanks also go to Megan Bardolph, who has read and commented on this research more than anyone else but who has always come to it with fresh eyes and new questions to move me forward. Thanks to Wendy Sharer in this same vein, as she has supported me in the challenging early-career years, serving as a much-needed reader and mentor. Many others have read and shaped portions of this work along the way as well, and I want to thank them, including: Leah Senatro, my writing group members Gesa, Patty, Erin, Jim, Rose, and Pam; my 2016 RSA Research Network group led by Byron Hawk; my 2014 Feminisms and Rhetorics mentoring group with Andrea Lunsford; my grad school writing group with Megan, Meghan, Brittany, Ashley, Stephanie, Ben, Liz, Jamila, and others I have certainly forgotten here

(I'm sorry); anonymous reviewers of journal submissions; and attendees at numerous conference presentations where I have presented portions of this work. There is a huge amount of invisible labor that goes into producing a book like this, and I wish there was a better way to acknowledge it all here.

I am indebted for financial support from the University of Louisville School of Interdisciplinary and Graduate Studies—and just about every other kind of support, mentorship, and friendship from the dean of that school, Beth Boehm. She helped me to expand my thinking about how these schools intersect with the full range of educational institutions, kindergarten through graduate school. I have received additional support for this project from Santa Clara University's provost's office, College of Arts and Sciences dean's office, and the Filson Historical Society. The most recent readers and sponsors of this work have, of course, been my editors, Elizabeth Wardle and Kristine Priddy, who have given me a chance to bring this volume to life, as well as Kelly Ritter and an anonymous reviewer who gave several rounds of priceless feedback and suggestions for revision. It is an honor to be the inaugural volume in the Writing Research, Pedagogy, and Policy series, and the location of this book in that series will extend and enrich the arguments here.

Most of all, thanks to my sisters, my families, my husband, my new baby, and my cat for getting me through the day-to-day reality of it all.

A SHARED HISTORY

Introduction: High Schools, Higher Learning, and Our Histories

Education discourse in the United States today—from the federal administration to the professional literature to the statements of teachers and students themselves—presupposes clear definitions, distinctions, and relations between the high school, college, and university. A *high school* is a public or private school providing "secondary education" to students aged fourteen to eighteen. Following high school, *college* provides "higher education," usually entailing a general education curriculum, electives, and an area of specialization called an academic major. A *university*, by turn, is an institution that, along with general undergraduate education, provides specialized instruction in graduate programs or professional schools. The whole system is understood as hierarchically organized and progressive in rigor and specialization across a student's academic career.

But these terms and definitions have not always seemed so apparent, especially in the nineteenth century. That period was one of sweeping educational transformation in the United States, during which the public high school first emerged and these commonplace conceptions initially took shape.

Following on the heels of the Common School Movement, which established the first public schools in the country for basic literacy and numeracy, education reformers developed the nation's first public high schools in cities like Boston, Philadelphia, and Baltimore in the 1820s and 1830s. From there, the idea spread to cities across the Midwest,

South, and West, with some 44 high schools established by 1860, 160 by 1870, 800 by 1880, and 2,526 by 1890, according to the estimates of educational commissioner William Torrey Harris in 1904.[1] While these numbers have been the subject of much debate, the trend of high school building was undeniable by the turn of the century. And yet, what this trend meant within the larger educational landscape and, more importantly, to local communities was less clear. This uncertainty was due to a lack of clarity about what a "high school" was and how it related to existing educational institutions.

Newly established and still developing their own educational missions, nineteenth-century American high schools had few distinguishing characteristics to define them as a type, beyond their position at the upper level of common schooling and, generally, their public funding through taxation. Instead, their curricula, pedagogies, missions, and even degrees and credentials overlapped with academies, seminaries, normal schools, and colleges. High schools' relationship to colleges was especially confounding, as numerous educational historians of this period attest. As scholars like William Reese note, the term "high" was simply a relative indicator: it referred to the schools' relation to the lower schools, indicating an extension of public educational provision into what was variously called the "higher branches" of knowledge, "higher learning," or "higher education." Sometimes this was merely a year or two of study beyond the elementary grades, especially for the preparation of teachers, and sometimes it entailed a full classical course of instruction terminating with a bachelor's degree. Thus, the term "high school" is somewhat of an anachronism, and carries with it associations and assumptions today that simply do not map onto the nineteenth-century educational landscape.[2]

The term "college" was only slightly more definite. Many historians have debated about the status of specific colleges and college types—particularly women's colleges and small liberal arts colleges—*as* colleges. Some academies and seminaries offered more advanced education than nominal colleges, and most colleges enrolled more students in their preparatory departments than in their actual collegiate courses. But beyond a question of reconciling individual institutions, historians have further observed "the close relationship between and even the identity of preparatory and collegiate institutions" in the nineteenth century that confounds any attempt at categorization. The lack of differentiation was in part due to the fact that the curriculum that had defined collegiate instruction was under revision during the century, from a classical curriculum to a modern English curriculum. The expanding instructional offerings at a range of institutions left the definition of college unmoored.[3]

Other institutions fare no better. Normal schools, offering both academics and teacher training, had a similarly unreliable relation to the high school and the college, often offering preparatory, review, and collegiate courses of study. Not fitting readily in any of the currently available categories of elementary, secondary, and higher education, their status in the academic hierarchy has received much comment among historians of rhetoric and composition, who have compared them to various other institutions in discussions of their writing instruction.[4]

Even professional schools of law and medicine, which did not require a bachelor's degree for admission, had an unclear relationship to high schools and colleges. This is the result of professional education's undetermined connection to the liberal arts curriculum that had largely defined the college (and high school) and an as-yet undeveloped hierarchy between secondary, collegiate, and university (or professional) study. It is also a result of the fact that many institutions of higher learning—from the high school and academy to the college—tended to be what historian Roger Geiger calls (speaking specifically of colleges) "multipurpose" institutions, providing a range of academic and professional programs in teaching, business, and the like. As such, they challenge our current educational terminology, which has framed the distinctions between institutional types as fairly discrete and self-contained.[5]

Because of the lack of differentiation, "higher" schools played a significant role in the teaching of college-level writing, just as did the well-documented preparatory departments in colleges to which first-year writing is intimately related.[6] Students in high schools were taught "rhetoric and composition"—by that name—as a discrete subject area in the curriculum from at least midcentury. They focused on a broad range of written and spoken literacy practices, and performed them in the classroom and in public contexts within their community. High schools even taught their students how to *teach* writing, which connects them to the history of normal schools and the closely related field of English education.

In short, there are numerous intersections between secondary and tertiary education of which we in rhetoric and composition have yet to explore the implications—that they had similar audiences, as age ranges were not standardized; that they had comparable goals, especially as high school was understood as terminal education for a great many students; that they shared theorists and practitioners, as many faculty moved between high school and college positions over their careers and wrote texts for a variety of audiences; and that they even had indistinguishable titles and identities at times, prior to the assertion of a hierarchical and formalized leveling of instruction by the end of the nineteenth century that determined the high school to be not only separate from but also preparatory or at least subordinated to a college education in what Christine Ogren calls the "academic procession" of both rigor and value in the U.S. system.[7] In these and many other ways, historical high schools trouble the secondary–college divide, and both in spite of and because of the difficulty they pose to these categories, they cannot be easily dismissed as part of the college-building impetus of the nineteenth century, and as part of the history of college-level writing. In fact, as I will suggest, the instability of the high school–college divide has persisted into the present.

And yet, high schools remain largely overlooked in histories of rhetoric and composition. While we have expanded our disciplinary purview to include the history of rhetorical and writing practices at the widest array of institutional and extracurricular sites, we draw a curiously persistent line at the secondary school. Of course, important historical work has been done on nineteenth-century schoolbooks, pedagogical traditions, and public commencements from the schools (particularly academies). This work implicitly and explicitly invites us to shift our gaze to traditions and practices adjacent to the college writing classroom. And yet, even in these accounts of texts, teachers, and writers, their presence in the high school writing classroom is somewhat incidental—peripheral, almost spectral, seldom addressed directly. Not only do we not write and publish stand-alone histories of high schools, we neglect them in otherwise comprehensive lists of institution types in almost every volume on nineteenth-century instruction in our field, mentioning our discipline's connection to colleges, universities, historically black colleges and universities (HBCUs), women's colleges, normal schools, and even academies, often with one glaring omission.[8]

The most notable exception to this trend of passively overlooking the history of high schools has been in the work of Lori Ostergaard and Henrietta Rix Wood. Wood's *Praising Girls* studies high school girls' public writing at the turn of the twentieth century, establishing the significance of high school rhetoric and writing to historians in the field. Likewise, the recent edited collection from Ostergaard and Wood, *In the Archives of Composition*, gathers local histories specifically from U.S. high schools and normal schools to elaborate the history of rhetoric and writing. As Kelly Ritter reminds us in the introduction to that edited volume, "'Writing' does not emerge, fully formed, out of first-year college students (whether at the community college, the four-year comprehensive, or the research university, private or public). Writing happens in secondary schools, and *has* happened in this location in rich and vital ways for nearly two hundred years."[9]

Further, though, writing in the historical high school is not only important because of how it *influenced* college writing, but also because of the ways it *constituted* college writing in some historical cases, in terms of its pedagogies and purposes, its rigor, its uses for students and communities, and even its cultural and institutional status—that is, the ways it troubles the very definition of "college writing." Positioned at the highest branches of the common school system, high schools were conceived as an upward extension of the common school principles, democratizing higher learning as the common schools had democratized basic literacy acquisition. In this way, Ostergaard and Wood point out in the introduction to their collection on normal schools and high schools that both were referred to as "the people's college"—"a phrase that suggests both their egalitarian nature and the diversity of their students."[10] While suggesting egalitarianism and diversity, this phrase also, of course, suggests advanced study. That is, while some high schools prepared students for college (purposely or incidentally), they were also often framed as an *alternative* to college for those who would not attend an exclusive or distantly located school, providing collegiate work in their own backyards. Not being clearly subordinated to colleges, early high schools instead could be (and were) *compared* to colleges in their provision of advanced liberal education and degrees, suggesting the need to reevaluate our assumptions about what it means to study the history of college writing.

This is not to say that differences between high schools and colleges were nonexistent or meaningless. Certainly, broad institutional trends exist that make it meaningful and efficient in many cases to draw this distinction. Those trends include patterns of differential access based on race, gender, and class, for instance, and I foreground the confounding relationship between high schools and colleges both to trouble our reliance on those categories and in order to demonstrate the role of racialized, gendered, and class-based privilege in determining an institution's status. As I demonstrate, the actual curriculum or educational practices of schools has been less salient to the evolving definition and value of educational institutions than the embodiment of the students therein. Rather than flattening the complexity of these determinations, I relish the messiness of the discursive work of imagining and upholding them. I hope that temporarily setting aside the common institutional categories and looking at our history from the perspective of this overlap itself provides new insights into the role of writing as a subject in higher schooling that may prove useful to better understanding the teaching and learning of writing on both sides of this ostensible divide.

In particular, the emphasis on institutional overlap provides renewed perspective on the current issue of dual-credit and concurrent enrollment courses that have been of great interest to the field. The classification of these and other programs (such as Advanced Placement and International Baccalaureate) under the umbrella of "accelerated learning" models is quite telling and concerning to many experts in writing studies who understand the value and importance of ongoing writing instruction and practice across a vertical curriculum—and not merely as a "gatekeeping" requirement to complete, the earlier the better. The "accelerated" model for writing instruction is not an inspiring one to many of us. But concerns about the blurring of boundaries between high school and college that also often attend discussions of these programs find themselves on less dependable ground in light of the history here. Parsing the different pedagogical, ideological, and professional concerns that attend this trend will only prove helpful in addressing it effectively, and I hope to contribute to that work with this study.

In this volume, I use the history of Louisville's nineteenth-century public high schools to demonstrate that high schools were a site of rich negotiation of the means and ends of higher learning, with particular implications for our histories of composition and rhetoric instruction. Elaborating a legacy of productive confusion around these institutional titles and roles, I trace how the suppression of the high school's value coincides with the colleges' and universities' efforts to assert their own distinction. Because the boundary between these institutions and their constituent parts has been unreliable and locally negotiated, I argue that the difference between high schools and colleges has been less demonstrable, stable, or evidence-based, and more ideological—that this is, in many cases, a distinction without a difference. And, as Sharon Crowley has put it, "Distinctions and boundaries are never disinterested: when someone is named as a witch, a factory worker, a rustic, or an illiterate, someone else profits from that distinction . . . no body is disinterested."[11] As I will argue, this distinction has major implications for how we think about a course like First Year Writing, the notion of something like "college-level writing, and the bodies that perform it." We are not disinterested.

Inventing the High School: "Drudgery of a Kind Most Wearisome"

As demonstrated by the words of the educational historians above and elaborated throughout this book, advanced educational opportunities in the nineteenth century were not clearly demarcated and defined. As the educational system expanded by the turn of the nineteenth century, however, the popularization of high schools and the development of universities changed the definition of "high school" and "college." As Marc VanOverbeke explains, it was during this time that efforts to articulate a reliable system of educational leveling in the United States—from elementary to secondary to postsecondary institutions—were only just beginning, and those efforts established our current academic hierarchies and the notion of educational progression across academic levels.[12] National reform movements led by legislators, school leaders, and college faculty alike advocated for clearer definitions of each institutional type, with more reliable standards and articulations between them, and the newly emerging comprehensive research university at the top of this system. Historian Richard Angelo explains this development in terms of university professional schools:

> In the years following World War I the baccalaureate curriculum *became* central to the formal educational experience of those who attended the university. . . . As first one and then another of the refurbished professional curricula dislodged themselves from their longstanding equality with the classical

> A.B. and took up their new position "above" it, the expanded and updated baccalaureate curricula, like the university itself, became "post-secondary" to a formal degree unparalleled in the 19th century. The attorney or the physician who never studied for a Bachelor's degree was already something of an anomaly as a result, like the dentist or pharmacist who completed only a year or two of high school.[13]

Mariolina Salvatori explains this transformation and its effects in terms of the field of education and the status of pedagogy. She explains how new university departments of pedagogy in the 1880s made a case for their existence and necessity precisely *against* the work of normal schools and over and above the work of high schools, subordinating the scholarly work of teachers in the schools. That is, because they were largely duplicating the efforts of teaching and teacher training that had been occurring in the high schools and normal schools, the university departments redefined the work of teacher training to reflect their own model and exclude these other models. Thus, the establishment of a "beginning" of departments of pedagogy at the university level was advertised as being "different from and in opposition to departments of pedagogy in normal schools" and high schools. In short, the assertion of a beginning for these new departments, as Patricia Donahue puts it, "produce[d] difference where difference was not apparent before."[14]

This arrangement and its consequences were not unique to the development of pedagogy departments or professional schools, but instead extended across the systems of American schooling. In particular, the model of universities defined by a focus on theory, research, and knowledge production, increasingly proposed as detached from matters of practice, brought with it new ideas about who (and what) constitutes expertise in American society. Michael Katz explains that "until the late nineteenth century, most experts and expert knowledge had been produced outside universities. By capturing the process through which they were produced and transferring the actual production of much new knowledge from outside their walls to within them, universities staged one of the great coups in the history of capitalism."[15] In short, the university research departments took higher learning and knowledge production as their domain, and in this process, they created and asserted a difference from other institutions of higher learning (like high schools, seminaries, normal schools, and even colleges)—and their faculties and students—that did not exist previously.

The famous Harvard reports of the 1890s speak to the state of institutional overlap, the investment college administrators had in dissolving it by annexing intellectual work exclusively for the college, and the consequences of these efforts. Widely linked by historians of rhetoric and composition to the establishment of writing programs in U.S. colleges, the Harvard committee's reports recognized the uneven preparation of college applicants and recommended a firmer divide between secondary and college standards. Asserting a distinction that was more aspirational than factual, the committee sought to elevate college composition work above the "drudgery" of student themes by promoting a vision of composition work at the secondary or preparatory level *defined* by this drudgery:

> It is the University, not the Preparatory School, which has to do with "style" and "individuality" . . . The province of the preparatory schools is to train the scholar . . . in what can only be described as the elements and rudiments of written expression,—they should teach facile, clear penmanship, correct spelling, simple grammatical construction, and neat, workman-like, mechanical execution.

Composition teaching at the secondary and grammar level, according to this report, "demands . . . drudgery of a kind most wearisome."[16]

Historians of rhetoric and composition have tended to accept the significance of this committee's recommendations as indicating a developing sense of standards for college writing, along with what Donna Strickland has called a "managerial unconscious" for managing the labor of college writing programs. That is, we have looked at this moment as one of our own disciplinary beginnings, recognizing the work of composition theme reading and the need to manage that labor. We tend to accept the professed attempt to raise the standards of high schools (even if we recognize the critique of high schools to be somewhat dubious). What we have so far underexamined is the role reports such as these play in *creating* and *maintaining* this division between secondary schools and colleges and the writing practiced and produced therein. We don't tend to observe how this discourse serves to suppress the standards of writing in high schools almost by definition. In this way, when Strickland rightly notices in commentary like this the efforts to "dissociate the college composition course from mechanical work in order to more decidedly associate it with intellectual work," she and others still overlook the simultaneous effort to associate the *high school* with this mechanical work and to dissociate *it* from intellectual work.[17] The sword cuts both ways.

The assertion that high schools need to be clearly divided from colleges is as much about the concern that high schools are competing with the work of colleges as it is that the college will be reduced to "a mere academy" or high school itself. But the high school, in particular—which has come down to us as a site assigned the "drudgery" of English language instruction preparatory to college—posited itself as an alternative to the traditional American college as a form of higher learning. To this end, high schools took on a modern English curriculum (featuring modern languages and sciences) in place of or in addition to a classical curriculum because of the growing belief that the English subjects were a valuable area of advanced study for those outside of "the professions"—traditionally, law, medicine, and clergy. As part of the English curriculum, the writing instruction in at least some high schools was theorized and rigorous long before it was taken up as the purview of most colleges. There is evidence that high school writing instruction before this time (and undoubtedly persisting throughout it as well) was particularly holistic, integrated, inquiry-based, student-centered—and rhetorical. As we will see in the case of the Louisville high schools, faculty emphasized "practice" as a key to a practical English education, positing an expansive notion of possible uses and applications of school learning well beyond mechanistic, time-bound, or solely career-centered use—much less drudgery—and instead attending to the student's own development, needs, and interests in learning as a lifelong process.

Thus, in these higher schools writing was part of a "practical" collegiate curriculum that, along with natural sciences, reflected a challenge to the primacy of the classical curriculum—a challenge that would eventually come to shape the curricula at more traditional colleges as well, as they, too, adopted the modern subjects by the end of the century. Attempts to articulate a national educational system, then, weren't just addressing "failure" or lack of standards of the high school, but instead were a matter of reconciling different political and pedagogical philosophies of higher learning, including the disjuncture between the classical and modern curriculum that plagued colleges and high schools alike for several decades. Thus, the reality of high school and college articulation is one of general mismatch, and competition—with high schools, at times, even exceeding the standards of colleges in relation to writing instruction and other modern subjects. The history of writing in high schools powerfully challenges our dominant narratives about composition's beginnings.

Disciplinary Boundaries and Beginnings

By bringing the story of high schools into our disciplinary purview and highlighting the ways they may have connected with, contradicted, complicated, or constituted the story of pedagogical developments of value to our field, my aspiration is not to promote a new sense of our *beginnings* so much as draw attention to a *before* that is also of value and meaning to our field. In her reflection on the problem of beginnings that closes the volume *Local Histories*, Donahue draws on Edward Said to articulate the ways in which marking any beginning is a constantly shifting goal: "The boundary a beginning creates as a way to separate itself from what preceded it can only be temporary; its conceptual dependency on what comes 'before' will be marked in numerous ways . . . As Said himself says, a critical purpose of a beginning is to produce difference where difference was not apparent before."[18] Donahue's comments underscore a particular limitation of demarcating origins for our discipline: beginnings construct boundaries and foreclose connections with what comes before in ways that have implications for what comes after. The production of "difference where difference was not apparent before" applies well to our understanding of higher learning in the nineteenth century and the eventual assertion of the high school–college divide.

While I am not interested in staking claim to an origin, the assertion of a significant "before" is important to how we conceive of our discipline through its histories, and how we forge connections with others outside of that discipline. The practices associated with the common schools represent just such a "before." In observing that our histories have largely continued to overlook and undervalue a vast range of theories, practices, and traditions that stemmed from the lower schools, I further assert that this omission is neither obvious nor inconsequential. Instead, it reflects and reinscribes assumptions about our discipline's relationship to pedagogy, education, and the high school itself that it is time to reconsider, particularly as it affects the work of composition teaching today.

I argue that our efforts to uphold this historical distinction between high schools and colleges belies our more democratic ideals as a discipline and reinforces the devaluation of teachers and teaching (particularly at the K–12 level) that many in our field have tried in other ways to work against. At its core, I see our reliance on this divide as born of an anxiety about the status of rhetoric and composition in the academic hierarchy, and our field's ongoing investment in establishing ourselves as a serious research discipline—in part, by asserting our distinctiveness from the work of K–12 writing teachers.

Our acceptance of the centrality of the college and subsequent devaluation of the high school is difficult to evidence because it most often manifests in omissions, gaps, silences, and lost opportunities. By and large, we simply don't consider the histories or practices of high schools, which are understood as firmly—by their very definition—outside of our disciplinary purview. Instead, high schools have been the purview of education researchers and teachers. Thus, we have marked our own beginnings by marking difference with what came before—whether that is what came before in our disciplinary history, or in our students' individual life histories. As the other against which college writing can define itself, high school language learning has been intentionally devalued in university discourse over the course of its history. Particularly in light of the significant overlap between institutions that will be explored in this volume, I understand our historical efforts to impose (and police) distinctions between secondary and college contexts as self-protective and not ideologically sound.

Historians of rhetoric and composition are one group that has been inadvertently complicit in the devaluation of the high school in the ways we frame the significance of our histories of pedagogy and composition for our field: through our assumption of the stability of "college" teaching and scholarship. Part of what is at issue is that in each new "recovery" of disciplinary pasts and precursors we are tacitly required to justify our historical interventions in terms of existing disciplinary narratives, terms, and value systems, and our justifications at times foreclose the value of other interventions. Jacqueline Jones Royster and Jean Williams explain:

> As in other officializing processes, as existing histories of composition acquire "official" status, they participate in the making of metaphors and the symbolic systems of reality by which we

> draw the lines of the discipline and authenticate what is "real" and not, significant enough to notice and not, or valuable and not. These constructions set the default boundaries, and, in effect, determine the range of what can be rendered in composition history in "mainstream" or "traditional" terms, and what is consistently rendered in the terms of exception or "other."

This is powerfully true of the notion of the "college" and "college writing" as it has circulated in histories of our field.[19]

For example, in her important recovery of the history of normal schools for rhetoric and composition, Kathryn Fitzgerald expands the scope of our disciplinary inquiry to include normal schools, identifying in the European pedagogies circulating there an alternative pedagogical tradition for composition that contrasts with the dominant pedagogies of Eastern colleges. In comparing these pedagogies and values to the tradition of rhetorical instruction in the colleges, though, Fitzgerald expands our scope to include normal schools without fundamentally challenging the disciplinary values and structures that had excluded that history in the first place.[20] To put it another way, she justifies our examination of normal schools by aligning them with colleges, thus keeping the ostensibly reliable category of colleges as the appropriate center and touch-point of the discipline.

Indeed, it is Fitzgerald's assertion of normal schools as comparable to colleges—*not* to secondary schools—that leaves her open to the critique by Ryan Skinnell, who attempts to uphold the distinctiveness of colleges. According to Skinnell, attempts to compare normal schools to colleges or universities are misguided because "normal schools were established in completely different social and educational environments than virtually all colleges and universities, elite or otherwise," and are particularly differentiated by the fact that "they were not exclusively post-secondary institutions."[21] In reality, though, very few institutions were *exclusively* secondary, a great majority relying heavily on preparatory departments for the bulk of their enrollments throughout the nineteenth century. In fact, it would have been exceedingly rare to require a secondary course for college admission throughout much of the century, which would seem to be the requisite criteria for defining colleges as "postsecondary" at all. Thus, though Skinnell uses this claim to argue that normal schools were, therefore, not akin to colleges, I argue that this instead points to the ways that the distinctions between *any of these* institutions is less clear or useful than even Fitzgerald supposed. That is, both she and Skinnell take the divide between secondary and college education as more reliable a criterion than it is from the perspective of this project.

In place of a narrative of division and distinctiveness that relies on the suppression of the value of high schools (as well as normal schools) in relation to colleges, this book brings the high school and college back together in a shared history in order to consider the development of writing instruction from the perspective of this overlap.

I am not suggesting there are no differences between institution types. And I'm not suggesting that we need to locate the origins of college composition in high schools. Instead, I want to look to high schools to better understand writing across "higher learning"—to attend to both difference and sameness in more cautious and curious ways. I want to ask what happens when we look at the tradition of college-building and the fate of composition from the perspective of the high school, focusing on these overlaps rather looking around them. I use Louisville's history here to help ask that question.

Why Louisville?

In *A History of American Higher Education*, John Thelin reveals much of our common knowledge about institutional traditions and legacies to be, in fact, backformations—attempts to shore up contemporary schools, policies, or practices by aligning them with a sense of revered history. As he explains, the triumphal history of college- and university-building in this country can seem smooth and obvious from a certain vantage point only because some of the messier aspects of the story have been obscured through revisionist histories that have an investment in conveying tradition and longevity. Thelin cites the University of Louisville as an example of a university that has revised its own history in this way, asserting a longer historical legacy (traced to the founding of Jefferson Seminary in 1798) in order to "contribute to civic or state pride." He uses this example to "illustrate that historical writing about higher education is constantly subject to new estimates and reconsideration."[22]

Though Thelin does not explore the point, it is not only the seminary but also the *high schools* in Louisville that are significantly connected to—and also perhaps purposefully obscured in relation to—the history of the university as it developed. In fact, it could even be argued that, ironically, it was a high school that offered the only courses that would qualify the University of Louisville as a university in its early days, by our current definitions: essentially a professional school at first, offering courses only in medicine and then law, the University of Louisville offered its liberal arts core curriculum through the "academical department," which was coterminous with Male High School. Outside of the Male High School, which separated from the university in 1860, a proper undergraduate college for the university did not exist again until 1907. Changing names some seven times before working out its institutional identity as a high school, the status of Louisville's Male High School remained complicated by the fact that it conferred bachelor's and even master's degrees until 1912.[23]

The history of Louisville's Female High School runs parallel to Louisville's Male High School, beginning with an 1851 charter that designates a school tax for the "support of the Public Schools and High School for females of said city, and the University of Louisville." Plans to establish a female high school were circulating prior to any specific mention of a male high school but in tandem with developments of the "academical department" of the University of Louisville that would become Male High School, suggesting Female's alignment with this collegiate project.

While always designated a high school, Female's institutional position and status is similarly complicated by its advanced collegiate curriculum. As late as 1905, Emma Woerner (who would later become the first principal of Louisville's Atherton High School for girls in 1924) was able to enter University of Kentucky as a junior based on her academic accomplishments at Female High School. The high school's status was also complicated by the fact that it offered a teacher training course that served as a privileged credential for teaching in the city's schools, and it was at several points in its history proposed as a normal school for the city and even the state. When the Louisville Normal School was established in 1871 (as the oldest normal school in the South and one of the oldest in the nation), it continued to have a close relationship with Female, serving as a professional extension of that school.[24] In short, we can see even from this brief overview that the definitional boundaries between institutions of higher learning in Louisville in the third quarter of the century were unstable.

And yet, the nomenclature was not without purpose or effect. Christie Anne Farnham explains in her study of women's colleges that some schools across the South specifically avoided the term "college"—opting for "collegiate" or other variations—to avoid the public and governmental scrutiny that colleges attracted. Such scrutiny included both ongoing social criticisms about the appropriateness of college for women and the necessity of having a charter passed in state legislatures for the granting of college degrees, which may have proved troublesome in light of ongoing educational controversies. Farnham goes on to argue that the flexible naming conventions and the "incremental process" of expanding course offerings at academies to include college courses led to important gains in the expansion of higher education for women, in part due to the inconspicuousness of these schools: "The female college, then, did not represent a startling disjuncture, but rather a continuous progression in the slow, upward climb toward equal opportunity between the sexes."[25]

I argue even further that the female college didn't necessarily represent "a continuous progression" at all, but instead represents the uneven, inconsistent process of cultural change that includes false starts, reversals, and surprising innovations. Particularly for traditionally underserved groups, such as women and African Americans, historical high schools were sites of surprising educational innovation and opportunity that have been broadly overlooked by rhetoric and compositionists, providing a context for these individuals not only to pursue higher learning and professionalization but also to write and speak publicly about their lives and their positions in society in the second half of the nineteenth century. White women students in Louisville were being trained in rhetoric, composition, and elocution, performing their own original compositions in front of mixed-gender public audiences from 1858, while also actively pursuing professionalization as teachers.

Beginning in 1876, African American students in Louisville were similarly afforded opportunities for advanced education and rhetorical practice through their training as teachers in the "A" Grade of the Central Colored School and, by 1882, in the Central Colored High School. Though lagging twenty years behind the establishment of high schools for white students in the city, Central was one of the earliest public high schools for African Americans established in the United States, providing a rhetorical education comparable to that of some local colleges. In an era of segregation and overt discrimination, high schools remained at the vanguard of higher learning for African Americans into the twentieth century.

These opportunities were at least partially enabled by the status of the high school as part of the common school system—specifically *not* a college—and the rhetorical construction of its students as "girls" and "boys," and as future teachers in service of the community. In this way, the criteria that seem to exclude such schools from a consideration of college writing are the same that secured students' access to collegiate learning at the site of the high school. That is, the ability of these high schools to fly under the radar of racist and misogynist cultural critics to provide higher educational access has, ironically, left these schools off the radar of rhetoric and composition scholars as well. Attending to the stories of U.S. high schools, then, adds depth and complexity to our understanding of historical literacy and language practices, especially as it sheds light on the schooled rhetorical practices of countless young people not represented in histories of colleges and universities. Though high school attendance was far from universal throughout the nineteenth and into the twentieth century, it was still much more common than college attendance, particularly among women and African Americans.[26]

Louisville serves as an especially instructive example for understanding the diffuse work of and justifications for high schools for different populations of students because of its particular location, programs, and structure. Long an important hub of commerce at the Ohio River Falls and the Louisville and Nashville Railroad (commonly called L & N)—at the border of both the American North and South, as well as the East and West—Louisville was also a hub for cultural exchange across regions, merging many cultural norms from the South with social and educational programs from the North and East. Perhaps because of its location at a key intersection for commerce and culture in the nineteenth century, Louisville's public high schools reflect (and refract our understanding of) most every serious educational development of the second half of the century—college- and university-building, the development of English education as the dominant curriculum for higher learning, student-centered pedagogies and educational theories, the development and transformation of normal schools, the introduction of manual education and its mutation into vocational education, the advent of the research university, and the spread of advanced education for women, African Americans, and working class students, to name just a few. While public school systems around the country each negotiated some constellation of these issues—and the questions of race, class, and gender they also entail—Louisville is remarkable for its almost comprehensive engagement with educational trends of the time. Further, the persistence of the school system's racial, gendered, and programmatic segregation into the twentieth century ironically provides an opportunity to examine separately the discourse surrounding and value accrued to each program and group of learners and teachers.

Thus, Louisville provides insights into the ways local communities negotiated educational values and priorities on the ground, complicating our sense of national or even regional trends. The attention to the discursive and material construction of this one school system allows us to capture some of the messiness and overlap of institution-building and pedagogical theorizing at this time of educational flux and change. As a local history, it helps us to resist binaries and easy categorizations in our constructions of the rhetorical past. At the same time, as David Gold has argued, local histories "must not simply recover neglected writers, teachers, locations, and institutions, but must also demonstrate connections between these subjects and larger scholarly conversations."[27] In this way, *A Shared History* uses the Louisville history to better understand the larger conversation about high school–college connections, providing historical insights into the writing instruction, practices, and values of nineteenth-century high schools in general, as the educational ideals and realities of "higher learning" were being worked out.

Louisville also draws our attention to the work of high school teachers as innovators and theorists of writing pedagogy and education writ large. The Louisville high schools produced several notable educators who rose to national acclaim over their careers. For example, professor William N. Hailmann—who taught natural science at both Male and Female—authored several volumes on education and pedagogy, and is most famous for his innovations in the kindergarten movement. Likewise, Abraham Flexner, author of the eponymous Flexner Report on medical education as well as other volumes on the American college and university, was both a student and teacher at Male High School. Based on his experiences in the Louisville schools, Flexner went on to become nationally influential in identifying and addressing the issue of institutional overlap across higher education. Both of these educators theorized and practiced student-centered, active pedagogies for authentic learning decades before Dewey would do so, though their work remains largely or entirely unknown in our field. In short, our tacit (and superficial) disciplinary interest in "colleges" has produced gaps in our scholarship, which will be enriched by a more nuanced understanding of the currency of these terms in their own time and a more flexible sense of disciplinary territory.

Recognizing both the local and the national contexts of these developments, I use microhistorical analysis to dialogically weave together local, concrete description and abstract narrative throughout. As Bruce McComiskey argues in the introduction to his edited collection of microhistories, this methodology "is ideally suited for the complexities of a discipline like composition, which emerged and developed in local sites yet also shows signs of more general social and historical influences." In the same way, American high schools like those in Louisville and the composition instruction they embraced also emerged at the intersection of local and global forces. In the language of microhistory, the Louisville high schools prove to be what is called an "exceptional normal" in the history of composition in higher learning, the historical value of which "lies not in its uniqueness, but in its exemplariness."[28] It is a seemingly exceptional case that gestures to an overlooked trend—a case that makes us reconsider what "normal" is.

Indeed, Louisville is just one example, one site in which the shape of higher learning was being negotiated among school leaders and communities as they expanded public schooling opportunities. Most every other major public school system from this period has a strikingly similar story—from New York to St. Louis, Baltimore to Cincinnati, Chicago to Philadelphia, public high schools were being developed to provide higher education to local students. Like Louisville's, the work of these high schools overlapped significantly with the work of normal schools and colleges. They sometimes merged with or became colleges (as in the case of the New York Free Academy), and other times remained marked as high schools (like Philadelphia's Central High School, which remains confounding in that it continues to confer bachelor's degrees to this day). In each case, their institutional identities were fraught and much discussed.

Thus, the new normal that emerges here is the significance of early high schools and their rhetoric and composition instruction in the landscape of higher learning, challenging our tacit acceptance of the distinction between historical high schools and colleges, and our sense of the perpetually inadequate American high school rendered in documents like the Harvard reports of 1892. Overall, if our lack of attention to high schools in the history of U.S. higher education has seemed obvious and rational from the perspective of the present or from the perspective of our field's master narratives, microhistories of high schools help us to challenge received paradigms in favor of more complex and nuanced historical accounts.

As we currently try to rethink higher education—in relation to individuals and society, to liberal arts and career preparation, to access and standards—we can see that the story unfolds unevenly. Even very widespread values and ideas take a long time to take hold in practice, and the experience of most students and institutions are not reflected in master narratives or even broadly regional accounts. Local and micro-histories can help us to position ourselves in relation to these complexities in order to understand the stakes of our histories and our present practices and values. They remind us of the ways writing programs and practices are understood differently by local stakeholders and are put to various social and personal uses. Providing an alternative perspective to ongoing disciplinary conversations about the meaning of "college writing," its history, and its relationship to writing in the high schools, this book recovers a time when other possible outcomes for the organization and spirit of higher education were possible. It demonstrates that, as Katz argues, "There is nothing inevitable about the shape of higher learning. It is . . . the result, if not of planning, of human agency. It is the product of compromise, conflict, and, above all, choice."[29]

We are facing such compromises, conflicts, and choices again (or, rather, still) today, bringing the "boundaries" between high school and higher education back into view in significant ways. Most pointedly, public discourse about college readiness, accelerated learning models (such as Advanced Placement, dual-credit and concurrent enrollment), and ongoing conversations about basic writing and the role of first-year composition within our own field each bring the ostensible high school–college divide into view. While there may be well-reasoned support for or against any of these programs, appeals to the ostensibly intractable distinction between high school and college-level writing have never been reliable. My hope is that attention to the history of local negotiations and morphology helps us not necessarily to defend programs like dual enrollment but instead to think about what a different set of assumptions and perspectives might help us to accomplish in high school and college writing classrooms, and how it might help us to reconfigure the relationship between them toward more productive ends.

Because *A Shared History* takes seriously the role of high schools in the history of college writing, it bridges a gap between the fields of rhetoric and composition and education, which too seldom collaborate around their shared histories and investments in writing studies. As much as we have our areas of expertise and bases of local knowledge across institutional spaces, we also have shared areas of investment in composition. We would benefit from more teachers working together to articulate shared writing outcomes and trajectories of broader learning experiences for our students within their own local contexts and structures. Challenging assumptions about the "obvious" differences between high schools and colleges pushes us to seek more operational (locally enacted and changing) definitions through ongoing research, practice, theory building, and collaboration.

As we continue to hone, expand, shift, and otherwise morph our disciplinary identities and institutional locations, it becomes increasingly untenable to disavow or even benignly neglect our connection to teachers, the schools, and their histories. Local and microhistories—tracing the complex institutional and pedagogical work that has been undertaken in individual schools and cities—can help us to complicate such divides and celebrate the messiness of our intersecting histories and beginnings. Embracing nineteenth-century high schools as part of a shared past to which we can appeal, we can work together to articulate more operational definitions of "college-level writing" that can hold up in the face of institutional changes and challenges.

In the chapters that follow, I have begun this work by constructing a history of the rhetorical instruction and opportunities of Louisville's higher schools from their early days through the last quarter of the nineteenth century. Each chapter proceeds in rough chronology through distinct but interconnected aspects of this development that contribute to a rich ecological perspective on the political, social, economic, racial, and gendered aspects of rhetorical education being negotiated for an increasingly diverse student body across the last half of the century. While mostly organized chronologically around the shifting educational trends that emerged over time, the chapters also tend to compartmentalize the discussions of each high school in turn, highlighting the ways each school and their differing student bodies—white men, white women, and African American men and women—were influenced differently by the processes of institutional overlap and distinction described.

The chapters in section 1 focus on the founding and early years of operation of the city's first two high schools, Male High School and Female High School, for white men and women. In chapter 1, I begin by discussing the city's early experiments in higher learning and the justifications for establishing the high schools. In particular, I highlight the gendering of teacher training and collegiate learning and the impact of those associations on the purposes and titles assigned to public high schools.

In the next two chapters, I flesh out the high schools' curricula and pedagogies, attending again to differences and similarities in these first two high schools. In each school, the formal curriculum aligned with that of many colleges, blurring the boundaries between these institutional types. In chapter 2, I illustrate the similarities through an examination of textbooks and student writing, attending again to the gendered implications of such porous institutional boundaries.

At the same time, an examination of the educational philosophies of the schools shows that the high school also broke from the college tradition in key ways. The high schools' political position as part of the common school produced valuable alternative pedagogies for "college writing" in the early years of their operations. The shift to pedagogy in chapter 3, focusing on significant figures such as the schools' principals and one noted faculty member who published his pedagogical philosophies for local and national education audiences, sketches the contours of a broader pedagogical tradition for writing in the high school while also emphasizing local variations in practice that further trouble categorical claims.

In the second section, after a brief interchapter that uses the Civil War as a fulcrum around which to pivot, I explore changes and challenges faced by the high schools in the last quarter of the century. In chapter 4, I introduce the curricular transformations to Male High School and Female High School following the war, particularly the introduction of the "university" model and the subsequent fragmentation of the general education curriculum. There, I introduce the challenges leveraged to the status of the high schools, arguing that the critiques of the schools emerged (unexpectedly, perhaps) as a result of the high schools' ambiguous relationship not to the *college* but to the emerging model of the *university*. This discussion focuses largely on Male High School, as it is that school that was most acutely impacted by this shifting educational and political context in its formal relation to the University of Louisville.

In chapter 5, I introduce the history of the Central Colored High School, which was established after the transformation of the other Louisville high schools was well underway, though the teachers there similarly drew on the institutional ambiguity of "higher" learning in their efforts to train rhetorically savvy citizens and teachers through the end of the century. I emphasize the impact of racism in shaping the social significance and curriculum of this high school.

In chapter 6, the penultimate chapter, I shift the reader's gaze toward the final decades of the century and the fate of high schools in relation to national reform efforts. Using the experiences and educational writings of Abraham Flexner, a former student-turned-educational-reformer, as a touchstone, I trace the challenges posed to the high schools through national and local articulation efforts, focusing specifically on the consequences for writing instruction.

Finally, in the closing chapter, I discuss the implications of this history for both historians and teachers of writing shaping research, pedagogy, and policy today. Recognizing that the complex interface between the two broadly conceived categories of high school and college persists into the present as well, manifested in the variability of learning and teaching practices both across *and within* institutions and classrooms, I address the specter of dual-enrollment programs and argue that the history outlined in this volume invites us to fundamentally alter our disciplinary discourse about these programs, shifting from a concern about blurred standards and educational leveling to a renewed interest in the local and nuanced pedagogical work occurring in specific classrooms, between and among specific learners and teachers.

Throughout, I attend to writing by and about the students and teachers in these schools, when possible, focusing on the ways these individual stories highlight larger ideological and political shifts in the landscape of higher learning in Louisville and beyond. For example, at three different points I closely narrate the controversies surrounding the principalship of the high schools, demonstrating how each of these seemingly personal, highly local controversies points up the larger ideals of higher learning that were shifting and settling uneasily throughout this period—and the material effects those shifts had on real teachers and learners on the ground.

Together, the arguments forwarded in each chapter demonstrate the value of examining diverse sites of higher learning as sites of pedagogical innovation, rhetorical opportunity, and citizenship training of significance both to our rhetorical histories and to the ways we address reform efforts in higher education today. The term "higher learning" is key, establishing a shared context for the rhetorical and writing work that we do—and have been doing—in various institutional contexts for nearly two centuries. If the establishment of "beginnings" for both rhetoric and composition and departments of education has entailed the assertion of "difference where difference was not apparent before," my hope in this book is to make that difference less apparent once more.

PART ONE

Establishing the First "Higher Schools" in Louisville

CHAPTER 1

The Idea(l) of the High School

The significance of the high school to the history of college writing is grounded in these schools' identification as "higher schooling" and in the particular admixture of political and intellectual ideals that undergirded this identification from their earliest beginnings. Given the complexity of the educational project and audience of these schools, those ideals were multiple and sometimes countervailing—including both the democratic principles of the common schools and the highest intellectual and cultural aspirations of collegiate learning, and thus both public goods and individual gains. Adding to these broad educational and political ideals, appeals to more pragmatic considerations such as the need for teacher training also fundamentally shaped the identity of the emerging public high school, with distinctly gendered implications.

It all began with the advent of public education systems beyond pauper schools. Beginning in the 1820s, U.S. education reformers in New England like Horace Mann famously took on the project of expanding basic educational access through the establishment of common schools, free and open to the public, which were to provide a common or shared educational background for citizens. The premise of the common schools was that all citizens in a democracy should have basic literacy and numeracy skills in order to participate in the work of the republic. The trend spread, as cities across the North and East began establishing funds and organizing systems to provide free public education to their youths.

In time, the high school grew from the roots of these common schools, constituting the "higher branches" of the public school system.

Sometimes this meant only a handful of courses or a teacher preparation program offered beyond the lower grades, sometimes even in the same room. In general, though, a high school course was considered a three- or four-year general education curriculum. The trick was that what constituted "general education" in the higher branches was under revision. Prior to the nineteenth century, general education in the higher branches entailed the classical curriculum of traditional colleges, drawing from traditions in Europe. The classical curriculum, including Latin, Greek, rhetoric, and mathematics, was believed to produce the "mental discipline" and cultural knowledge necessary for the traditional professions of law, medicine, and clergy. This classic collegiate learning was exclusionary almost by design; knowledge of the ancient languages and histories was a mark of honor, and a degree was a private and individual acquisition. In short, higher learning had long distinguished a person from the knowledge that is common or shared. So, whereas the common schools provided basic literacy and numeracy to develop students as citizens and efficient workers, and were therefore framed as a public good, higher schooling had been an individual good, leading to personal accomplishments and professional opportunities. But, with publicly supported and widely available higher learning in high schools in many cities and across some states, that was changing.[1]

The high school offered higher learning for "the people," and so school leaders (often under acute public pressure) sought anxiously to determine what subjects were best suited to preparing people as citizens and workers. The classical curriculum, it was determined by many, did not do this, and so schools were experimenting with new models and curricular reforms to meet the needs of a changing student body and a modernizing society. The public high school found a viable model to follow in the "practical" English curriculum, which offered an array of "modern" subjects including English and the sciences.[2] Like academies and an increasing number of colleges, high schools embraced these modern subjects—but without wholly releasing the hold of the classical curriculum, particularly Latin. Thus, they often offered a sort of hybrid curriculum, featuring both classical and modern "tracks," or amending the classical curriculum with the inclusion of some number of English and science courses. To further complicate matters, colleges themselves were revising the classical curriculum to embrace more of the modern English subjects. So, whereas the classical collegiate curriculum had once been taken as a fairly reliable indicator of institutional mission or type, the curriculum itself actually became an increasingly unreliable and changeable feature in an institution's profile. Given the confused relations between curricular programs and purposes, institutional titles were also used interchangeably to indicate (an admittedly indistinct and ever-shifting) relation to the enterprise of higher learning.

In this chapter, I focus on these issues of naming, tracing the ways Louisville schools were defined and redefined in relation to various educational and political purposes in the years leading up to their establishment. In doing so, I hope to productively blur the lines between institutions and remind readers of the many other possible definitions that might have become dominant as stakeholders determined the contours of higher learning for Louisville and cities across the United States. These definitions and distinctions would come to shape not only the role of writing instruction but also our ideas about education itself—and the identities of writers and teachers—by the end of the century. At this early point, though, the meaning of "high school" was still open to negotiation.

Public and Private Goods: Higher Learning in Louisville before High Schools

An early convert to the common school movement, Louisville, Kentucky, established its first free public schools in 1829, nearly a century before much of the rest of the state. However, these early public schools only included what were called "lower schools," which offered basic education to about an eighth-grade level. After that stage, students desiring more formal education would need to attend a private academy, seminary, or college. This division of publicly and privately provisioned education at the lower and higher levels speaks to the differences between the purpose and audience conceived for education at each level—that is, higher schooling was broadly understood to serve a purpose different from common schools.

Prior to the development of public high schools, such higher learning was provided by paid academies, subscription schools, colleges, and a robust network of Catholic and other religiously sponsored schools in Louisville. Take, for example, a notice for a "female high school" run by Mr. and Mrs. Atkinson that circulated in the *Louisville Morning Courier* at midcentury, inviting Louisville's public to "entrust to their care a large number of lassies, from the bounding and graceful age of ten, and younger to 'sweet sixteen,' and twenty." Similarly, the classified ads of an 1855 issue of the *Daily Courier*, the year before Louisville's public high schools opened, feature no less than eight high schools, institutes, and seminaries, and even a "regularly chartered college" for young women, not to mention the many opportunities available for young men.

Not far from the city, there were also famous academies like Science Hill Female Academy in Bardstown, Kentucky, and colleges like coeducational and integrated Berea. Thus, Louisvillians had opportunities to access higher learning, and the communities that hosted these schools often paid some money to support their establishment, representing an early investment in publicly supported higher schooling. But while these academies and private high schools already procured public support for themselves, W. Bruce Leslie explains that "what set the urban high schools apart was . . . obtaining guaranteed annual support rather than initial grants, state literature funds, and sporadic 'top up' funding."[3] Thus, while Louisville, like most major cities of the time, already boasted a wide array of academies, seminaries, and colleges, the idea of an ongoing commitment to publicly funded schooling was a new proposition, and one that had to be justified to the public.

In Louisville and elsewhere, this idea was persuasively tied to republican ideals asserting that it is both a national interest and a democratic responsibility to provide universal access to education for all white children. The idea was established in relation to the common schools earlier in the century, and the scope of this "common" education was now extending into the higher branches. Specifically, as historian W. G. Walker observes in relation to the Illinois public schools, the language of Jefferson's 1779 "Bill for the More General Diffusion of Knowledge," which established the democratic importance of public education, can be heard to resonate throughout many subsequent appeals for public higher schooling. An article in the *Daily Courier* explained in this vein: "We rejoice in the prosperity of private schools: the more good schools we have the better for our city." But, the article continued,

> In our opinion there are no schools so thoroughly republican, none which minister so directly to the mental growth of the community, as public schools, schools supported not by

> members of charitable associations or of one or another religious denomination, but by the whole people. These are emphatically the people's seminaries, and as such they commend themselves to the regard of all frends [*sic*] of education.[4]

Supporters commonly used terms like "people's seminaries" and "people's colleges" to describe the nation's public schools, particularly the higher schools—this language serving as an implicit critique of traditional seminaries and colleges, which were framed as more exclusionary or elite, while simultaneously raising the status of the high schools to the level of these more established institutions of higher education.

But these "people's colleges" were slower to develop in Louisville. The beginnings can be traced to the Jefferson Seminary, which had been chartered in 1798. The seminary had been established by some of the city's earliest leaders, within just a few years of the founding of the state itself. But the seminary, which taught the English branches along with Latin and Greek and higher mathematics to both male and female students, did not catch on in the community. Instead of a "people's college" it was framed by citizens as an elitist enterprise that only served to alienate students from their parents—it was not seen as the public good that Louisville's people were seeking. Indeed, that was not even its aim: the seminary was intended as a "select limited academy," and the faculty was reportedly frustrated with even the limited number of underprepared students who were being admitted.[5]

Unable to reconcile its vision of what and whom to teach throughout its operations, the seminary was closed in 1829—the same year that the common schools of that city were established. Not coincidentally, the state allocated a portion of the assets from the Jefferson Seminary to establish a "high school" in Louisville at that time. As their "high school," the city established the Louisville Collegiate Institute in 1837 (at the same time as they established the Louisville Medical Institute), the name of which soon changed to Louisville College, and the college eventually inherited that portion of the seminary estate set aside for the high school. Thus, the idea of the college and high school were overlapping from the earliest experiments of public higher learning in Louisville.[6]

The college was renamed University of Louisville in 1846, when several medical schools and a new law department were merged under the control of the city, making it one of the earliest municipally owned and run universities in the country.[7] Significantly, though, this school was no people's college either—and would hardly be considered a college at all by today's standards, as the collegiate department itself never flourished. Instead, the school initially provided only professional training in medicine and law, with no general liberal arts curriculum, as admission to such professional schools did not require a bachelor's degree. The limitations of this school's programming was a point of contention, as citizens and school leaders advocated for the establishment of programs of more broad and general interest to the community.

Part of the problem was that the college—though owned by the city—had for a number of years been in possession of the medical faculty, who were making their livelihoods as professors there. Though the medical faculty had been in possession of the university property and endowment, critics argued that they did not have a particular claim on these educational resources over the interests of liberal arts programming for the broader public. Those who advocated for the establishment of liberal subjects did so on a definitional point, arguing that "the establishment of a '*college*, with law and medical departments,' was the original purpose of the foundation—the advantages to be derived from the college or academical department, being, obviously, the efficient motive to the grant."[8] In this way, supporters of the liberal arts asserted that the academical department would better fulfill the true definition and purpose of the "college" endowment than the medical and law schools did. A "college" was defined here by the provision of liberal, academic subjects, not professional specialization.

In order to support an academic department at the university—also commonly referred to as a Free High School—it was proposed in 1850 that a rent or tax be levied on the medical department. The project, as described by the *Louisville Morning Courier*, was to "establish a Free High School, as the academical department of our University, where a thorough course of instruction should be provided in the English language, in the elements of philosophy and physics, and in the modern languages, with a view of giving our youth a liberal education for the counting room, the work shop, or the farm."[9] The choice of careers here would have been strategic, indicating to readers that this college (i.e., high school) would serve a broad, democratic audience drawn from the common schools, not a more narrowly defined, professional audience.

Still, the proposal proved controversial. While the editor of the *Louisville Morning Courier* considered it "right and just" to levy a tax or rent on the medical department for these purposes, the *Louisville Journal*, perceiving injustice to the medical faculty, characterized the proposal as "idiotic" and "insane." It was the perspective of the former that won out, who framed the project as "more legitimate and more beneficial to the citizens, than the Medical School," again appealing to the common school roots and purposes of this institution of higher learning. To that author, the purpose of a university was wrapped up with its public ownership and the "usefulness to the people" and "public benefits" to be accrued from it.[10] In this way, the higher learning associated with the high school, which was previously considered a private good in relation to the seminaries and colleges, began to take on resonance as a public good. The high school, then, though a "lineal descendent" of the Jefferson Seminary and Louisville College, was forging a different path, "its usefulness and standard of scholarship being improved as its name was made less sounding."[11]

Through this debate—specifically, the conflict surrounding the privately operated medical school on municipal grounds—the idea of the public high school came to represent a new kind of liberal arts college for the people of Louisville, set against the values of specialization, professional training, and private gain associated with the medical and law programs. But the school was still not a reality. More support was needed to make the case for advanced liberal education in the public schools.

Growing Out of and Serving the Common Schools: The Role of Teacher Training

As I have established, the positive reception of the public high school idea hinged on its provision of general education and its explicit association with the common schools in the expanding city school system. This association was confirmed through a revised city charter in 1851 stipulating taxes for the "support of the Public Schools and High School for females of said city, and the University of Louisville"—all three entities being presented as parts of one holistic enterprise. In a report of the school board from the same year, the high schools were described—following Jefferson's famous plan—as comprising the final stage of a public education system: each city ward would have one school, divided into male and female departments, and also into primary, secondary, and grammar departments. When qualified, students would be promoted through the system to the grammar departments, where "they can remain until prepared to enter, the boys the academical department of the University, and the girls the Female High School." In this way, the academical department of the university and the Female High School were proposed as equivalent opportunities for young men and women, respectively, to pursue advanced education from within the common school system. As late as 1896, a historian of Louisville explained of Female High School that "the curriculum is very thorough and it sustains to the graded schools the relation of a college, the former serving as preparatory schools for it."[12] Significantly, though, the term "college" and a full collegiate curriculum was withheld from female students, indicating that the term had more to do with the identity of students than with the status or function of the school itself.

The charter and plans did not accomplish much at first. By 1855, the Committee on Examination and Control were still making their appeal to the board, insisting that "these two schools are now imperatively demanded." They rested their case on the "large number of pupils in both the Male and Female Grammar Departments, [who] are fully prepared for admission to such schools," arguing that "when the hearts of pupils are thus filled with the love of study; when they are fired with this noble enthusiasm, every lover of learning, every friend of ingenuous and aspiring youth, must fervently desire their wishes should be granted; that every possible opportunity for wise mental development should be presented." Framing supporters of the schools as "friend[s] of ingenuous and aspiring youth"—thereby casting the students not as college men and women but schoolboys and schoolgirls in need of patrons—they made it hard to argue against this cause. The *Daily Courier* editor drummed up further urgency in his claim that the high schools were necessary to the very functioning of a democratic state, arguing that their establishment was "the last interest among a free people that should be permitted to languish, for upon the education of the masses rests all the vital principles of a free government, and no people have ever been more ready than the citizens of Louisville to show that they recognized this truth."[13]

But resistance persisted as citizens and workers, understanding the promises and perils of the literacy myth, considered the personal impact that expanded educational opportunities might have on their own lived experiences. Whereas the wealthy of many cities resisted giving up their monopoly on higher education, the poor resisted the taxes that would be imposed to support the schools, especially as many of the poor would not actually have the time and privilege to go on to higher school.[14] Thus, the cause of advancing higher learning was fraught.

But the president of the school board added a crucial perspective to this debate, saying that the high schools would not only be supported by but would themselves support the common schools. That is, they would provide teachers for the community.

> It is a matter of great importance to place, as soon as possible, the advantages of the High School within reach of pupils whose past course gives a guarantee that they will faithfully improve its privileges, and to whom we may hereafter confidently look for thoroughly educated men and women, to fill vacancies which may occur; and to keep the teacher's ranks constantly supplied with intelligent and accomplished instructors.[15]

Though the idea that higher schools would produce teachers for the rapidly expanding school system is presented here as an auxiliary concern, it becomes elsewhere a central rationale for the schools. As superintendent George W. Anderson would write of the high schools in 1860:

> This system must advance to completeness . . . we must have not only educated men, but we must have educated teachers; men, I mean (I include women also), who have been taught the art of teaching, the most important and highest of all other arts. To attain such teachers at all times and most conveniently, they must be made such by us, and made at home.[16]

The production of teachers had been a major concern for a rapidly expanding public school system, which exerted an almost constant strain on the local supply of teachers. Each year, more students were enrolled in grade school than ever before, and cities and towns struggled to keep up with demand. Attendance at the first public school in Louisville, which had opened in 1829 for all white children aged six to fourteen, had quickly reached 250 in one room. To manage these large numbers, the school had been operated on the Lancasterian or monitorial system of instruction, whereby only a handful of teachers oversaw the work of hundreds of students, with the help of unskilled monitors. Moving away from the Lancasterian system, a new building was opened shortly thereafter, with male and female departments and smaller classes, and other school buildings followed. By 1840, there were fourteen Louisville public schools (excluding Louisville College), with an aggregate attendance of 1,227 pupils. By 1850, the city was up to five grammar schools and eighteen primary schools, with a total of 4,303 pupils and forty-three teachers. These numbers would only continue to grow, to 13,593 pupils and 267 teachers in 1873.[17]

This pattern of growth was consistent with other major cities in the United States, a great many of which established high school and normal departments for their public school systems in the 1850s and 1860s, often citing the need for teacher preparation as part of their justification and assigning that responsibility to female schools. The school board of New York, for example, was thus advocating for the establishment of a high and normal school for girls in 1866, the same year that the city's Free Academy for boys was converting into a fully chartered college. Even in coeducational schools, normal departments tended to be explicitly associated with women students. Chicago's co-educational high school was authorized in 1856 along with the provision of a normal department to supply teachers for that city's schools. The range of studies was to be expanded in 1866 in order that "the large class of young men seeking a liberal education in our city may be able to gain it here," at the same time as a new high school branch was established as the training branch for the normal department, primarily for female students. Similarly, St. Louis established its normal school (especially for girls) around 1867, having operated a co-educational high school since 1853.[18]

In Louisville, Female High School required all students to take an advanced course in teaching theories and methods from 1857, until a normal school was established separately from (but in close relation to) that school in 1871. Male offered master's degrees to those who practiced for three years in the "professions," which explicitly included teaching, though that option was seldom, if ever, exercised.[19]

Thus, though the teacher-training function would come to be attached primarily to Female High School (and later Central Colored High School as well), the need for teachers served as a powerful exigence for providing public higher learning to both male and female students. To this end, newspaper reports appealed to the General Council to establish the long-awaited high schools in order to advance the educational interests of the growing city and its public school system. Again combining appeals to both the individual high school students' needs and the school system's needs, the *Daily Courier* explained,

> There are many young ladies who are anxiously waiting for the opening of that school, that they may go on with the more advanced studies and prepare themselves to become accomplished teachers. The good influence of such an institution, combining in itself the advantages of a high and a normal school, will be incalculable. It will be felt in every department of our school system.[20]

Producing teachers for their own schools was a powerful appeal to many citizens. This trend can be observed in the policies of Kentucky's State Normal School (formerly the literary department of Transylvania University), also opened in 1856, with eighty students from across the state, which offered instruction to one student from each district with the provision that they return there and teach one year for every year of instruction.[21] This local interest is partly due to the fact that, in Louisville and across the South, educational advocates were suspicious of Northern educators. Aware of the claims made for literacy and higher learning as shapers of morality and political ideology, administrators sought to control that process locally. State superintendent of education J. D. Matthews underscored this local focus (along with a regional distrust that went with it) when he wrote of the importance of forming "early associations and the most enduring attachments of youthful training" in "institutions of learning, founded in their midst, and with their own treasure, and for their accommodation."[22] Particularly in the years leading up to the Civil War, regional distrust was an important factor in establishing local public schools in Kentucky, especially public high and normal schools that would feed back into the public school system.[23]

In addition, the interest in providing teachers and higher learning was inflected by religious sectarianism, particularly anti-Catholicism. As one paper reported, Protestants of Louisville in the first half of the century often sent their children to Catholic schools and female seminaries because "there are no good Protestant seminaries for young ladies."[24] This was a concern to many Protestants, who saw the Catholic influence in education as a threat. In this way, the establishment of public schooling in Louisville can be seen to be responding not just in favor of free education (which was notably available at many of the Catholic schools, in particular) but also *against* Catholicism. This anti-Catholicism is further evidenced by a report that on July 12, 1855, several teachers were dismissed "on account of their foreign birth and Catholic proclivities. The affair created much feeling in our community."[25] This dismissal occurred one year before the opening of the male and female high schools, and the public "feeling" about it on both sides must surely have shaped the development and identity of those schools.

Clearly, the democratic principles of increased access and preparation for a wide range of careers to serve the community were not innocent of other motives and biases. But out of this context of conflict on the verge of civil war, the Louisville public high schools emerged as institutions that would in many ways redefine higher learning in this community. Drawing on a range of institutional missions and forms to address the various and changing public needs, these were "multipurpose" institutions with a modern, hybrid approach to higher learning that was permeating not only the new schools but also more traditional colleges across the last decades of the nineteenth century.[26] As I will demonstrate, this institutional hybridity caused confusion for the leadership of the schools, once they were finally established, but it also constituted a distinctive and valuable tradition of higher learning for the city.

Establishing the High Schools: The Politics of Naming and Defining Their Work

In the fall of 1856, after the protracted debate of the previous decades, the first free public high schools of Louisville were at last established, unimaginatively named Male High School and Female High School. Male High School opened in a new building in the central part of the city, on Ninth and Chestnut Streets, with forty-two students. It was an impressive building with a large pillared entrance and a domed roof on the site of "university square" (fig. 1.1).[27] Female High School opened with sixty-nine students in an existing building at Center and Walnut Streets.

Both schools were open to all white youths of the city who passed a satisfactory entrance examination. These exams were basic, with a brief test in grammar, arithmetic, and geography at Female and examination

Fig. 1.1. Artist's rendering of original Male High School building. This illustration was included in the *Annual Report* of 1860 along with drawings of other public school buildings across the city. COURTESY OF JEFFERSON COUNTY PUBLIC SCHOOLS.

in grammar, geography, history of the United States, arithmetic, and algebra at Male. Throughout the second half of the nineteenth century, institutions of higher education could not afford to have stringent admission requirements, as the proliferation of colleges and high schools meant that schools were competing for students and, hence, were often forced to accept students with only minimal preparation and from a range of ages. While this was a source of concern among school leaders, minimal requirements can also be understood as ensuring greater access to students with various levels of preparation and perpetuating the uncertain boundaries between high schools and colleges that some students and teachers used to their advantage.

Controversy surrounding the principalship of Male High School at the time of its establishment points to the unique and, at times, confounding status of the high schools. The controversy is telling because it centered not on the qualifications of individual applicants but on questions about the very nature and shape of the school system itself. Namely, two different men considered themselves principals of something called a "high school" at the time. According to principal William W. Harney of the Fifth Ward school, he himself had been elected and appointed by the board, and had acted as principal of the high school for a year already—from within the ward school building of which he was principal teacher, prior to the opening of the Male High School building. As he explains in one of numerous newspaper reports on the matter,

> The High School, when organized, was placed in my ward building, and in the very rooms in which my Grammar School had been held. . . . In everything but name it had been a high school for more than a year, and was so spoken of by a prominent member of the Board. Excepting French, there was no new branch of study introduced. It was emphatically my own school, and, until the expiration of the session, there was no one ever hinted that I was not, in name as well as in fact, the Principal. It was only after the year's work was done that I was informed that I was not so.[28]

The controversy here is as much about what a high school *is* as it is about who runs it. Harney is contesting the definition of the high school by identifying that the courses he had taught in his school were the same as those of the newly established high school, making his own school a high school "in everything but name." He asserts his own claims, therefore, as the incumbent principal of Male High School when it opened officially in 1856. But the board disagreed. It was William F. Beach who was appointed principal that July, immediately preceding the opening of the Male High School. According to news reports, Mr. Harney was offered the position of professor of languages, but he took this offer as a slight, given that he already understood himself to function as the principal of that school.

The confusion here is telling, as it illustrates how unfamiliar and unstable the idea of a "high school" was. A fundamentally relative term, was a high school something other than the "higher branches" of study, wherever they were taught? Or was it a particular institutional type and site? If it had the institutional coherence suggested by its formal establishment in 1856, what was the relationship of the high school to the existing idea of the college or "academical department," with which it was identified? What was its relationship to the ward schools? The controversy over Harney's appointment highlights these important questions.[29]

For his part, president of the board of trustees George W. Anderson argued that Harney was never principal of Male High School, because that position did not exist. He explained in another newspaper editorial: "Mr. Harney never occupied in the Collegiate Department of the schools the place to which Mr. W. F. Beech [sic] has been elected, viz. Principal of the Male High School. That position has just been conferred; it was never before conferred." In short, for Anderson the position of principal of Male High School was attached to the Collegiate Department specifically separate and distinct from the existing schools. While clearly differentiated from the lower schools though, it was largely or entirely undistinguished from a college. Anderson goes on to describe the relationship of the high school to a college as merely a matter of internal improvement: as soon as it was found that the school was "making good progress, and awakening a profound interest for its future success among our citizens," the board would take "initiative steps to assimilate it as rapid as it is found advisable to all the characteristics of a well and thoroughly organized College, having in view the bestowal of Diplomas."[30] In short, to Anderson the standards and goals of this high school were distinct from those of the ward schools, though largely indistinct from a college.

But while the difference between such a high school and a ward school seems well-defined enough to Anderson, it was clearly not obvious to Harney and others what this "high school" was all about. Hence, what is at issue here is the as-yet slippery definition of high school—a term Harney asserted applied to his ward school "in everything but name"—and its relations both to the common school system of the city and simultaneously to a more aspirational idea of college, "having in view the bestowal of Diplomas." The great deal of ink expended in the course of this conflict reveals the active negotiation of these key terms and the educational ideals they represented as the public high school shifted the very foundations of higher education in Louisville and beyond.

The appointment of a principal for Female High School was also complicated, as that school went through three different appointments in just over six months. The first principal elected for the position in April, J. C. Spenser, had declined it by August to "occupy a more lucrative and responsible station" in New York. Another candidate, Prof. William Kinne, who was corresponding with the board from a position out east, was elected in September. However, the minutes from the board meeting on October 20, 1856, report a letter sent by Kinne to the principal of Male High School "suggesting political difficulties, which might arise, should he take charge of the Female High School." The board resolved to revoke their offer, "stating that the Board have no use for his services and that the Public Schools of Louisville have nothing to do with politics." Professor E. A. Holyoke was elected principal in October.[31]

Kinne's "politics" cannot be discerned from the board minutes, but according to the *Daily Courier*, "He is conscientious of slavery, and does not wish to emigrate to a State where his politics would not suit." Commending Mr. Kinne for his "honesty," the newspaper goes on to remark that "it would be well if some other school masters had remained at home in Connecticut," such as the editor of the *Louisville Journal*, who "came from the State of wooden nutmegs and yet preaches his abolitionism." In an otherwise unrelated event that year, a Mr. Brady, principal of a public school in Louisville, was tarred and feathered by the school committee for writing a report to the Oxford, Ohio, *Citizen* critiquing a slave auction held on Christmas Day in Louisville. He was subsequently "compelled" to resign his position and leave the city.[32] As this demonstrates, politics were certainly not kept out of the schools, despite school leaders' professed intention to do so.

At the same time, Female High School, significantly, did not elicit the same debates about its status as Male High School. Instead, its controversies reflected the larger political climate and concerns circulating also in the ward schools, and, though posited as parallel and even equivalent to Male, Female was itself never considered a college. Thus, while school leaders asserted that "in our city, at least, the importance of female education is fully realized" and "girls are there given equal advantages with the boys, and fully qualify themselves to adorn any sphere of life, whether it be of the light graces of cultivated literature, or in that more solid learning which fits them to battle with adversity or to reason away unfounded and pernicious prejudices," there is room for doubt.

The dubious equality is evidenced not only to the differential naming of these ostensibly equivalent institutions, but to material differences in their appropriations and operations. For example, the (male) principal of each school was paid the same salary (twelve hundred dollars in the first year), but instead of "faculty," Female High School typically had "teachers," and those teachers were never paid salaries at the level of the faculty at Male. The cost per pupil at Female in 1861, for example, was $51.32 (with 94 students), compared to $69.19 at Male (with 114 students). The students were not taught Greek, the most collegiate of subjects, and received diplomas rather than degrees. The school was also allocated less funding than Male, and was perpetually housed in inadequate facilities throughout much of the century.[33]

The fact of the matter is that the status of Female High School was, from the beginning, defined by its audience—that what was "high" for women was not the same as "high" for men. In Louisville and elsewhere where gender-segregated high schools existed, the women's high school remained *a* high school, while the men's high school was called *the* high school and often offered a more advanced course of study and degrees.

This pattern persisted in other cities as well. All-male schools such as Baltimore's Central High School (later Baltimore City College) merged with or became colleges, while others, like Philadelphia's Central High School, remained marked as high schools but conferred bachelor's degrees (a privilege that school retains to this day). In each case, the corollary women's high schools in these cities remained high schools, neither obtaining charters to convert to colleges nor granting academic degrees. This was by design. In Baltimore, school leaders went so far as to assure citizens that, by confining to the English branches of study, the female high schools would *not* be equivalent to the men's, which was unequivocally "the highest school of our system." In Philadelphia, by a similar turn, Central High School, for men, conferred bachelor's degrees, while young women up until 1860 had only a normal school, the purpose of which was expressly "not to give an extended course of instruction to all the pupils of the Female Grammar Schools" but only to train teachers for the public schools. In New York, the Free Academy for boys was converted to a City College in 1866, while still no high school for women existed.[34]

In this way, the assertion of Male High School as a college should be acknowledged as necessarily exclusionary and political, not merely as reflecting their differential curricular aspirations or achievements. That these "equivalent" institutions were distinguished in their naming and the allotment of resources based on the gender of their student body reveals the designation of "college" status to be a highly problematic criterion for those interested in representing an equitable history of higher learning in the United States.

At the same time, in a climate of skepticism about women's higher education, Female's status as a "high school" (*not* a college) and the provision of teachers that came to attach particularly to women's high schools served as a political advantage for the students as well, offering access to higher learning and rhetorical opportunities that may not have been available to many of them under the auspices of a "college." The politics surrounding women's higher education varied by region, but were everywhere limiting. In the South, where women who could attend school into the higher branches were of such wealth and pedigree that their education was understood as a cultural attainment and not a threat to the sex-segregated workforce, women's colleges were common. Some of these schools offered a full collegiate course of study, including Latin and Greek. In the Northeast, by contrast, women students typically could access two forms of higher learning: an "ornamental" education featuring arts and music alongside academic studies, and teacher training, which was offered with a distinctly "practical" bent that did not often include classical subjects, rhetorical instruction, and opportunities for public performance. But, as Christie Anne Farnham explains, the *combination* of cultural training and professional opportunity was rare for women in college. In this vein, historian Karen Graves suggests that high school students in St. Louis were afforded greater opportunities to develop as "female scholars" prior to the development of a differentiated curriculum that aligned education more directly with gendered professional goals and posited educated women as a threat to a sex-segregated labor market.[35]

Students in early high schools like Female actually benefitted from the uncertain status of the high school, where they could learn advanced academic subjects and also become teachers. Thus, the high schools' confounding connection to other educational sites—the common school, normal school, and college—was not only an issue of naming, but instead of policy and practice as well, inviting us to consider not only what a college designation may afford, but also what it has constrained historically. As we will see, the history of something like a "college composition" course becomes complex and contested in these institutions that trouble the commonly accepted distinction between high schools, normal schools, and colleges in the United States.

CHAPTER 2

A Polished, Practical, or Profound Education: Collegiate Curricula in the First Ten Years

> The curriculum of studies pursued, embraces whatever is requisite to a polished, a practical, or a profound education—belles-lettres, languages, dead and modern, mathematics, physical science. All these branches are taught thoroughly, and by able and accomplished instructors. They are, together with our equally invaluable common schools, the chief ornament of our city
>
> —*Superintendent George W. Anderson, 1861*

Given their relation to both common school principles and collegiate traditions, the high schools were actively engaged in the debate about how best to educate the nation in the higher branches: a polished, a practical, or a profound education. What is the purpose of higher learning? To prepare students for college or for life? How did that purpose differ for men and for women?

Since preparing students for college meant something quite particular at midcentury—the study of Latin and Greek—the emergence of this popular distinction between preparing for college or life was itself an implicit critique of the "narrow erudition" of the classical curriculum, which was not seen as providing students with the knowledge and skills needed for business and life. While the famous Yale Report of 1828 and subsequent supporters had staunchly defended the classical curriculum as the best possible way to develop mental discipline in students, the need to articulate such a defense is telling: the classical curriculum was in decline.

The alternative to the classical curriculum was the English curriculum, popular at many academies, which was comprised of Latin, mathematics, rhetoric and composition, science, history, and modern languages. This approach substituted courses like English grammar and modern languages for Latin and Greek to develop mental discipline while teaching subjects considered closer to the lives of everyday Americans. Deemed more modern and practical, the new curriculum promised to improve prospects for white-collar employment while cultivating character.[1]

And yet, many schools continued to offer a classical curriculum because that was considered, by tradition and reputation, the cultural knowledge of most worth. If the public school systems intended to extend their offerings into the "higher branches" of learning—indeed, the *highest* branches, which they did—that meant offering the classical collegiate subjects. Thus, as the form of general education was shifting from a classical curriculum to the more modern English curriculum, many large, urban high schools offered both, trading on the prestige of the collegiate tradition even while they were in the process of altering it. And many colleges followed the same model. Indeed, as Charles Eliot explained in 1869, "The experiment of conducting parallel classical and scientific courses in one and the same institution is by no means a new one. It is merely being tried afresh on a large scale and under new conditions in this country, after having failed in Europe." Thus, high schools were in line with changes that were occurring across higher schooling.[2]

Louisville high schools provide an excellent case study in the local negotiations of these curricular transformations. Growing out of and contributing teachers to the common schools that had been established under public control for several decades, the institutions that would become the Louisville high schools were also intricately and significantly connected to the work of the developing university. The promise of Louisville's school superintendent George W. Anderson that high schools pursue "whatever is requisite to a polished, a practical, or a profound education—belles-lettres, languages, dead and modern, mathematics, physical science"—reflected this split identity: institutions on the border of higher and lower education, balancing public and private gains, and tradition and reform.[3] Because of this split identity, both rationales for and critiques of the schools responded to a complex of ideas about the means and ends of higher learning—and of rhetoric and writing instruction.

Within both the classical and English curricula of the high schools, the role of rhetoric and writing was central from an early date. While colleges of the time have been criticized for focusing exclusively on declamation and recitations, consummately practical high schools like Louisville's emphasized regular practice in original composition and delivery on a range of subjects, seemingly regardless of the course of study students took. Thus, high schools accommodated multiple student purposes. The resulting high school curriculum—particularly the teaching of writing—reflects the value of practicality in higher learning, especially in relation to preparing people for civic participation.[4]

In this chapter, I trace the role and status of rhetoric and composition instruction at Male High School and Female High School from 1856 through the 1860s to more closely examine how such schools complicate and contribute to our disciplinary histories. Using assigned textbooks for each school and sample student essays shared at commencement exercises in 1860, I analyze the schools' work in relation to nominally college-level curricula of the time and to the scholarship on rhetoric and composition within our field, attending to the ways the high schools aligned themselves with traditional higher learning to build credibility and support in their community, as well as how they represented an alternative to that tradition. I begin here with an examination of Male High School, which was overtly collegiate, before discussing Female High School, the status of which was limited by gendered strictures and complicated by its strong teacher-training mandate, though it nonetheless leveraged its identification as a high school to provide advanced rhetorical and professional opportunities not available at most women's colleges.

Rhetoric and Writing at Male High School: A Collegiate Curriculum

The promise of a practical liberal education for the city's youth secured support for Louisville high schools. But, for all of the appeals to the practicality and democratic ethos of the high school, Male High School opened in 1856 not with a reformed, modern English curriculum, but with the most narrow and elite curriculum available: instruction only in ancient and modern languages and mathematics. Mandeville Thum of the Committee of Examination and Control only lamented the "imperfect system of collegiate education as yet afforded" in the Academical Department in 1857 because the professorship of Rhetoric and English Literature was vacant at that time. The next year, Professor Holyoke, principal of Female High School, was engaged to provide "temporary aid" in teaching boys elocution, composition, and belles lettres, or literature, thus rounding off the school's provision of a collegiate curriculum.[5]

William N. McDonald, who held a master's from the University of Virginia, was hired as the first professor of Rhetoric and English Literature at Male by the following year. Little evidence survives of what McDonald taught in his rhetoric and English literature courses, but we do have a list of the textbooks he used for these courses. Though offering only an imperfect proxy for what was actually taught and learned in any school, text adoptions go far towards establishing a school's self-conception and conception of its students' needs and goals. The course textbooks selected for that year reflect a new emphasis on rhetoric and elocution, primarily in the first years of study.

Students used George Payne Quackenbos's *Advanced Course of Composition and Rhetoric* and Epes Sargent's *Standard Speaker* in the first year, along with assigned declamations in the first two years. These are examples of what Jean Ferguson Carr, Stephen L. Carr, and Lucille Schultz call expository textbooks, which are explicitly instructional. Such texts use "typographical features to mark the various uses, or relative importance, of different passages, usually printing illustrative examples in small type and rules and definitions in large type or boldface. They often number paragraphs or sections for easy identification and cross reference, include 'exercises' keyed to the exposition of various principles, and may have 'lessons' instead of 'chapters.'" With their emphasis on organizing and conveying information to the learner, these are the kind of nineteenth-century textbooks that have been critiqued by subsequent commentators for their lack of rhetorical theory.[6]

Quackenbos's *Advanced Course of Composition and Rhetoric*—which was Male's first rhetoric textbook and the text most commonly used at both Male and Female in their first ten years, as well as the most popular rhetoric text elsewhere in the United States in its time—is a noted example of this type of expository textbook, widely criticized by subsequent historians of rhetoric. Robert Connors critiques Quackenbos's *Advance Course* as reflecting "a sort of pedagogical vacuum" precipitated by the boom of college building. Lucille Schultz similarly notes that Quackenbos was "considerably less innovative and more rule-bound" than the rhetoric books she analyzes from the lower schools.[7] But for all of the complaints about the undertheorized and derivative nature of such rhetorics, it is also true that they were the norm among college classes at this time, as both Connors and Schultz acknowledge. The modifications to rhetorical theory in Quackenbos (who liberally redacted Campbell and Blair) were intended to make rhetorical principles accessible to an expanding and diversifying student audience in the higher branches. Thus, the use of Quackenbos aligns the high schools' curricula with common practice in colleges, at a time when both were expanding rapidly.

Other books in use at Male further blur the distinction between high school and college courses. For example, in the upper two years of study, students used Robert Gordon Latham's *Handbook of English Language*, which is half history and analysis of the English language and half exhaustive catalogue of grammar, syntax, and orthography rules, marketed "for the use of students of the universities and the higher classes of schools." As Carr, Carr, and Schultz posit, this broad sense of audience (comprised of both high school and college) was not unusual: "Early in the century, many rhetorics advertised themselves without discriminating among use at schools, academies, or colleges or for private study."[8] This is due to the fact that—as Louisville high schools demonstrate—the differences between these institutions were not clear.[9]

The rhetorical curriculum in the upper years of the high school became even more traditionally collegiate in the coming years, with students studying Campbell's *Rhetoric* and Kame's *Elements of Criticism* in their junior year, and Whately's *Rhetoric* and *Logic* in their senior year in 1859. Though not as popular as the work of Hugh Blair, these texts were among the most popular rhetoric treatises in colleges across most of the century. According to Sharon Crowley, Campbell's *Philosophy of Rhetoric* was "apparently deemed appropriate for more advanced students" and "was in use at many American colleges throughout the second quarter of the nineteenth century, and it enjoyed some popularity as late as the 1880s." Richard Whately's *Elements of Rhetoric* was similarly popular, having been "included in rhetoric curricula almost immediately upon its American publication in 1832, and it dominated those curricula throughout the 1850s and 1860s, remaining in use in some schools until about 1900."[10] Thus, Male was again solidly in line with its collegiate peers in its adoption of texts in rhetoric and composition.

Male High School initially offered this traditional, uniform collegiate course of study—featuring Latin, Greek, mathematics, and rhetoric—until 1860. In what is perhaps an interesting twist of irony, the school then changed its curriculum to include differentiated courses of study beyond this traditional collegiate course—the very same year that it was officially chartered as a college. That is, the high school moved away from the most traditional version of the college curriculum the year it actually became a college. At that time, the course options were expanded to three: students now chose between the original four-year classical course, a four-year English and scientific course that replaced the ancient languages and literatures with courses in advanced mathematics and sciences, and a partial diploma course for those who could attend the school for only two years. Completion of the classical course resulted in a bachelor of arts degree, the English/scientific course in a bachelor of science degree, and the partial or business course in a certificate of graduation. With only small alterations, this arrangement persisted for the next several years, through the war.

During this time, "Rhetoric (with exercises)" was taught with the aid of Coppee or Newman. Both texts were popular in Eastern colleges during the 1860s. According to Crowley, Coppee's *Elements of Rhetoric* was in use even to the end of the century, and "draws on a mixed rhetorical and logical heritage." The other text used, Samuel Newman's *A Practical System of Rhetoric*, is acknowledged as the first popular rhetoric textbook authored by an American and one that Robert Connors frames as a more "thought-oriented" college treatise than other question-and-answer based textbooks of the time.[11]

Rhetoric and composition was a regular feature of all of the courses of study, with each program (whether classical, English, or partial) featuring composition, rhetoric, and/or declamation each year, with little variation in emphasis or rigor besides the necessary abbreviation of instruction in the two-year partial course. That is, composition was integrated throughout all years of study.

The freshman course of study in rhetoric and composition was admittedly simplistic and surface-oriented, as reflected in the examination questions. The questions emphasize definitions and memory, with little opportunity for application or analysis. Students were asked to identify or define different parts of language, to describe (rather than compose) sentences, and to demonstrate knowledge of the history of the English language, including of how many words it consists (fig. 2.1).

But the complexity of textbooks and occasions for practice became more advanced as students proceeded through their four years of instruction. As Principal Grant avers,

> It will be observed that the Curriculum of study, in each course, is very extended for the time devoted to it. No one at all acquainted with the practical working of the school will suppose that the system of instruction is for this reason superficial. Whatever a student is required to learn *at all*, he is required to *learn thoroughly*. The less important parts of the various subjects are often supplied by carefully digested lectures from the various Professors, abstracts of which are written out by the pupils for the inspection of the lecturer. By this means no superficial habits are acquired, and the pupil receives the benefit of a more extended course of study, than could be otherwise accomplished in the same length of time.[12]

Students practiced their writing and speaking skills, among other ways, in widely celebrated public examinations and commencement ceremonies, attended by the public. Transcending the work of simple assessment, the public examinations were widely attended and reported on in the local newspapers, evidencing a community role for the high schools and an opportunity for meaningful rhetorical engagement for the students. Though most student writing from the school has been lost to history, two addresses delivered by students at the 1860 commencements are among the few extant examples of this work, as those speeches were preserved in the annual school board report of that year.[13] Across these two speeches, we can observe the traces of some of these students' literary and rhetorical training, and gain a glimpse into the personal histories of Male High School students in the early years of the school.

Francis A. Seymour, Address

The first speech, an untitled piece by student Francis A. Seymour, represents a standard epideictic oration that explores the notions of pleasure and pain—and painful pleasure—in the experience of his four years'

10

FRESHMAN CLASS.

RHETORIC AND COMPOSITION.—Begun.

1. Explain the meaning of *clause*, *phrase*, and *sentence*.
2. Give the rules for the use of capital letters.
3. What are synonymes and their use in language? Give examples.
4. What is the natural order of an English sentence?
5. Mention various ways for the transposition or inversion of a sentence without changing its meaning.
6. What do you mean by purity? and how may it be violated?
7. Define propriety and precision.
8. Name the four essential properties of a perfect sentence, and explain what is meant by each.
9. What are figures in language? name the various kinds.
10. Define *euphemism*, *autonomasia*, *tautology*, and *pleonasm*, and give an example of each.
11. Define *metaphor*, *prosopopœia*, *antithesis*, and *simile*.
12. Of how many words does the English language consist? What part are Anglo-Saxon? and what is the character of the Saxon element of our language?

FRESHMAN CLASS A & B.—First Day.

ALGEBRA.

1. Divide $x^4+x^2y^2+y^4$ by x^2+xy+y^2.
2. Divide $\frac{x^5+y^5}{x+y}$ by $\frac{x^4-x^3y+x^2y^2-xy^3+y^4}{x^2-y^2}$
3. Given $\frac{ax+b}{c}+\frac{bx-c}{a}=\frac{dx+f}{b}$, to find x.
4. What fraction is that to the numerator of which if 4 be added, the fraction will be $\frac{1}{3}$; but if 6 be added to the denominator its value is $\frac{1}{5}$?
5. Change $\frac{9+2\sqrt{(10)}}{9-2\sqrt{(10)}}$ into a fraction having a rational denominator.
6. Find the value of x in the equation $\frac{x-\sqrt{(x+1)}}{x+\sqrt{(x+1)}}=\frac{5}{11}$
7. Find x and y in the equations $\left\{\begin{matrix} x^2+2xy+y^2+2x=120-2y \\ xy-y^2=8 \end{matrix}\right\}$

Fig. 2.1. Freshman examination questions in rhetoric and composition for students of Male High School, printed in the *Annual Report* of 1860. COURTESY OF JEFFERSON COUNTY PUBLIC SCHOOLS.

school attendance. The personal topic allows Seymour to draw on his own experience in his composition, while the use of oxymoron allows him to celebrate the varied emotions attendant to this experience, if rather euphemistically. Across the speech, Seymour demonstrates an understanding of his rhetorical context, the public and celebratory nature of which occasions the praise and celebration of the school's work.

In its hyperbolic praise, this speech closely echoes the language and values of the school's leaders: a discourse that was established in advocacy efforts before the schools' founding and continued to reverberate in public ceremonies such as this throughout much of the century.[14] Drawing on the discourse of democratic necessity in support of higher learning, in particular, Seymour takes pains to involve the community in the students' sense of achievement, asserting that,

> While contemplating . . . the benefits received, we would not forget the source from which they have been derived; but with gratitude would remember that to *you*, the *generous public*, citizens of *Louisville*, we trace their happy origin. You have established in connection with your excellent common school system, higher departments, so that the youthful mind may be fed, not only with such food as is absolutely necessary for the support of the intellectual constitution, but also with those nutritious dainties and delicacies which add so much to the comfort and enjoyment of life.

Providing both what is "absolutely necessary" and the "nutritious dainties and delicacies" of life, the school is positioned as striking that ever-crucial balance between practicality and cultural development for the city's young people. And it is the community that they have to thank for this opportunity. In recognizing this point, Seymour effectively shores up the community's support for the schools, a shrewd move and one that continued to be necessary for most public high schools throughout the century.

In addition to providing youth with such opportunities, Seymour recognizes also a "higher motive" for public support of the schools that "cannot prove otherwise than beneficial" to the community itself: "Next to the *Bible*, and religious influence, our *common-schools* do MORE for the preservation of *law* and *order*, and the elevation of society, than any thing else." In other words, schools preserve civilization itself. It is on this note that Seymour closes, comparing the work of the schools to the intellectual work of the ancient Athenians and predicting that "doubtless, ere long, *America* will be the GREECE of modern times."[15]

Thus, Seymour uses his rhetorical opportunity to further marshal support for his newly established school and the broader school system of which it was part. He draws on the discourse of democratic necessity and community pride established by the school administration and alerts audience members to challenges and opportunities in the prospects of this new school. In these moves, Seymour's speech reveals, if nothing else, how immersed students would have been in the discourse of school reformers, aware of their tenuous privilege as students of this free high school. Thus, even if he writes in abstract terms, Seymour is clearly writing about something he knows well, applying his rhetorical lessons to a subject of meaning and significance to him and his audience alike.

In concert with this speech, Seymour's biography helps us to understand some of how a high school education was experienced and received in his day. Seymour, who was one of only four graduates of Male High School in 1860, was the son of a river pilot from England. According to census records in 1850, Seymour's family was living at that time in an expensive home (worth ten thousand dollars) in the Seventh Ward of the city, near a boatman, tobacconist, school teacher, and others, most with some three to six thousand dollars in real estate, so they were slightly more wealthy than their neighbors at the time. Their relative privilege likely played a role in Seymour's ability to attend and, also quite significantly, to complete a full high school course. And the high school was not the end of Seymour's own educational development either. Following this graduation speech, Seymour went to medical school at both the Kentucky School of Medicine and University of Louisville, served as a surgeon in the Union forces during the Civil War, and would go on to become professor of physiology in the University of Louisville's medical department, returning as a celebrated community member to deliver the alumni address at the high school's graduation in 1869. Seymour began his own medical practice in 1880 and eventually moved to California to practice, becoming president of the Los Angeles County Medical Association in 1885. In short, he enjoyed a long and celebrated career, which was presaged by his attendance and public recognition at Male High School, just as the school's leaders and supporters had hoped, and as his own speech had promised.[16]

Robert A. Holland, "Peculiar Motives to Intellectual Exertion in America"

If Seymour's speech exemplified the epideictic genre, reminiscent of the discourse of schoolmen in his own school system and across the country, the speech of his classmate Robert A. Holland grew from a different tradition, also circulating in his high school. Holland's speech reflected training in a more distinctly literary and oratorical vein, quoting frequently from celebrated authors and modeled not on the epideictic speeches of schoolmen but on the forensic speeches of famous historical orators. The speech telegraphs much of its intent to its audience through its title, which is repeated also in the speech's opening lines: "*peculiar motives to intellectual exertion in America*." The speaker must have assumed this title to be a shared cultural referent, initiating as it does in miniature a version of Edward Everett's oft-anthologized 1824 oration to the Society of Phi Beta Kappa on the same topic.

Almost point for point, Holland moves through his own version of Everett's speech, addressing each "incentive" in turn, discussing the role of politics in supporting or thwarting the development of literature and the particular role of our own "vast extent" of territory, shared language, and institutions in advancing knowledge in the United States. At each turn, he succinctly captures the analytical and patriotic tone of Everett's argument. He adds to this the self-referential significance of his own context, celebratory of his and his classmates' own intellectual exertions.[17]

But it is with his final "incentive to intellectual exertion" that Holland surprises his audience, diverging from Everett's established model to discuss a motive of his own: "the extreme loveliness of American women." "What greater motive to exertion need the young men of America," he asks, "than the smiles and good wishes of the daughters of this Republic." He closes with a lengthy excerpt from Thomas Campbell's "The Pleasures of Hope," ending in the famous couplet: "The world was sad, the garden wild,/ And man the hermit sighed, 'til woman smiled." A poem very frequently included in anthologies and language textbooks across the first half of the century, the lines are here juxtaposed comedically with the heretofore serious academic topic from a reputable model.[18] Thus, we see the stamp of Holland himself as an author and orator come through in the juxtaposition of literary referents and themes to comedic effect.

Though Holland, like so many of his classmates, never graduated from Male, his training there did not go unused. Instead, he went on to enjoy a "deserved and enviable reputation as an orator" in his capacity as reverend of the Methodist Episcopal Church. A notice in anticipation of one of his lectures just six short years after his speech characterizes him as "a natural orator with powers of description that are truly wonderful, and there is a fascination of manner and utterance which never fails to captivate his hearers." The author of the notice doesn't fail to mention, too, that the speaker is "one of our high school boys, of whom we are justly proud." The next year, following a lecture at the state capitol, a correspondent averred: "We know of no equal to him of his age, and of but very few of any age who equal him as a popular speaker."[19]

A profile of the reverend written a decade later describes his rather remarkable trajectory following that speech of 1860. At the time of the profile, Holland was twenty-seven years old, which means that he would have been sixteen years old for the 1860 Male High School address. Just a year later, at age seventeen,

> He preached his first sermon in this city . . . , taking the hearts of his hearers completely by storm. The beginning to his ministerial career [excited hopes which] have ripened into full fruition beneath the accomplishment of his mature manhood. Nor Bascom, nor Mills, nor Payne, nor Spurgeon, entered the pulpit with a [better chance of] distinction and success.

From this notice, we can presume that Holland did not graduate because he went into the ministry at this early age. After a time in the Confederate army and several years at the Methodist Church, he was making headlines again for his decision to move to Baltimore as part of an Episcopalian church, which spurred "much newspaper gossip, both religious and secular," in his city and beyond. Having moved to take the position, his propensity for writing continued to serve him well throughout his professional life.[20]

The son of a wealthy and respected doctor from Virginia, Holland had been well positioned for a successful life as a member of the clergy. During his years in school, his family (with four thousand dollars in real estate and six thousand dollars in personal estate holdings) lived in the

Fourth Ward near a banker, barber, clerk, coal merchant, and others, each of whom had considerable personal wealth and real estate. Holland's family had one female domestic worker from Ireland in 1860, another indicator of their status. Given his family's position in the community, Holland was poised for academic and professional success, which was further assured by his attendance at the new Male High School.[21]

These two students—Seymour and Holland—though representing only a very small sample of student writing and experience, prove to be somewhat representative of Male High School students in the early years. First, they are representative in their successful career trajectories, both pursuing professions traditionally linked with a college education—in medicine and the church. This speaks to the relative privilege of those who could afford to attend high school as well as the increasing exchange value of a high school education (if not yet a diploma or degree) as a credential, which persisted for a time. The graduation rate between them (at just 50 percent) is even fairly representative, with very few of even the most successful students persisting to graduation.[22] And, of course, the variety of their rhetorical productions is also representative, usefully demonstrating the flexibility of the rhetorical and writing instruction at the school. Though we are at a loss for not having additional samples of student writing, these specimens—along with the catalogue of textbooks used to contextualize their development—provide valuable insights into the practice of collegiate writing at the "university of public schools."

Between the regular practice of composition and elocution and the broader rhetorical instruction it provided, this "college" complicates our sense of firsts for the discipline, featuring as it does not only an introductory writing course but also ongoing instruction and practice in rhetoric and composition throughout the various courses of study. Clearly, these high schools represent a long tradition of rhetoric and composition instruction.

To the extent that we recognize this instructional tradition, the common narrative of composition's history has been that the high schools, which had long been teaching composition, were now shirking their duties, bringing the course reluctantly into the higher branches. But high schools like Male that conceived of themselves and functioned as colleges suggest an alternative reading that has thus far been largely overlooked. Here, this long tradition of composition instruction is posited as an alternative collegiate tradition within higher learning—one that has long valued writing instruction as part of the English curriculum and not focused exclusively on the classics. From this perspective, in beginning to teach writing, colleges were not innovators addressing the failure of high schools but instead were belated adopters of English writing instruction as they shifted their own curriculum from the more traditional classical curriculum to the modern English courses by the end of the century. From the records of schools like Louisville's Male High School, we know that these advanced high schools have a long tradition of teaching collegiate writing and rhetoric to their students. And those opportunities also attended Female High School in Louisville, challenging our sense of trends and firsts in the history of women's higher schooling as well.

Rhetoric and Writing at Female High School: Academic and Professional Training

Though not designated a "college," Female High School also evidences exciting developments in advanced composition and rhetorical practice. In contrast to Male's delayed adoption, Female always featured rhetoric and writing as central to its work, offered both in discrete courses and as an integrated practice across the curriculum. Thus, the provision of writing and rhetoric instruction was conceived as a central criterion for higher learning in both of these schools early on.

At Female, rather than separate courses and degrees drawing from the classical and English curricula, one uniform course study in line with an English curriculum was offered through roughly the first decade of operation, with only moderate room for elective studies introduced thereafter. In this uniform course, students studied a curriculum comparable to many women's colleges of the time, featuring Latin, French, mathematics (algebra and geometry), sciences, history, and rhetoric and composition. Technically, the school did not offer a full four-year course of study at first, but instead only a three-year course along with a preparatory year. But already in the intermediate, or preparatory, department in 1860 students were studying some of the same books used in colleges, alongside others of a more distinctly secondary or preparatory nature. For example, their geography textbook was advertised for "advanced classes, and is well adapted to the use of Colleges, Academies, Seminaries, and High

Schools." Similarly, in English, they studied George P. Quackenbos's *Advanced Course of Rhetoric*, a textbook used at Male and popular in colleges across the country—even if it is also criticized by modern scholars of rhetoric and composition as being a "less theorized" nineteenth-century rhetorical tradition, as discussed earlier.

Quackenbos's text is further notable here for having been characterized by Nan Johnson as having "persistently defined the rhetorician as male" and "discussed the ethics and epistemology of rhetoric with the male as the universal prototype."[23] In using this text, Female implicitly challenged the notion of rhetoric as the sole province of men, inviting women students to see themselves reflected even in these overtly gendered constructions of the rhetor. Students used this textbook in this preparatory year and again in their second year of study.[24]

In their first and senior years, Female students studied Greene's *Analysis of English*, which focused on sentence building and analysis of full sentences and is identified as the "progenitor of the modern idea of discipline through grammar and of language books." In other words, grammar in texts like Green's promised to replace ancient languages in the tradition of fostering "mental discipline," which was a concept key to nineteenth-century colleges.[25] The use of Green's text is thus complicated to unpack, as its status is wrapped up with the collegiate tradition of mental discipline as well as the history of grammar instruction and language in the lower schools. While Green's text is discussed by the turn of the century as foundational to the development of grammar instruction in the lower schools, in its own time it was also in use at schools like Michigan's Hillsdale College that embraced the use of English grammar for developing mental discipline. The various uses of this text speak again not only to the "low standards" of colleges but also to the frequent overlap between these types of schools, their texts, and their curricula as their form and function were being worked out.

In addition to lessons from these texts, students in all grades also had weekly in-class exercises in composition throughout this time, and wrote essays at home every three weeks. Principal E. A. Holyoke, also professor of Rhetoric and English Literature, described the language instruction as entailing "constant practice in impromptu compositions" and "the simpler principles of rhetoric." The impromptu compositions, in particular, came to be a hallmark of the school and a feature of the annual commencement ceremonies, at which students composed and read them.

In a time when even women at progressive colleges (like Oberlin) were barred from reading their essays at graduation, it is notable that high school students in places like Louisville were being trained in rhetoric and elocution, reciting their own original compositions at graduation in front of mixed-gender public audiences from their first commencement ceremonies in 1858.[26] Consequently, some of the opportunities at the women's high school even transcended those of college.

The practice of extemporaneous composition, particularly during graduation exercises, was a celebrated element of the school's curriculum, mentioned in newspaper reports and highlighted in the annual school board reports. As in the case of Male High School, a selection of these compositions is preserved in the annual report of 1860 (labeled "essays" rather than "addresses," as they had been at Male), providing a valuable glimpse into the writing of these students. While Schultz and others have argued that nineteenth-century school-based writing "was not a site for play, for resistance, or for writing about writing," these texts show students making these very moves in a school exercise, if not a classroom proper. Though we don't know the circumstances surrounding the production of these essays, the essays bear the traces of students' schooled literacies and challenge our understanding of rhetorical opportunities of both women and school students as necessarily constrained.[27]

Laura Burke, "Letters"

Laura Burke's essay, "Letters," explores a topic close to Burke's own experience, involving reflection on the act of writing itself across different types of letters and their purposes. This essay draws frequently on commonplaces to forward its argument that letters are deeply meaningful and socially situated communication. Using a range of rhetorical devices for playful and persuasive effect, Burke writes:

> We can always tell the letters of a friend. They are frank and unstudied, with a warmth of feeling glowing throughout, as it wells up from the heart and drops upon the page. The letter of a man of business, short and ceremonious, with words like quarter and half-pound papers of coffee, tea, and spice, and sentences measured as men measure calico, very much stretched, and yet too short. The Lawyers! What a pity that we should pay for what we cannot read! Stiff, formal, and sharp, like his

> scent of a fee. What a dread missive is the Doctor's, reminding us of the pestle and mortar, and giving us the chills scarcely less than one of their bills or their pills!

Across the three pages of her brief composition, Burke not only discusses the characteristics of the personal and professional letters mentioned above—from a friend, businessman, lawyer, and doctor—but also narrates the reception of letters in a range of specific contexts: an old man learning of the death of friend, a "laboring man" receiving a letter from a debt collector, a "coy little miss" spiteful that she did not receive a letter from her suitor. She punctuates each of these scenes with apostrophe, delivering sermon-like pronunciations—"Blessed be letters!"—as she narrates these scenarios.

Burke draws on the traditional authority of shared cultural experiences and universal "truths" rather than recounting any personal experiences. And yet, even in her use of a universal "we" that distances herself from the piece, Burke is notably writing not on "justice" or some other abstraction or topic far from her personal experience, as nineteenth-century school themes are often thought to do. She is writing about something she would have known well, and is also writing about writing itself, both of which demonstrate the movement identified by Schultz and others toward personal topics drawn from students' lives by the end of the century.[28]

She is also writing about a topic her textbook—Quakenbos's *Advanced Course of Composition and Rhetoric*—invited her to consider in its section on genres. In that section, Quackenbos dedicates several pages to the conventions of letter writing and directs students to compose letters for practice. Though he does not invite students to write a piece contemplating the idea of letter writing as a whole, Burke's piece echoes Quackenbos's enumeration of the varieties or principal kinds of letters, including newsletters, letters of business, and letters of friendship, among others. While demonstrating knowledge of the different discourse styles across personal and business contexts, Burke also demonstrates her knowledge of common rhetorical strategies, such as in her use of metaphor, apostrophe, and rhyme, all of which she was reading about in her school text.

We know school leaders approved of Burke's academic performance both because her essay was selected for inclusion in the school board report and because she was hired as an assistant at Female High School the year she graduated, and held the position until 1862. Born in 1844, Burke was just sixteen when she graduated and began working at Female. She most likely stopped working because of her impending marriage to Edmonds J. Howard, a wealthy shipbuilder, in 1863, though she remained involved with the school as an alumna. For example, Burke returned to the school to read from Longfellow's "Miles Standish" at the 1864 commencement ceremony.[29]

Rachel H. Gibbons, "Disunion"

By some contrast, Burke's classmate Rachel H. Gibbons took a notably different tack in her own composition, beginning her delivery on a serious and even ominous note: "Daily, hourly, simultaneously, from the four corners of our agitated country is echoed the word Disunion; and everybody, from the glib-tongued politician to the white-headed school-boy, is trying to excel everybody else in the 'length, pitch, and power' of his vociferations." In these opening lines, with the invocation of a serious political issue facing the nation on the cusp of civil war, Gibbons's essay "Disunion" would have certainly grabbed her audience's attention. Following this introduction, Gibbons even more shockingly moves from describing the potential revolution to asserting that "there are many now, not only willing but impatient to take part in the 'irrepressible conflict,' and among that many, we graduates apparent stand pre-eminent, for nowhere has the subject of disunion been discussed with so much vim, as within the walls of our dilapidated school-house." In the tense political context of antebellum Louisville, where the allegiances of citizens were famously divided even within families, Gibbons tells her audience that the women of Female High School had decided they "didn't believe in unions."[30]

From references to how the war would affect national economies and commodities such as molasses, to allusions to the War of 1812, Gibbons shows she is well versed in the stakes of the debate she is invoking. She is also impressively adept at the form of delayed revelation she is practicing, as the audience comes to realize the true meaning of "disunion" in her essay: "We have met to-night with one aim, one purpose: the union must and shall be dissolved . . . we have decided to settle the affair by *diploma*cy." The union that is breaking, in other words, is the union formed among the girls during their time at high school.[31]

From the point of this revelation onward, Gibbons cleverly maintains the tone and language of political satire while providing humorous details about her own school days:

> As I gaze for the last time on my perpendicular, polished desk, and think how often tears and drops of ink have chased each other over its surface, I can but wonder that the final split did not occur sooner than to-night. Here by the window—I always had a propensity to get near windows—have I spent some of the most weary, not-to-be-forgotten hours of my life. When the soldiers passed they would be so near that I could hear their measured tread on the street below . . . but if I moved an angle of 45 degrees, I was told to complete the triangle ACB.[32]

Gibbons uses juxtaposition to highlight both the proximity of and the divide between school life and the public world, identifying her desire for "freedom" as the cause of the separation, or "disunion." Throughout, she expertly blends political commentary with a humorous treatment of her own personal experiences at high school.

Even though she is not, ultimately, producing deliberative rhetoric, as she would seem to be doing at the outset of the piece, she is playing on her ability to do so if she chose. Gibbons herself recognizes the uniqueness of her apparent move into contemporary deliberative rhetoric in her statement that "one would have supposed, from the number and nature of our debates, that we had been translating the eloquence of modern legislative halls, instead of that which echoed from the Roman forum." In other words, she recognizes that young women were imagined to be studying ancient rhetoric, and not engaging in contemporary political debates, and that she would be beyond the bounds of her schooled discourse in doing so. By shifting her rhetoric from the deliberative to the epideictic, she diffuses the tension surrounding her display of rhetorical ability, while still demonstrating her facility with engaging the terms of contemporary politics. In particular, satire and humor provide Gibbons a way into a discussion of contemporary social issues when straight political commentary might have been beyond her reach. In using satire to describe herself and her schoolmates, she makes fun of herself, but also makes fun of "statesmen, editors, poets, stump-orators, news-boys" and the entire masculinized public world, a marker of her sense of freedom in writing for this occasion. "Cease your clamor," she tells them, dismissing them as readily as they would have dismissed her own "crisis" upon leaving school.[33]

Gibbons's essay is a near-perfect example of Schultz's "writing at the edges of school." Drawing on the work of Anne Ruggles Gere on the "extracurriculum" of adult writing, Schultz explains, "extracurricular texts that students composed, either outside of school or at the edges of school, reveal that in these peripheral spaces, students wrote in ways that went beyond textbook directives: they assumed the persona of a writer and wrote with attendant authority about their own experience of writing." Gibbons's essay is written both at and *about* the temporal edge of school—graduation. It is also deeply rooted in extracurricular discourse in its almost overwhelming number of popular culture references, alongside more traditional literary sources. Without marking her references, quotes, or allusions for her audience, Gibbons could assume her audience would be in on the joke when, for instance, she quoted from the Declaration of Independence, Shakespeare, or even from English hymn writer Isaac Watts. She draws on these different registers of discourse strategically, as is most apparent in her reference to the comic magazine *Yankee Notions*, which she pits purposefully against more literary sources: "How many eloquent things I might say, suited to the occasion, if I only possessed the pen of Shakespeare or the ink-stand of Prentice; but, classmates, in the language of the amorous swain of six years, though 'My pen is bad and my ink is pale, My love for you shall never fail.'" The "amorous swain" here referred to is a fictional young woman with very poor spelling writing to her "dere henry." The epistolary exchanges between the young woman and her beau were featured in an 1854 issue of *Yankee Notions*, and this epithet became a popular signature line for letters during the Civil War as well.[34] Thus, even as she invites her classmates to "throw our dusty books to the four winds," she brings the graduates and the audience together in their shared cultural knowledge, just as the common school system promised.

But as much as her speech relies on cultural references from a shared white middle-class culture, Gibbons is also using available means to assert agency in the determination of her and her classmates' educational futures. Her essay ends with an emphasis on the individuality and varied futures of her graduating class of nine: "Tomorrow will find us with separate hopes, separate ambitions, and rejoicing in the motto,

'E pluribus *nine*-um.'" Even in the moment of reaffirming the shared bond between graduates, Gibbons insists on the diversity of futures for all nine of the young women graduates of Female. Unfortunately, the future of Rachel Gibbons herself seems to have been cut prematurely short, as records suggest she died in 1861, just a year after this promising graduation speech. We cannot know to what uses she would have put her rhetorical training from Female High School.

Marie B. Radcliffe, "Women and Dreams"

We know more of Burke's classmate, Marie B. Radcliffe, who picked up on the note of individuality and independence in her own essay, "Women and Dreams." Radcliffe was twenty-one years old by the time she graduated from Female and wrote the essay "Women and Dreams" for her commencement, and just as Radcliffe's age blurs the line between our ideas of high school and college students, her essay most clearly challenges our assumptions about acceptable topics for young female writers and speakers in its forceful criticism of the limitations on women's minds and lives at the time.

In a clear move into the realm of deliberative rhetoric, Radcliffe argues in her essay that women should be allowed greater access to quality higher education and professional opportunities. To do so, she raises popular criticisms of women's educational potential and refutes them through appeals to logos and a shared religious ethos. Drawing on the authority of commonplace religious values, for instance, she writes: "If a woman's mind and talents were thus cultivated and developed, then we should have fewer aimless dreamers, and more active, brave, and earnest women; and if in their ranks were seen a physician, a lecturer, a writer, an artist, it cannot be unfeminine, it cannot be wrong, for God gave them their talents, and he doeth all things well." In other words, if we are to agree that God endows humans with gifts for a purpose, then extended occupational opportunities are a natural outgrowth of the intellectual development of women, and women's work should not be confined to the home and school. This is a familiar line of argument for women's rights in the nineteenth century, evident also in the notion of Republican Motherhood and related claims for women to enter the teaching profession earlier in the century. Just as extending education to women for use in the home (as mothers) enabled the argument that they were fit for the school (as teachers), so too does it enable the argument for women entering other professions. Of course, this was an implication of women's higher learning from which early reformers like Emma Willard specifically distanced themselves, and a claim that remained fraught throughout the century.[35]

If the move to extend women's occupations was not provocative enough, the models of women's achievement Radcliffe holds up—including Elizabeth Blackwell, Harriet Hosmer, and Rosa Bonheur—drive Radcliffe's progressive politics home in no uncertain terms. Blackwell was a teacher and abolitionist who in 1849 became the first woman to receive a medical degree in the United States. Her professional achievement spurred national debates about women's rights and responsibilities in the pages of magazines and newspapers. If the many references from the essay of her classmate, Rachel Gibbons, are any indicator, the women at Female were well versed in these contemporary debates, especially as they took place in the pages of popular periodicals. By invoking Blackwell, Radcliffe was evoking this whole rich cultural debate about women's sphere. And her other examples are no less striking.

"Who," Radcliffe asks, "would withhold their smile of approval" from these women and from the female authors of the day? The answer, of course, is that many did; but Radcliffe challenges her audience and asks: "Why, when a woman of genius modestly asks for the blessing of the world and a place for her name on the scroll of fame, she receives only the world's unloving frown?" She outlines the discouraging effect this public criticism has had on women of talent, using such rhetorical questions to implicitly argue for women's greater potential and challenging her audience through appeals to "common nature" to recognize the injustice of the restraints on women's work.

Work, of course, can include work in the home, but we don't get to that possibility until the last half of her essay, when she acknowledges that there are also a great many dreamers with "no brilliant genius" who "wish the fire-side their only throne, and murmured blessings their only applause." These women, too, Radcliffe goes on to say, need education to develop their minds and hearts to conduct their work and lives nobly, and to face the possibility of a change of fortune or future loneliness. Although Radcliffe knew that a majority of women would marry and focus most of their intellectual energy and attention on keeping a home, she argues that educated women can get happiness and fulfillment from their own minds that will enrich their lives at home well into old age. Those without a rich intellectual life, on the other hand, are depicted at the end of their lives "sitting by their lonely fire-sides, nursing the broken dreams that wander like ghosts through the darkened chambers of memory, muttering the soft, sweet words whose last faint echoes died long ago when faith and love expired."[36]

This conception of the value and purpose of education says much about the culture and atmosphere at Female High School. While Radcliffe's ideas may have been drawn from any number of extracurricular sources, their mobilization in the context of Female's commencement ceremony demonstrates a remarkable level of tolerance on behalf of both the school and the audience. A reporter from the *Daily Democrat* remarked that Radcliffe's reading "was the best of the evening. It had more earnest feeling, more mature thought, than the others" ("Commencement Exercises"). One of the only criticisms was from George D. Prentice, editor of the *Louisville Journal*, who praised the essay while also noting that it displayed "a maturity of thought very rare in young girls. The strong-mindedness was, indeed, an objectionable feature, emanating from so lovely a girl, whose business in life is to brighten a fireside, and not to discuss women's rights."[37] The fact that others did not voice objection to this "strong-mindedness" and that Radcliffe's essay was preserved and distributed in the school board's annual report demonstrates that such an intervention was welcomed or at least tolerated as part of the rhetorical education of Female students.

Radcliffe did go on to "brighten a fireside," marrying the year after her graduation and raising six children with Reverend Thomas D. Butler. However, she was never one to "wish the fire-side [her] only throne, and murmured blessings [her] only applause." Instead, she continued to publish frequently throughout her life, in both magazines and books, and to speak in public meetings of the Women's Christian Temperance Union and elsewhere. In his introduction to a posthumously published volume of her poems and essays in 1884, Radcliffe's husband, Reverend Thomas Butler, proudly describes Radcliffe's active public life, relating in particular one story of her well-known rhetorical prowess:

> She accompanied me to an annual meeting in the country north of Grand Rapids, where brethren and sisters spoke to me with regard to asking her to preach at the meetings. As I had to go, after the first day of meeting, to fill an engagement at Charlotte, I told them that they had my consent for her to preach,

> provided she did not speak in the open air meetings. When we met again at home the next week, I learned that she had preached four successive evenings in the public hall.

Hence, we learn that Radcliffe maintained her involvement with women's issues, her public writing and speaking, and her resistance to imposed social restrictions until she died. And these commitments took root during her time at Female. The significance of this first commencement speech is evidenced by the fact that it is referenced by Radcliffe's husband in the introduction to *Poetry and Prose by Marie Radcliffe Butler*, where Butler also playfully cites the critical report on her essay from Prentice in the *Louisville Journal*. Thus, the essay and its reception clearly mattered to Radcliffe and her family. In reading it, we witness a young woman negotiating the borders of classroom and public rhetorical spaces, using her school-based knowledge and the opportunity for public engagement provided by the commencement ceremonies to make a political intervention through her writing.[38]

These opportunities and the educational focus of the school shifted across the century, and Female's curriculum underwent changes already within its first decade of operations, following the transformation from "female scholar" to "domesticated citizen" traced by Graves in St. Louis high schools. While Female's principal Holyoke celebrated the "advancement of [Female's] course of study" in 1860, his successor, George Chase, was demonstrably anxious throughout his own annual report about the extended time and intensity of study Female required when he took over in 1863. Chase determined that "the course of study hitherto pursued is too heavy for the period allotted for its completion." The new principal explained that "Industrious girls, in numerous instances, have sustained a creditable rank in their classes at the expense of injury to health; while too large a proportion fail to pass examination, many of whom, becoming discouraged, give up their intention of completing their course of study or go to private schools." Thus, the school was deemed too rigorous for young women. As a result, the course of study was altered for the ensuing academic year, including the condensing of rhetoric to only the second year of study and addressing subjects like history and literature largely through weekly lectures.[39]

The curricular changes had much to do with the school's historic role as a normal school for the city, as women were already taking on a majority of the city's teaching posts. By 1855, there were twenty-six male teachers in the schools, compared to fifty-six female teachers. These numbers grew to thirty-five male and sixty-four female teachers in 1860. The cause of this pattern in Louisville as elsewhere was, at least in part, the low salary paid for teaching: as superintendent George H. Tingley explained, the average salary for a teacher, fifteen hundred dollars, "will not obtain the services of the very best talent, because men of ability can earn more in business, or in other professions."[40]

While few Male students went into education, all nine of the first graduates of Female became teachers after graduation, as did a great majority in the decades following. As early as 1859, Principal Holyoke had experimented with offering a formalized normal course of study, with explicit instruction about how to teach for all students. By 1863, teacher training was firmly established at Female (though it does not always appear in curriculum lists). When the separate Normal Training School was established in 1871, nearly half the graduates of Female matriculated to it. In fact, graduation from Female was a requirement for admission to the Normal School at many points in its history.[41] Thus, teacher credentialing played a clear role in the mission of the high school, although at times it fit uneasily with the school's academic mission.

While both Holyoke and Chase consistently advocated for teacher training as part of the project of Female High School, and teacher training remained part of the general academic curriculum until the establishment of a separate normal program in 1871, the location of teacher preparation in the curriculum changed, reflecting debates as to what training was needed for teachers: a thorough academic one, or a brief, practical one focused primarily on the skills of teaching. Under Holyoke, the school took the former approach: students had studied teaching in their senior year, graduating with a privileged credential for teaching in the city's schools. The senior class of the school was known as the Normal Class, and four of eleven graduates in 1863 went into teaching (as well as a great majority in the years before).

Where Principal Holyoke marked the highest class of students as the "normal" or teacher-training class, Principal Chase made the change to designate the first two years of high school, or lowest classes, as the teaching track. That is, the first two years of study would be all that was necessary for teachers, and advanced academic branches would be added in the final two years. Chase's explanation for this change reminds us of how exceptional a full high school education was at this time, far exceeding the necessary requirements to teach in the schools. He stated, "It is hardly to be expected that the majority of those who seek the benefit of the School, in order to qualify themselves for teachers, will remain for a longer period than one or two years; it, therefore, seems desirable that the studies of that period should be those of a Normal School, especially for the benefit of such pupils." Indeed, teachers in many schools of the time were as yet expected merely to have completed one grade above those they were to teach; other normal programs were explicitly identified as comprising one year of study beyond the grammar schools, which would be typically an eighth or ninth year of study, not a full high school course. The tension, as Superintendent Tingley put it in 1868, was the belief that "the ability to manage a school and skill to teach, with average scholarship, are more desirable than the highest literary attainments, without a knowledge of the practical methods to be pursued in the school-room." The school attempted to maintain this balance up through the establishment of the normal school in 1871.[42]

In light of Chase's new conception of teacher training and the curriculum, the new course of study at Female was slightly reduced, covering largely the same subjects as previously, but with higher mathematics, French, philosophy, and sciences concentrated in the higher grades in 1863–64. The study of rhetoric and composition seems to have taken the brunt of this reduction, as rhetoric becomes somewhat inexplicably attached to the study of the French language in this new course schedule, and the study of composition is removed from the regular list, included only as a note indicating that "exercises in Elocution and Composition shall be required of the pupils through the entire course of study; and on Wednesday of each week, lectures on topics connected with History, Literature, or Science, may be delivered by the Principal, Professors, or persons invited by them."[43] Extracting composition from the rest of the curriculum in this way would become a regular feature in many of the Male and Female course catalogues in ensuing years, indicating both an integrated approach to writing instruction across subject areas and a potential devaluation of the systematic study of these areas as subjects in their own right, especially as the schools emulated the traditional college curriculum.

Himself a professor of Latin and Mental and Moral Science, it is perhaps unsurprising that Female's principal Chase would value the study of rhetoric and composition less than his predecessor, who had served as instructor of English literature and rhetoric in addition to the principalship. Also unsurprising is that the study of Latin retained a central position across all four years in the new curriculum. Despite opposition across the realms of higher learning, Chase urged that it was "indispensible" for the study of sciences, mathematics, logic, rhetoric, and, especially, English, as a form of mental discipline. He particularly argued for the value of Latin to the learning of those subjects that it most directly displaced, asserting that "a thorough knowledge of this language is incalculably valuable to the teacher" and "greatly facilitates progress in English studies." Quoting a report from the Boston schools, he argued that "English Grammar, for instance, becomes a light task after the Latin Grammar is mastered." In what he sees as a synthesis of subjects under the umbrella of mental discipline, it is the intention of the principal that, through the curricular changes, the school's motto, *Esse quam videri*—to be, rather than to seem—"shall truly indicate [the school's] character as one where thorough mental discipline and practical education, rather than showy accomplishments, may be secured."[44]

Latin retained its place in the curriculum at Female for several decades, and it was presumably this new curriculum that was praised the next year in the *Louisville Journal* (which notice is reprinted in the subsequent annual school board report) when they write:

> The Course of Study in this institution is most thorough and comprehensive—of such a character as to fit a female for any position in life—imparting to the mind the strength of a practical education and the grace of elegant accomplishments; the course of four years including thorough tuition in Ancient and Modern Languages, Natural Sciences, mathematics, Vocal Music, &c. We cannot too warmly recommend this noble institution to the confidence and fostering care of those who are interested in the cultivation of the mind.

The balance between "practical education and the grace of elegant accomplishment" characterized the goals of both academies and women's colleges of the time. In this way, as in many others, the women's high school shared much in common with the women's college.[45]

While collegiate rigor cannot be determined solely on the basis of a particular textbook, sample composition, or write-up in the local newspaper, the significant overlap between high school and college that emerges here is documented elsewhere as well, particularly in the frequent reports complaining about the unclear distinctions in the final decades of the century. At the least, courses in the first two years of college very often overlapped with the last two of high school. Particularly insofar as persistence and graduation rates at colleges remained low, students at Female High School studied a course comparable to that of a great many students in American colleges, revealing a tradition of scholarly achievement often overlooked in histories of higher education.

But for all their similarities and overlaps, there were also differences in the pedagogies and educational philosophies of high school and college rhetoric and composition instruction. After all, though conceiving of themselves as teaching the highest branches, the alternative educational philosophy of the high school—growing out of the common school—represented an alternative pedagogical tradition to that of recitation popular in more established colleges. As a result, the high schools "did college" differently—and they did something that was akin to "college writing" differently too. The following chapter, then, will look not to the curriculum but to the *pedagogies* of the high schools, which draw on educational traditions from the common schools even during their most rigorous collegiate years. It is here that the most exciting traditions of composition instruction and the most striking possible futures for collaboration across the "high school–college divide" circulate.

CHAPTER 3

Practical Rhetoric and Progressive Pedagogies in the High Schools

> The great bane of our present school system is the deplorable fact that the teacher's work is measured by the quantity, disregarding the quality almost entirely. The teacher's purpose is to dispatch so many pages a day; he measures his pupil's progress by the number of questions answered in an hour. On the other hand, the young men or women, desirous of showing that they have received a liberal education, mention the number of subjects they studied in the various schools, or the number of text-books they have "gone through." . . . They think that to become masters of their language it is enough to recite a grammar, a rhetoric, etc.; that to be a philosopher is to have memorized and recited a mental and moral philosophy, etc.—in short, they mistake the tools for the work, imagine that, having heard of the elephant, they have seen it; and having seen it, they have obtained possession of it.
>
> —*William N. Hailmann*

High schools—as the "people's colleges"—prided themselves on offering a "practical" English curriculum for the people. But insofar as the classical curriculum remained the gold standard of college learning throughout much of the century, the high schools and colleges of the

South and West continued to shape themselves in its image, drawing on the social capital associated with those subjects by offering an English curriculum *alongside* the traditional classical curriculum, or as a modification of it (removing Greek but retaining Latin), rather than in place of it. Because many high schools themselves offered a classical curriculum similar to that available in colleges, then, the high school can be read as an intervention not into *what* should be taught in higher learning but *who* and *how*. The *who* entailed a broad democratic sample of white students from all economic backgrounds. To emphasize this point, the principal of Male advertised "how generally the different classes of citizens are enjoying the benefits of this school" by publishing in the annual report a list of parents' occupations, including grocers, lawyers, various merchants, ministers, widows as well as butchers, printers, masons, farmers, and others in 1860. He repeated the practice in 1864, citing a majority of clergymen, carpenters, lawyers, laborers, retired people, widows, merchants, and farmers among the parents and claiming in relation to the list that "all classes of our citizens are represented in the School; yet no distinctions are recognized, except mental and moral excellence."[1] Of course, the ideals of meritocracy gloss over the realities of unequal access and privilege—particularly in relation to the as-yet excluded African American population. Nonetheless, the schools were beginning to imagine what the "people's college" might look like. So how did they teach these students?

Key to understanding the pedagogical atmosphere of the high school is the notion of "practical" higher education and student-centered learning. Practicality emerges as a keyword in nineteenth-century America across various cultural contexts. From the transcendentalists to pragmatist philosophers to local legislators, we see traces of this term and its value evoked at all levels of social discourse across the century. It becomes part of what James A. Berlin calls the "noetic field" of this time—part of the underlying value system and epistemology that produces rhetorics and pedagogies. This trend is tied to changing orientations toward time, labor, and social relations in the antebellum years, especially with the growth of scientific knowledge and values, and becomes increasingly pronounced in educational discourse in the last quarter of the century as industrialization and urbanization began to pose new social problems that were increasingly addressed through public schools.[2]

Practical education was particularly linked with the notion of universal education and common schooling in a rejection of what was framed as an aristocratic and exclusionary tuition-based system of academies and colleges and their classical curriculum and pedagogy, as discussed in chapter 1. As part of a national interest in universal education and the expansion of higher education through high schools, normal schools, colleges, and the eventual establishment of land-grant universities, an emphasis on practical education was often linked explicitly to notions of democratic and civic participation.[3]

The comments of George W. Morris, president of the Louisville board of trustees, reflect this trend. He writes, "One of the most frequent objections urged against the system of education in this country is, that in the common schools and academies, too little of that kind of instruction is imparted that has a direct bearing upon the practical things of life, while in the classical institutions it is lost sight of altogether." But he assures the school board and public that,

> I need hardly say that this objection is not applicable to [the Louisville schools] . . . [A]ll the essential and practical branches of English education are taught in our public schools, after which the pupils of these schools, on being found qualified, are transferred to the high schools, the design of which is, by a more thorough course of mental, moral and physical training, the better to prepare them for the engagements of active life.[4]

In short, practical education in the high schools was meant to ready students for a broad range of civic and professional engagements. In this way, high school posed an explicit critique of traditional college, which was increasingly under fire for teaching students a narrow array of classical subjects detached from practical life and the work of most citizens.

In its emphasis on student needs, activity, and progressive development, this pedagogical approach was set against earlier educational models that posited students as vessels to be filled with knowledge, which no longer seemed adequate to prepare students for leadership in a time of change. In its emphasis on "active life," the new curriculum was also at odds with the traditional notion of higher learning as "train[ing] aristocrats, a class of men whose education was intentionally made to be unrelated to the affairs of the larger society, resting instead on eternal principles." In place of an elitist approach to higher learning, the high school explicitly sought to develop a curriculum that would foster thorough and practical knowledge. Female's Principal Chase echoed this interest in his decision to place the motto *Esse quam videri* ("to be, rather than to seem") on the seal of the school, to "truly indicate its character as one where thorough mental discipline and practical education, rather than showy accomplishments, may be secured."[5]

Practical education was also intimately linked to science. Just as Annie Mendenhall has argued that "*Real*, *practical*, and *scientific*—terms circulating at the time among progressive educators and in rhetoric textbooks—became buzzwords" at land-grant institutions like Ohio State University, they were also buzzwords at public high schools, where educators similarly sought to develop reliable procedures to teach writing and rhetoric—and indeed all courses—"scientifically." Setting the value of science and practicality in opposition to the traditional collegiate curriculum, the Committee on Examination and Control thus explained the need for a science professor in the high schools in 1857:

> The necessity for such instruction is now beyond dispute. The exclusive attention to the dead languages and the more abstract mathematics, has yielded to the imperious requirements of a practical age. Men are no longer educated for a life of useless metaphysical abstractions for the cloister. Intelligent usefulness is the demand directly made by the spirit of the day. The Professorship of Natural Sciences is needed to supply this want.[6]

This attention to natural sciences was characteristic of the emergent English curriculum, which entailed attention to the vernacular and modern languages, a decreased emphasis on (though often not complete dismissal of) classical languages, and the incorporation of science and more applied mathematics. These subjects were touted as practical for students who were not going to college, but also eventually became the norm at more elite institutions and colleges as well, which adjusted curricula and entrance requirements to promote articulation with the public high schools and appeal to a broader range of students.[7]

Historians of rhetoric have long discussed this move toward practicality as well. In the realm of rhetorical theory specifically, the emphasis on the practical precipitated a movement away from abstract rhetoric in textbooks, which ran parallel to similar changes in educational philosophy being drawn from Europe. As Albert Kitzhaber explains:

> Beginning in the lower schools, where the new European theories of education were first felt, and extending gradually to the colleges, the aim of rhetorical instruction became that of teaching students to write acceptably, rather than loading them down with a mass of principles to be committed to memory... As a result, rhetorical doctrine was simplified, with the aim of pruning it of unessentials and thus making it practical.[8]

In other words, rather than reading and memorizing theoretical principles about rhetoric, the focus of rhetorical instruction became the production of written and spoken texts.

The Louisville case seems to support Kitzhaber's characterization of rhetorical theory to this point. But Kitzhaber goes on to outline a sort of theoretical impoverishment that resulted from this emphasis on practice: "Since the rhetorical instruction of mid-century had been chiefly theory without practice, the tendency at the end of the century was to urge mainly practice without theory, or at least with a bare minimum of theory." More precisely, what emerges in Kitzhaber's study is a new theory "of a more mundane sort" that was focused on "superficial correctness in mechanical details" that becomes ossified as the theoretical approach into the twentieth century, largely through a tradition of grammar instruction.[9] Berlin and Crowley each similarly trace the development of nineteenth-century rhetoric into this "current-traditional rhetoric," which entailed a reductive emphasis on surface correctness in writing, such as seen in the texts of A. S. Hill, Barrett Wendell, and John Franklin Genung.

But this story of theoretical impoverishment and current-traditional rhetoric is not the only available interpretation. For example, challenging these negative assessments of nineteenth-century rhetoric, Nan Johnson argues that these "practical" rhetorical traditions actually extended the New Rhetoric "by synthesizing the epistemological, belles lettres, and classical rationales to justify a broader range of rhetorical practice," thus promoting a more encompassing and synthetic vision of rhetoric which claimed "the status of science, practical art, and civil servant" and was deeply responsive to its own historical moment. So, though the rhetorical and pedagogical traditions that emerged by the end of the century may be less than inspiring from our vantage point, Johnson asks us to seek to understand the social and epistemological forces that shaped these theories and practices for their own time.[10]

Building on Johnson, I argue that the European educational theories that Kitzhaber mentions almost in passing should be recognized as an important influence in writing instruction and practice, especially in schools around midcentury. These theories are crucial to understanding the pedagogical approach of the schools. Rather than articulating a stifling set of criteria for the product of that practice (as rhetorical textbooks began to do), these European educational theorists (focusing especially on the lower schools) are significant because they attempted to base practice around developmentally appropriate activities, with an emphasis on process—an emphasis on practice as activity, as discovery, as learning. They did not represent "practice without theory," but instead theories promoting practice.[11] Their opposition to the teaching of complex rhetorical treatises, then, can be understood not as atheoretical, but based on a theoretical interest in starting from what the student knows and guiding her through the perception and application of theoretical knowledge—an inductive rather than deductive approach, based largely in emerging theories of child development, psychology, and evolution.

Against the pedagogies of recitation and memorization, schools embracing these European pedagogies emphasized scientific experiments and hands-on learning over book learning, and writing practice based on student experience and growing out of a student's desire to communicate with others. The sense of the practical was not just about helping students produce acceptable prose compositions, or about preparation for a job, but more broadly about developing skills students could practice and use in life, particularly the ability to observe, understand, and judge new information, to apply it to their own self-directed learning, and to communicate with others in speech and writing. The writing students produced in school was an occasion for practicing such observation, understanding, and judgment.

Lucille Schultz and Kathryn Fitzgerald have each documented this distinctive tradition of writing instruction in the schools. In her examination of nineteenth-century textbooks, Schultz argues that these European pedagogies were the reason why "some of the earliest examples we have of writing assignments based on the concrete and the familiar—and in some cases on personal experience—were generated not in the colleges but in the schools." Similarly, Fitzgerald traces the intellectual tradition of European pedagogy in normal schools, which serve as a precedent for "contemporary attitudes about composition theory, methods, teachers, and students."[12] Each in their own contexts, these scholars shed light on the influence of European pedagogies in American schools and texts.

The constellation of reforms to formal education posited through these European pedagogies and other modern reforms revolving around student-centered activity came to be known broadly as the "New Education." Broad and multivalent, this movement encompassed the ideas of Johann Heinrich Pestalozzi, Friedrich Froebel, Jean Piaget, and, later, John Dewey, who drew on the philosophies of Locke and Rousseau to articulate classroom practices for student-centered learning. New Education was closely related to the kindergarten movement, but its grounding in empiricism and scientific inquiry aligned it also to the reforms of the undergraduate college and scientific school in the second half of the nineteenth century. These collegiate reforms were outlined by Harvard's Charles Eliot, who published in 1869 a widely noted article in the *Atlantic* with the title "The New Education" that explained the practical and scientific impulses transforming higher learning and the need for a reformed school system in support of these changes.

In the lower schools the New Education is perhaps most strongly informed by the work of Swiss educational theorist Johann Heinrich Pestalozzi (1746–1827), who is best known for developing what came to be called "object teaching." This pedagogy emphasized the natural learning patterns of the child, teaching not from precepts but from concrete objects and observation. Against memorization and strict discipline, Pestalozzi believed that students have a natural desire to learn about the world that need only be directed by the teacher. In this way, object teaching involves providing students with tactile objects and guiding the student to observe and analyze their properties. For instance, by observing a sheet of paper, young students might explore the concepts of whiteness, smoothness, plane surfaces, rectangles, etc. By comparing that sheet of paper to a window, students might further develop the concept of opaque versus transparent, flexibility versus rigidity, etc. Later in their educational development, students were invited to explore more complex objects and phenomena, including written texts, but always with the focus on student-centered apperception and analysis as the guiding forces of each lesson.

In this chapter, I trace the influence of the New Education and object teaching in the operations of the Louisville high schools to argue that the high school was a key interface between pedagogical innovations from the public schools and curricular traditions of the colleges, promoting a tradition of advanced composition and rhetoric instruction distinct from that of many of the colleges featured in our disciplinary histories.

The New Education and William N. Hailmann

Discussions about object teaching circulated often in the Louisville schools at midcentury. Quite notably, though object teaching was considered a pedagogy for younger children, these conversations frequently were led by the high schools' own William N. Hailmann, science professor at both Male and Female from 1857 to 1864. An influential voice in shaping the curriculum and teacher training in this city, Hailmann is frequently cited in the school board reports and minutes, and his ideas are reflected in the disciplinary and curricular values of the schools. After leaving Louisville, he went on to become an administrator at schools in Indiana, Wisconsin, California, and elsewhere, and became a celebrated voice (along with his wife, Eudora) in the kindergarten movement. He is best known for promulgating the theories of the New Education, particularly through publication of an educational history that covered Pestalozzi and Froebel, a translation of Froebel's works for English-speaking audiences in America, and a magazine, *The New Education*, dedicated to these and related educational ideas.[13] Hailmann also published two treatises on "object teaching" for the Louisville schools, one of which is published in the annual school board report of 1861, and the other published by a New York firm in 1867. While his publications on object teaching were formulated for the lower schools, Hailmann himself maintained that the principles of this pedagogy should be extended through higher education and into adulthood—a position that put him at odds with notable schoolman William Torrey Harris of St. Louis, with whom he had well-publicized professional disagreements.

As a natural science professor, Hailmann may seem an unlikely figure in the history of rhetoric and composition. However, Hailmann was clearly less interested in subject areas than he was in the learning process, and that process is in many ways a rhetorical one: students "must be taught not only to think, feel, and form plans; but also to speak, act, and execute with the necessary directness, energy, and power of endurance." He writes, "The principal aim of school education is to teach the pupils *how to form ideas* and *how to express them*. The amount and kind of knowledge gained are only secondary considerations, important ones, indeed, but considerations that will take care of themselves, if the power to form and express ideas has been properly imparted."[14] Thus, Hailmann attempts to theorize the "natural" order of learning, which—as a scientist who believed in observation and rationality—he says begins with sensory observation.

His theories of learning are also theories of rhetoric. For example, his discussion of "how to form ideas" is recognizable as a discussion of invention, attending to imitation, memory, comparison, analysis, and other common terms from rhetorical theory (seemingly via Campbell). Though not without its limitations, his treatment of invention is itself notable during a time of "stylistic rhetorics" that often neglected or altogether abandoned a consideration of invention as a rhetorical canon. As Crowley explains this trend, these "stylistic rhetorics" usually "made a perfunctory acknowledgement of the traditional primacy of invention and then moved on to grammar and style."[15]

Focusing not on rhetoric per se, but on education and communication more generally, Hailmann's theory retains a central position for invention. Like other educational theorists, he is most interested in understanding the "natural development" of how students form and communicate ideas. Mental discipline pedagogies outlined this process as "attending, observing, memorizing," an approach later criticized by Dewey and others for its overemphasis on memory. By contrast, Hailmann emphasizes an alternative triad of "perception, conception, *judgment*" as the natural development of the faculties to be followed, significantly replacing the object of memorization with that of judgment. In developing judgment, the student is to follow the "natural" process of moving from the known to the unknown, simple to complex, concrete to abstract, whole to parts, and particular to the general—echoing Campbell's advice to "ascend from particulars to universals" in the acquisition of natural knowledge from the world.[16]

Building on these inventional procedures, Hailmann's discussion of "how to express ideas" covers aspects of arrangement, delivery and style, including correct and distinct pronunciation, correct emphasis, concision, elegance and beauty of expression and arrangement. His own work suggests his familiarity with and influence by eighteenth-century rhetoricians and their successors who, as Johnson points out, synthesized classical, epistemological, and belles lettres theories to frame their approach to style.[17]

Under the head of "how to express ideas," Hailmann also dedicates a full eight of sixteen chapters in his book specifically to grammar. Recalling Kitzhaber's characterization of late nineteenth-century rhetorical theory as concerned primarily with grammar, we might recognize Hailmann's lengthy articulation of grammar instruction as a rhetorical treatise in line with the trends of his time. At the same time, Hailmann insists that he did "not intend to write an exhaustive treatise on grammar" and instead aimed to "merely show, by means of a few practical illustrations and hints, how these subjects may be handled in obedience to the principles of the [object teaching] system."[18] In other words, Hailmann is not interested in promoting grammar *as* rhetorical education, but in using grammar as an example of a topic that can be taught *rhetorically* through object teaching. This means teaching grammar by engaging the students' perception, conception, and judgment about language use, not by expounding universal principles.

"Grammar," writes Hailmann, "is the art of *conveying* ideas correctly by means of language and of *understanding* ideas so conveyed by others: it is *the art of using language correctly* . . . it includes not only all modes of expressing ideas by language—reading, speaking, and writing; but also the power of interpreting ideas so expressed." While the emphasis on correctness here is pronounced, it is not manifested in the sample lessons by intolerance for error but by a dialogic exploration of language leading to "correct" naming and usage. Hailmann emphasizes the necessity of patience on the part of the teacher and repeated, varied exposure to ideas before students can be expected to understand and express them "correctly"—and in the face of error, not direct correction but a series of provocative questions is the course to be followed: "If the answer is incorrect, the pupil is skillfully led to discover his mistake himself and to correct it himself."[19]

At the same time, Hailmann's approach to writing pedagogy does focus rather narrowly on description, comparison, and contrast, and other didactic genres promoted for their ability to cultivate the abilities of observation and analysis in students. His emphasis on observation and analysis in shaping a text aligns with the trend in other textbooks of the time to promote formulaic writing that closely mirrored the process of intellection it was supposed to capture. As Crowley points out, "Any discourse that resulted from analysis would likewise be arranged so as to move from the particular to the universal." Thus, this approach does have the potential of slipping into current-traditional rhetoric. Further, Hailmann's emphasis on "elegance and beauty of expression" underscores the focus on surface features, seeking to "bring the pupil to a consciousness that language may serve him not only the purpose of expressing his ideas clearly, but also of presenting them in a pleasing garb, in an impressive manner."[20] In line with belletristic trends from eighteenth-century rhetoricians such as Campbell and Blair, the notion of presenting ideas "in a pleasing garb" suggests the potential that language is merely the dress of thought.

But Hailmann's system—reflecting the European theories of which it is born—also pushes against the flattened, surface-oriented discourse of current-traditional or even belletristic rhetoric. In particular, Hailmann's treatise goes far to de-emphasize error and correction, insist on the individual needs of student writers, and value moments of seeming idleness as part of the writing process. Like others involved in the New Education, he was dedicated to recognizing the capabilities of students, even young children, to observe, understand, and judge information taken in by their senses to thereby make meaning of the world around them. Through perception, conception, and judgment, students observe, understand, and apply and test their knowledge—they form and express ideas. In the end, educational theorists like Hailmann understood that this process could not be systematized and regimented. Resisting the sense of uniformity his own system could be taken to imply, he characterizes his approach as "systematically unsystematical" and "artificially natural."[21] His emphasis, then, is not on developing and communicating ideas in a recitation style, but on practice and application of these skills in response to real rhetorical and material contexts.

Hailmann concedes that advanced students would benefit from "the synthetic study of grammar with any good text-book and with any good teacher who, instead of following the textbook blindly or indolently, is ever mindful of the great principles of natural teaching and gives full scope to his inventiveness, that most important of all mental qualification to the teacher." While incorporating textbooks in the higher levels, then, the "conscious study of grammar in its narrow sense, as a *science*" that proceeds from there should not "work on the old routine plan of school grammarians" but should "still follow the method of combined analysis and synthesis—of combined discovery and application on the part of the pupil." Here, too, the teacher must "beware of the habit of *lecturing* and *explaining*, where this would save the pupils wholesome labor . . . Let the pupils set their minds to work—let them *labor* with their faculties—let them take difficult questions home again and again, until, by independent effort, *they* have explained them."[22]

Thus, in Hailmann's treatises on object teaching we find a rhetorical theory in its own right, providing insight into some of the pedagogical assumptions and values circulating in the Louisville schools and challenging the assumption of current-traditional rhetoric and its attendant pedagogies there. But just where and how do we see these pedagogical ideas circulating in the Louisville high schools?

Circulating the New Education: A Pedagogical Atmosphere

In bringing them into the high schools, Hailmann understood the pedagogies of the New Education to be a way of democratizing higher learning, making it appealing and relevant to a more diverse student population, which was a goal shared by him and the Louisville administrators. Quoting sociologist Herbert Spencer, Superintendent Anderson supports the extension of object teaching to the higher levels of schooling, highlighting the claim for this method as preparing lifelong learners. He argues that object lessons "should be extended to *a range of things far wider, and continue to a period far later than now* . . . . They should not cease with early childhood; but should be so kept up during youth as insensibly to merge into the investigations of the naturalist and the man of science."[23]

But Hailmann's theories are reflected most clearly in the remarks of Edward Augustus Holyoke, who served not only as the principal but also as the professor of Rhetoric and English Literature at Female (and briefly at Male as well) until 1861, just before his death. Because he served as instructor of rhetoric and English literature, his perspectives on the work of the school writ large apply with particular force to our understanding of rhetorical education there, and his vision is said to have had a lasting influence on the work of the school.

Born in Massachusetts, Holyoke was a descendent on his mother's side of the ninth president of Harvard College (1737 to 1769) and a line of noted Boston physicians. At least two of his brothers were Harvard graduates, though it is unclear whether Edward attended. According to one genealogical record (compiled by a descendent), he was instead trained at an art academy in New York City, after which he took a position at Munro Collegiate Institute in Elbridge, New York, before moving to Louisville.[24]

Holyoke may not have been the recognized scholar that many members of his family were, but, from all accounts, he led the school with great vision and inspired his students toward greatness themselves. As one writer explained in the *Louisville Journal*, "As a mere teacher of facts in literature and principles in science, the lamented Holyoke no doubt had many equals," but, the author continues, "there was a peculiar force in his character, a nobility surrounding his every-day life, and a charm in his manner, which fitted him more than ordinary men as the moulder of the female life and the educator of the female mind." In fact, he was said to be "truly Napoleonic" in this regard, "for he inspired all about him with an appreciating sense of their own worth—of the grandeur of the achievements which they were themselves capable of making." Reminiscences of one of his first graduates, from the class of 1858, support this characterization of "a man of marvelous resources and influence" whose "touch on the lives of his pupils was a call to earnest and untiring endeavor." As that student recalled, "He said that so small a class ought to make up in work what it lacked in time; and so we entered very enthusiastically into the spirit of the forty-eight hour day."[25]

A founding member of the Kentucky Association of Teachers, which he served as secretary, Holyoke was not only an inspirational teacher but also a serious academic professional dedicated to improving teaching and learning in his area. He established and edited the *Kentucky Family Journal* in 1859 and also gave public lectures on various artistic and literary topics meant to bridge the academic–community divide.[26] It is under Holyoke that the school is said to have begun its practice of hard study, particularly in Latin and writing. As one of his students explained, "Each day the hour of Latin prose was followed by an hour of English impromptu composition. The strenuous season of writing was not pleasant at first, but we lived to be grateful for the relentless enforcement of good spelling and correct style."[27]

While the "relentless enforcement of good spelling and correct style" certainly smacks of current-traditionalism, characterizations of his teaching here and elsewhere do not give the impression that he was merely focused on surface correctness or writing in isolation of meaning. Instead, we hear also in this "relentless enforcement" a potential for revision and continual improvement and an emphasis on ongoing practice, which surfaces over and over again. It is in this that Principal Holyoke's philosophies and pedagogies in approaching these studies reflected the values of Hailmann's New Education.

His philosophy most clearly aligns with Hailmann's in his remarks at the 1860 commencement ceremony, in which Holyoke speaks of the value of applied over book learning, the educative value of the home and the lifelong application of learning, and the variability of students' progress and educational needs. Echoing the major principles of Hailmann's theory almost to a point, Holyoke summarizes his vision for the school in progressive language that is worth quoting at length:

> We aim to do our part in making honorable, intelligent, high-minded women. We aim to cultivate common sense; and our whole course of instruction is designed to be truly *practical.* We wish them to become *accurate thinkers and reasoners*; and we pursue a short, but thorough course of mathematics, together with mental and moral philosophy. We wish them to know something of the *material world*, the world of vegetable and animal life, and a course in the Natural Sciences, in which *things as well as books* are studied, enables us to accomplish much in cultivating habits of *observation and reflection.* We wish them to be able to *communicate the knowledge they have gained*, and we instruct them in the great principles of language by means of a thorough instruction in the Latin and French, by *constant practice* in impromptu compositions, and by giving the simpler principles of Rhetoric. Almost daily *practice* in reading gives them the great principles upon which all good reading is based, though we cannot do what we would for want of early elementary practice. Above all this, however, we labor to make them *independent in thought and action.*[28]

Holyoke's insistence on practice, observation and reflection, forming and expressing ideas, and independent thought and action all closely resemble the values promoted by Hailmann, and challenge a reading of his writing pedagogy as stifling or current-traditional. Though it is difficult in this case to argue a causal connection between Hailmann's and Holyoke's educational theories, the coincidence of them suggests that the "spirit" of the New Education was reaching into the higher levels of learning in Louisville in the early years of these schools, with the justifications for these pedagogies and their extension being tied up closely with the notion of providing a practical education.[29] The evidence suggests that students at Holyoke's school were being trained to *use* their language, and were provided remarkable opportunities for meaningfully doing so.

Moreover, Holyoke's articulation of education as transcending the schoolroom and continuing into later life echoes Hailmann as well, with implications for his writing pedagogy. In the spirit of the New Education and its emphasis on practice and process, he challenges the commodification of education and rejects the idea of education as preparation for later life in favor of education *as life*. In his speech at the 1860 commencements, Holyoke thus admonishes parents to recognize this broader scope of education, promoting a sense of education as a lifelong process, not a product co-terminous with a degree or certificate:

> You cannot send your child to the school to purchase an education as you send him to the shop to purchase a garment. Education is not a thing to be had at a certain place, at a certain price, and from a certain man. It is constant, ever progressive. You are educating your child by your every look, and word, and act, as well—yes, far more than he is doing who teaches him algebra or Greek. The morning paper plays a more important part in the process than the text-book; and your fire-side, or the street-corner, than the school-room.

In this same way, Hailmann defines practical education by its development of human minds that can be useful and happy in their various pursuits in the classroom, in the workplace and at home. His goal is to "send pupils from school hungry for more and with sufficient power, energy, and endurance to obtain more—pupils who feel that their education can never be finished and who have the ability to continue it independently, not pupils who are glad to have escaped the odious school-house and to have 'finished their education.'"[30] Education, and particularly writing (i.e., learning to form and express ideas), is not preparation for life, but is itself characteristic of living.

This expansive notion of education and writing reflects an appreciation for extracurricular and civic rhetorical practice that pushes against the divide between home and school. Indeed, rich extracurricular education and composing, in the form of lyceums and parlor rhetorics, were features of this period. While scholars have most often acknowledged the significance of these rhetorics and movements to those without access to formal education, observing the language and values of the lyceum movement within the high schools also suggests the significance of that movement to those (women especially) who had enjoyed some formal higher education. And students at Female took up this invitation to continue to learn, to teach, to write, and to speak (even, in some cases, in public) throughout their lives.[31]

Beyond Treatises and Speeches: Other Evidence of Teaching and Learning

Both Hailmann and Holyoke were clearly defenders of active student learning and rhetorical engagement in and out of the classroom. But other evidence helps us to further understand what this value looked like in the schools and how it affected the writing students produced. For example, we can look to the public newspapers to see that the practice of active and publicly engaged learning and writing was established in the lower schools as well, particularly in the upper grades. The *Courier-Journal*'s "Educational" section, inaugurated in 1866, provided one forum for this work, publishing reports and opinions on educational matters as well as student compositions from the ward schools each week. Through this outlet, students were able to engage their assigned writing rhetorically, with an authentic sense of audience. They were taught to consider this audience, and motivated to think about the world around them as a source of potentially useful topics with which to engage. As one student explained:

> I have promised myself several times to write you a letter, and see if you would notice it. But our teacher is always advising us better to do anything without an object in view. Heretofore,

> I have been kept from writing to you, fearing I might not say anything worth printing or reading. However, the exercises in our school yesterday evening were so satisfactory to both teacher and pupils, that I know if I could tell of them in a good way, they would at least be interesting if not instructive.[32]

Thus, in these compositions, students related details from their own community and experiences, described their classrooms and writing processes, and commented on the act of being assigned writing topics. They even self-consciously modified their assigned topics to suit their own interests and experiences. For example, one student changed the assigned topic of travel to "fireside angels" to reflect the fact that she had never been away from home. Even in an assignment theme, then, there was space for her to take such ownership and liberties.

These compositions even became the site of lively public debate when one local man, who signed his letter only "Jay," wrote in to speak against the advancing education of women. "Jay" complained of women's education in "the various 'ologies' of the present enlightened age," characterizing women as "intellectual inferiors" and arguing that a young woman's "ignorance was really refreshing in these degenerate days when knowledge is so universal."[33]

We discover that the students clearly read the papers as well as writing to them, and within a month, students in the ward schools had composed and published numerous responses. These student essays elicited their own rejoinders in what became a debate over whether girls are as smart as boys that continued for several months.[34] Through these compositions, we can observe that education and schooling was of general public interest in the city at this time, and key educational questions were moderated through writing—and through the circulation of student writing in the local print press. In this way the shape and status of composition instruction throughout the upper grades was influenced by the value of authentic, engaged learning situations such as those advocated by the New Education.

Other educational features within the schools further supported this orientation toward learning. The format of the annual examinations of the high schools, for instance, reflects this interest in demonstrating authentic understanding and active thought rather than rote memorization. Oral examination questions were drawn from the audience, including from local businessmen and professionals. Students' responses, thus, could not come directly from memorization of their textbooks. As the Committee on Examination and Control of 1860 noted of Male High School's exams, "The classes in Mental and Moral Science, and Criticism, gave evidence not only of a thorough acquaintance with their text-books, but a comprehensive knowledge of the subjects. They also evinced an independent and philosophic accuracy of thought, a purity of taste, and an elevation of moral sentiment rarely found among students of the most celebrated colleges of the country."[35]

In addition to these oral examination questions, students at both high schools wrote compositions that were read aloud to the audience, as discussed in the previous chapter. As Lisa Mastrangelo posits, oral presentation "would have offered them the opportunity to emphasize their ideas over correct spelling" and "masked such factors as bad spelling or sloppy handwriting."[36] Thus, the presentation of these compositions de-emphasizes surface correctness in favor of attention to the larger sentiments, organization, style, and delivery of the compositions. This is in line with Hailmann's emphasis on grammar as important insofar as it facilitates communication and meaning-making and Holyoke's celebration of individuality and ongoing practice in language development, each of which depicts an atmosphere of writing instruction that goes beyond recitation and themes, reaching toward meaningful rhetorical engagement.

While proponents of the New Education criticized pedagogies of recitation and drill in favor of learning from and engaging with the real world, they did not forgo the use of textbooks altogether. They understood what we understand about textbooks: that their value depends on how the teacher uses them. Still, some of the textbooks used in the schools did align with the pedagogical values of the New Education. For example, Schultz points out traces of Pestalozzian object teaching in Parker's *Aids to English Composition*, which was in use at Male in 1866. Beyond merely reflecting the language or spirit of Pestalozzi, as other texts she examines do, Schultz notes that Parker's 1844 *Aids* actually includes a section dedicated specifically to object teaching that does not exist in his 1832 *Progressive Exercises*, demonstrating an emerging awareness of Pestalozzian object teaching even into the higher levels.[37]

Still, scholars have found much to lament about the majority of rhetoric textbooks in use at the high schools, and Parker's is no exception.

For example, Crowley noted the object lesson exercises in Parker as one of the means through which "subjects took on a life of their own in current-traditional composition theory." In particular, she saw the emphasis on observation as requiring that students have a broad range of experiences before they would "store up enough material to become a writer worth reading." Another problem for Crowley is the assertion in this approach that objects had exact mental equivalents as subjects of writing. She observes this trend in another popular text from the schools, George Payne Quackenbos's *Advanced Course of Composition and Rhetoric* (originally published in 1854, and used in the schools throughout their first four years), in which "subjects were supposed to be as easily discernible from one another as objects were, and they could be developed or covered as well." In a similar vein, textbooks by Coppee and Newman (both used at Male in 1863) each rely on a psychological model of invention, in which "the stuff invention works on is taken in from the outside world or from books and is stored in memory until called for. Without such a mental storehouse, invention is impossible."[38]

Undoubtedly, there are limitations to these texts, and some are more problematic than others. But the professed pedagogical values of the schools shed light on the ways even these more limiting texts may have been used. Though the rhetorical trend of the time may have relied on common limiting ideas about invention and composition, other documentary evidence discussed above suggests that faculty simultaneously understood the value of self-selected topics of significance to students, of de-emphasizing surface error and correction, of writing in a variety of genres of an authentic sense of audience, and other beliefs at odds with reductive current-traditional composition pedagogies. Thus, some of the critiques of these texts do not adequately consider the pedagogical tradition that undergirded either their creation or their use. The invention strategies in Parker's text, for example, might be read more sympathetically through the lens of object teaching and its attempt to confer autonomy and agency to the student. And rather than framing this textbook as an extension of the mental discipline pedagogies adapted for "exceedingly uninformed teachers" and courses such as had "never before . . . been offered on the college level," as Connors does, we might see in the same text a flexible resource for a "systematically unsystematical" pedagogical approach.[39] In short, the pedagogies of the New Education that were permeating the high school encourage us to reconsider how we interpret teaching materials and how we understand the writing practices in these sites of higher learning.

The Ambiguous Legacy of the New Education

In line with these pedagogies, the high schools taught writing as an integrated means for students to learn and think about their worlds, and as a public practice. In the case of pedagogy, then, it is the high schools' difference from rather than their similarities to colleges that are of note for contemporary scholars of rhetoric and composition. Because of their relationship to the common schools and their investment in a democratic, "practical" education, high schools taught composition and rhetoric from their earliest years, and they did so in an atmosphere infused with an interest in student-centered pedagogy that, by all accounts, rarely existed in colleges.

While the ideas of applied, individualized, student-centered learning clearly infiltrated the atmosphere of teaching and learning at the high schools in their first decade of operation, though, it's hard to say the New Education took hold in the practices of most other schools. As superintendent George H. Tingley Jr. put it, "That there is something good in Objects lessons is not denied, but the difficulty in having even a judicious course properly taught by a large majority of teachers is almost insurmountable." Significantly, the failure of the program in Louisville is attributed to Hailmann's own removal from the school system in 1865, when he left to start his own school in the city.[40]

Additionally, in the increasingly centralized and complex educational bureaucracies of the second half of the nineteenth century, the idea of student-directed learning, which is necessarily more open-ended, was increasingly in tension with efforts to standardize education across classrooms and schools. Early notions of practice and the practical merged with an interest in specialization and the value of job preparation in a market economy to produce a separation of manual skills from academic (arguably to the detriment of each). In this bureaucratic context, the value of practicality was also productive of writing practices such as those of the daily theme writing assignment and other approaches that did little more than practice for practice's sake, resulting in the much-discussed current-traditional rhetoric as well as reductively vocational programs that emphasized specific job skills over and against a more general liberal arts focus.[41]

Yet the early pedagogies of the high schools point to an intriguing tradition of writing instruction informed by these schools' position as both a part of and separate from the common schools. As part of the common schools, the high schools were ideologically attached to the value of democratic access and benefitted from the pedagogical ideas circulating in the lower schools, while as collegiate institutions they were also set apart. Drawing on the cultural and political value of both educational traditions in turn, the high schools sought to balance appeals to excellence with the value of access, such that "while they can be made free enough for all, they can, at the same time, by wise and judicious management, be made good enough for all."[42] That balance, however, proved challenging in the decades following the Civil War, as the rhetoric and writing curriculum transformed with the emerging belles-lettres tradition, and the high schools came to be in tension with the college and the emerging university model.

INTERCHAPTER

The Civil War Years

Within five years of their establishment, the Louisville high schools were facing a challenge far greater than the institutional uncertainty traced so far: they faced national uncertainty. The country was embroiled in Civil War, and border cities like Louisville were on the front lines. Remaining neutral throughout the war, Kentucky sent some 76,000 white men to serve in the Union, and 25,000 in the Confederacy, plus a total of 23,706 soldiers in the United States Colored Troops, which constituted 13 percent of the total number of African Americans who enlisted in the Union army. Louisville was itself the staging ground for six of the Colored Troop Regiments.[1]

The enlisted ranks also included members of Male High School, who enlisted mostly in the Union forces. According to Principal Grant, two instructors and "not less than thirty-nine under-graduates, in this institution, have enlisted—a few in the Confederate, but more in the army of the Union. At least five of them have fallen on the battle-field boldly contending for what *they believed* the RIGHT."[2]

On the home front, too, life in Louisville was indelibly marked by war, even if no fighting occurred there. Schoolhouses were being occupied by forces, removing classes into the basements of churches and other buildings. By July 1862, the board of education had instituted a form of "loyalty oaths" to ensure that faculty "solemnly promise that you will bear true allegiance to the United States . . . that you will discountenance, discourage and oppose succession, rebellion, and the disintegration of the Federal Union." Throughout

September 1862, tension rose as rumors and fears of a Confederate invasion circulated around Louisville; many people were evacuated from the city, the public schools were all closed for a time, and the city was put under martial law.

The impact of the war was enduring throughout the decade. The city having been a staging ground for the Union, troops remained in Louisville through much of the war and even after, looting and gambling and causing all manner of disruption to the citizens and businesses there. By 1863, these circumstances began to take their toll on the political sensibilities of the citizens: with "the passage of the Emancipation Proclamation and the recruitment of slaves into the Union army, and with thousands of Union soldiers inhabiting their city, bringing with them crime and gambling, Louisville began to openly support the Confederacy."

Kentucky officially declared the war over in February 1866, but, according to local historian Bryan S. Bush, "Louisville may not have noticed the change," as the city had become a military headquarters, retaining soldiers in the city through the 1870s. Highlighting the significance of the war to the state, historian Thomas Clark has observed that nearly half of the young men who came of age in Kentucky in the 1850s and 1860s were killed or disabled by the war. The effects of the conflict were felt in the schools as well, which sought to repair buildings and grounds damaged by the occupying forces throughout the next decade.[3]

And yet, the schools soldiered on, as it were, even thriving throughout the war years. In the months prior to the Union occupation and threats of Confederate invasion, president of the board George W. Morris averred that

> amid the general prostration of business in all sections of the country resulting from our national troubles, under which the educational interest has in many cities, North and South, been paralyzed, it is gratifying to know that in our own city the Public Schools are, in many respects, in a better condition at the present time than at any former period of their history.[4]

Even during the most troubled months of the war, the high schools benefitted from the fact that the two high school buildings were exempted from possession as military hospitals under martial law. And holding fast to their own buildings was not enough for these ambitious schools even in the war years: instead, the resolution for a new Female High School building was pressed before the board in every annual report throughout this period, until a building was purchased and renovated for this purpose in 1864, at the height of the conflict.

Despite the generally distracted condition of the city and country, and even the loss of students and faculty into the ranks, the schools seem to have taken the war in stride in other ways as well. A new literary society, the Athenaeum, was established at Male in 1863 (following the previously established Phi Gamma, which adjourned indefinitely in 1864). Throughout this time, the students of Male continued the publication of their monthly paper, the *Athenaea*, with monthly public readings. Annual commencement ceremonies were held throughout the war, and, according to acting superintendent J. P. Gheen in 1863, "Such was the desire on the part of the public to witness them, that long before the appointed time at which they were to commence had arrived, the spacious hall was filled to overflowing, and hundreds were turned away disappointed at not being able to gain admittance." Though Male's Principal Grant mentions the next year that "the public oral examination [of Male] was poorly attended, owing to the excitement incident to the then existing invasion of the State," it is notable that the public exam was, after all, still held during a time of military occupation and widespread disruption. Oddly, there is not even one mention of war (or, notably, the Emancipation Proclamation) in Principal Grant's or Principal Chase's reports for 1863. By 1865, even, Grant asserts rather casually that "no change in the usual course of the school has been made, except in omitting the weekly public lectures . . . on account of the nightly outrages, that, for a time, baffled the vigilance of both the civil and military police."[5]

By that final year of the war, though, the social impact of the conflict does begin to resonate, as Grant notes reflectively:

> The small number comprised in the Class of Graduates is a forcible illustration of the difficulties with which this Institution has had to contend during the past three or four years. The demand for intelligent boys to fill stations in business houses, to supply the places of those who have joined the armies during the late war, has been pressing and unremitting.[6]

But these struggles were, nonetheless, strikingly minor for new institutions growing up in an occupied city during the American Civil War.

The most important source of the high schools' success seems to stem from their position as a representation of democracy and American ideals for the citizens of Louisville: a symbol the citizens seem resolute to preserve and extend. As the superintendent put it (in typically effusive terms), the high schools represented to many Louisvillians those things that "exalt, embellish and humanize the soul." Indeed, their preservation and persistence through the war years was a point of pride, and in many ways goes hand in glove with the fact that they were politically and affectively significant as institutions of unparalleled higher learning for the city, open to all of its white children. In this way, they served a unifying function during a time of divisiveness. School board president George W. Morris explained the schools' expectations at the Male commencement in 1859: "We do not, indeed, expect all men to be philosophers or statesmen, but we confidently trust that by the diffusion of general knowledge and good and virtuous sentiments, the political fabric may be secure as well against open violence and overthrow, as against the slow but sure undermining of licentiousness." Thus, it was argued, the whole community stood to benefit from this higher learning as a source of social welfare and security, which proved to be a powerful appeal for galvanizing public support and interest in ever-higher schools.[7]

And yet, by the time the war had drawn to a close, the national transformation of the modern American high school was underway, shifting the plans and possibilities conceived for these schools in their early years. High schools were to be standardized, and their relation to other institutions of higher learning clarified. In Louisville, that transformation affected the two established high schools for white students and entailed the eventual development of a high school for African Americans and a manual training high school for white men as well. In each of these schools, the variability of local practice continued to confound attempts to separate and subordinate the high school to the college. Those practices and the challenge they represent to our current conceptions of high school-college relations are the subject of the second part of this book.

PART TWO

Higher Learning in Transformation

CHAPTER 4

The "Absurd Effort": The University Idea and the Changing High School

> [O]ur suckling freshmen and seniors scarcely in their teens, proud of their degrees of Bachelor and Master in Arts budding before their whiskers, enjoy a fool's paradise in thinking themselves scholars after a four years' course from their grammar schools . . . comparatively little thorough work can be accomplished by our Male High School until the absurd effort it has made so long to swell into a college is abandoned and it becomes in reality a high school for boys, with a principal instead of a president and assistants instead of professors.
>
> —*"Blue Monday," Courier-Journal, 1 Sept. 1873*

As I have demonstrated, the first two Louisville high schools exemplify the complex relations between nineteenth-century institutions of higher learning. The confounding definition of each institution continued and was even amplified in the last quarter of the century, as the field of higher learning grew and elaborated. During this time, the modern English curriculum emerged as the dominant curriculum across the field of higher learning. Meanwhile, educational institutions offered an increasingly broad array of studies and specializations (a bit of everything to everyone) as they sought to remain relevant. Geiger calls this the era of the "multipurpose college," when many colleges also functioned as secondary schools, normal schools, and even business or commercial schools. W. Bruce Leslie applies this same "multipurpose" identity to academies, which operated similarly. The same insight benefits our conception of the high school, as these, too, were "multipurpose institutions" serving a broad range of interests and pedagogical purposes.

The confusion produced by these various and expansive institutional missions was heightened as the American research university entered the scene in the 1870s. The model of the American university—traced variously to England, France, and, especially, Germany—signified advanced, specialized study and research beyond the general academic subjects traditionally taught in the undergraduate college and high school. It entailed a more independent and more comprehensive, while more specialized, form of education that gave attention to the wide range of new research in agriculture, mechanics, and science at the land grant institutions. As Harvard's Charles Francis Adams explained it in his 1869 editorial in the *Atlantic*, "It cannot be said too loudly or too often, that no subject of human inquiry can be out of place in the programme of a real university. It is only necessary that every subject should be taught at the university on a higher plane than elsewhere." Thus, the university was another fundamentally relative form, and its relationship to the American college and high school was yet to be worked out.[1]

With the advent of the American university, cultural and educational commentators such as Thorstein Veblen, Cornelius Broome, and others came to define college education less by what it *was*—i.e., the study of classical or English liberal arts, or the most advanced course of study—than by what it *wasn't*—i.e., specialized study. In fact, public and scholarly debates in the late nineteenth century were often less concerned with the distinction between high school and college programs—both of which were dedicated to providing a general liberal arts education that differed only in degree or focus, if at all—than they were with the distinction between collegiate liberal arts programming and specialization. Whether it was the specialized research of professional study, vocational training, or the study of knowledge for knowledge's sake, specialized education was an increasingly important and fraught issue, and different schools had different thresholds for what they considered to be "specialization." Thus, the upper two years of undergraduate college—what we might now call coursework in the student's major today—was part of this debate as well, as were the commercial and industrial programs emerging at the high school.

The incorporation of specialized study into higher learning had implications for colleges, normal schools, and high schools alike. In light of this new institutional model, high schools and colleges across the country sought to extend their course offerings still further, to embrace not only the general, liberal studies of the "college" but also the specialized research of a "university."[2] This exerted pressure on the already-strained general liberal arts curriculum, in order to make room in students' educational experience for this more narrow study and training. It also brought criticism on the emerging educational system as a whole, which some considered too time consuming for students. As Edward Krug observes, the advent of the university entailed "a powerful movement, led by men from the universities, to modify or shorten the period of college education itself," sometimes by combining the secondary and college work, as both were considered part of the general curriculum. Krug points out that "sometimes the proposal was to cut out the college entirely and have pupils move from extended secondary schools into professional studies or graduate work." Indeed, that was long the reality across the nineteenth century and beyond—that students were admitted to professional programs (including normal programs as well as law and medical programs) without an undergraduate education. To this end, schools like University of Michigan toyed with ways to remove the undergraduate college from their ranks, combining the high school and college into one.[3]

It is this same impulse to internally manage and contain the emerging academic/collegiate and university distinction that is captured in the history of "junior colleges" (later called "community colleges") as they emerged at schools like University of Chicago. There, William DeGenaro explains, William Rainey Harper "divided academic units into an 'Academic College' (freshmen and sophomores) and a 'University College' (juniors, seniors, and graduate students) and in 1896 renamed the two levels 'Junior College' and 'Senior College,' respectively." Having decided that "he ultimately wanted freshmen and sophomores removed from the intellectual space of the university campus," Harper was simultaneously setting up articulation programs for select high schools to fulfill lower credits and enable students to advance more quickly toward the "University College," or senior college, than those from "inferior" secondary schools.[4] In this model, the first two years of college were equivalent to the high school in providing the liberal arts, and the remaining college curriculum was increasingly directed toward specialized research.

In response to the new educational aspirations represented by the university, Male High School began to offer advanced studies in an expanded range of "university" studies above and beyond a separately marked high school course of study. It even took on the additional designation as the "university of public schools." Though Female High School did not follow suit in this transformation, both of these Louisville schools help us consider the stakes of enhanced specialization and the "university" development for the fate of higher learning, beginning with changes to the general education curriculum at both schools and the incorporation of other specialized programs going into the final quarter of the century.

In this chapter and across the second part of this volume, I overview the changes made to the high schools in the next few decades (including the establishment of a high school for African American students in the 1880s and one dedicated to manual education in the 1890s), positioning these changes in relation to the impulse toward both expansion and bureaucratic control that characterized this period of educational history. I begin here with a discussion of Male High School, which felt most keenly the impact of these shifting institutional distinctions, before moving on to discuss Female High School in the second part of this chapter.

A "University of Public Schools": Tensions and Contradiction

As demonstrated in the first part of this book, Male High School was founded on the promise of instructing local students in the highest branches of learning. Though it offered a fairly standard collegiate course of study, the fact that Male High School did not offer the full scope of advanced studies that was coming to characterize a university left it open to the criticism that it had not, in fact, succeeded in converting "into a college or University," as had been intended.[5] But, because this idea of a university was still embryonic, its relationship to the college and even the high school remained unclear. Some continued to conflate the terms, such as one commentator who argued that Male High School's "continuance in its present liberal course of study . . . actually elevates it to the dignity of a first-class college" and asserted that, thus, "Louisville has her University well established."[6] Here, the liberal course of study makes Male a college, and the association of that college with the law and medical departments is likely what establishes it as a university. Elsewhere, Male High School was "of so excellent a character . . . that there is no longer any need of an Academical Department of the University," and it was said that people had altogether lost interest in the establishment of a university. Because it is able to displace the need for an "academical department," that meant that to this writer the high school was not, after all, the same thing as the academical department—which means it was not a college, and not affiliated with the university. And meanwhile another report just two days later praises Male's "establishment upon the university principles" as "its most attractive feature," yet expresses doubt that it has fulfilled its promise as the crowning feature of the school system. The significance of each of these terms to the community is complicated to parse, but the force of the argument is clear overall: there was little consensus around the status and role of the high school, and changes to the broader landscape of higher learning weren't clarifying the issue.[7]

As elsewhere, a major force driving changes to the curriculum was the notion of specialization, which was exerting pressure on the curriculum of high schools and colleges alike. In this way, school board president William Morris expressed concern in 1869 about "whether in our zeal to impart some knowledge of every subject which the human mind is capable of analyzing, there are not well grounded apprehensions of failure to accomplish the true object intended." He resolved, "Let us adhere to a thorough, complete course of study in everything that is practical—that which will confer the greatest possible intellectual good upon the largest number." But what those studies were remained unclear.[8]

A proposal for a polytechnic department for Male High School that circulated in 1869 spoke directly to that question. This report was commissioned by the school board in order to explore the increasingly popular prospect of industrial or mechanical education in the Male High School. Perhaps surprisingly from a modern perspective, this proposal was predicated not on the idea that some students weren't suited to advanced academic study (and therefore needed vocational course offerings), but instead hinged specifically on Male High School's identity as a university and, as such, its aspiration to provide advanced, specialized study in every field possible. The high school, the authors of that report argue, is a special kind of common school, where

> the studies pursued are of a more special character, as fitting the students for particular pursuits. In High Schools, therefore, and especially in a High School like ours, designed and chartered as the *University of Public Schools*, we are in favor of placing its course of studies upon a broad and generous basis, and of allowing to the students the largest liberty of election which is consistent with a systematic course.

By this the authors intended not a general liberal arts degree, per se, but a broad elective system capable of preparing students for a range of specialized careers. "Life is too short to learn everything," they reasoned, "and, as teachers of our young men, for the short period during which they are under our charge, we shall act the most judicious part by storing their minds with such resources as are most likely to be available in the contingencies of their future life."[9]

Working with the notion of specialization that defined a university course of study, the report clarifies that they "do not design to lower, in any degree, its collegiate powers and standing, but to give it more of a university character by presenting to its students a broader field of studies from which they may choose." In designating this university course, in fact, they sought instead to "Raise industry to the rank of a profession." A high school committee would even complain in 1869 of having missed out on funds from the first Morrill Act of 1862 for not having higher agricultural and mechanical branches established at the school, further indicating the role of the university idea in these changes. Thus, the high school, as an institution of higher learning affected by the same impulse toward specialization manifested in the university-building efforts of other American colleges, offered increasingly specialized courses and electives by the end of the century—linked, undoubtedly, to the national shift to industrialization and concomitant shifts in social and economic arrangements occurring at the same time.[10]

As the avowed site of general liberal arts study, the high schools had previously been quite clearly against such specialization, as colleges had been. Speaking specifically against the pressure to specialize boys early in preparation for business or industry and to divide the development of mind and body, Male's Principal Grant had in earlier years insisted: "No system of education is worthy of the name that contemplates anything less than the thorough and harmonious development of *all the faculties*, mental, moral and physical. . . . Exclusive attention to one pursuit or study should be reserved for well-developed, vigorous manhood."[11] But while the idea of specialization had been resolutely kept from the high schools and colleges of midcentury, it emerged as a value in the final decades of the century, dramatically changing the course offerings at both high schools and colleges as well as at the new universities.

It is these ideas of specialization—introduced in the high school through its attempts to be a "university"—that paved the way for the subsequent emergence of vocational education by the turn of the century. The value and function of that specialized training took on a different meaning as the high school shifted in relation to the college. As the high school became subordinated to the college and university, the vocational programming offered there took on the role and status of early specialization, or "tracking," lamented by subsequent educational theorists.[12] That is, what once might have been considered professional preparation at the high school level was at odds with the coursework needed to gain acceptance to college. Thus, paradoxically, many of the characteristics that seem most clearly to mark high schools as subordinate and clearly *not* college-level by the end of the century (such as manual training, business, normal, and home economics courses) were in Louisville proposed precisely because of the school's status as a *university*. It is no surprise that citizens and even school leaders would be somewhat confused about the definition and status of a high school, college, or university in this context.

Changing the High Schools, Changing Writing Instruction

In the face of a changing educational landscape, the high schools negotiated their own shifting position, and not without some public criticism along the way. In particular, doubts persisted as to whether the course of study at both Female and Male was thorough and comprehensive enough—or perhaps *too* thorough and comprehensive. As Professor Grant explained in 1863, there was some concern about whether "the curriculum of studies is not so extended as to prevent thoroughness on the part of the students." He insisted, though, that "those who have taken pains to examine either the students, the School, or its graduates, will bear cheerful testimony, that no institution exceeds it in thorough and practical instruction and discipline."[13]

Both schools sought to strike a balance between the pressures toward "practical" education for a broad range of student interests and the provision of an advanced, collegiate education with the highest cultural value, balancing the new interest in independent study and specialization in their course as well. As previously, they often compared favorably to the work of colleges, which they continued to see as their peer institutions. Indeed, with their own practical and liberal curriculum, they often saw themselves as superior to other colleges. For example, Principal Grant explained this curricular balance as it was negotiated at the Male High School at this time:

> It is well known that in most colleges the "*hard study*" is mostly accomplished in the Freshman and Sophomore years. The student is less tasked by the recitations of the Junior or Senior years. Theoretically, it leaves him more leisure for reading and general culture, as his mind becomes more mature. Practically, it too often leaves him time for idleness and dissipation. This would be more frequently the case in an institution like this, where young men are surrounded by all the fascinating temptations of a large city. Constant and profitable employment is ever a great security against temptation, and in no way can a teacher so effectually guard his pupils against demoralization as to keep them fully employed.[14]

Extending the "hard studies" into the latter years of the course made room for academic specialization, as students were able to focus their studies on areas of personal interest.[15] This served to advance the curriculum of Male and Female in their early years of operation, especially as students did not have to focus time and energy on preparing for admissions exams to other institutions. College admission examinations took up a great deal of energy and attention in the curriculum of college preparatory schools, but a school focused on advanced, terminal study was able, ideally, to focus this time on learning instead of cramming. With this idea in mind, the high schools continued with their collegiate curricula in the ensuing decade, expanding their offerings in line with the changes unfolding at other colleges, including an emphasis on literature and belletristic rhetoric.[16]

Within their English curriculum, students at Male continued to focus on composition instruction in their first years of study, now using

Parker's *Aids to English Composition* and Graham's *English Synonyms* in their freshman year. Parker's *Aids,* though used early in students' freshman year there, is subtitled "embracing specimens and models of school and college exercises," and it saw success as a best-seller across both contexts, with thirty-three imprints from 1832 to 1879.[17] The use of this college text in the first years of the high school course suggests the school's composition instruction was relatively rigorous.

For a time, this focus on composition and rhetoric continued into the more advanced classes at Male as well. Even as the interest of belletrism emerged there, with students using Cleveland's *A Compendium of English Literature* in their sophomore year, the emphasis on rhetoric and composition is suggested by the use of Kames's *Elements of Criticism* in their junior year, and Coppee's *Rhetoric* and *Logic* in their senior year.[18] Kames's *Elements,* as Beth Innocenti Manolescu has argued, encourages a rhetorical, practical approach to the *production of* arguments "rather than simply the reception of beauty, sublimity, and so on."[19] Manolescu points out that *Elements* was noted in its own time as part of the rhetorical tradition, though it has not received adequate attention from rhetoric and composition in this regard. It would also be considered a solidly college-level text, as was Coppee's *Rhetoric.* Students were still also engaging in regular exercises in composition and elocution, which are pulled out of the list of courses, as before, represented in a notation stating that students would complete weekly exercises in composition and elocution in the first and last years of study, and of composition and declamation in the sophomore and junior years.

As a basis of comparison for understanding how these texts and areas of study circulated elsewhere, we might look at the College of Science, Literature, and Arts at Kentucky University—which was founded in 1865 by merging Bacon College with Transylvania University and moving the newly christened institution to the nearby city of Lexington. Based on the limited information provided in the table, we can observe that the university's curriculum for 1865 features a course of study and texts similar to Male's at the same time. However, it is also interesting to note the different ordering of the course, with Cleveland's *English Literature* as a sophomore-level course at Male and a senior-level course at Kentucky University, while Kames's *Elements of Criticism* is sophomore-level at Kentucky University but junior-level at Male, for example. And, though students at Male were not presently studying Quackenbos or Whately,

Comparison of Male High School and Kentucky University, 1865–66

	English, writing, and rhetoric courses in the Male High School, 1865–66	*School of the English Language and Literature in the College of Science, Literature, and Arts, Kentucky University, 1865–66*
Freshman	First term—Weekly exercises in composition and elocution throughout the year. Second term—Parker's Aids and Graham's English Synonyms; weekly exercises in composition and elocution throughout the year.	First term—Mulligan's Structure of the English Language; English composition and elocution Second term—Mulligan's Structure of the English Language; English composition and elocution
Sophomore	First term—Cleveland's English Literature; weekly exercises in composition and declamation throughout the year. Second term—Weekly exercises in composition and declamation throughout the year.	First term—Quackenbos's Rhetoric; exercises in composition and elocution Second term—Kames's Elements of Criticism; exercises in composition and elocution
Junior	First term—Weekly exercises in composition and declamation throughout the year. Second term—Kames's Elements of Criticism; Weekly exercises in composition and declamation throughout the year.	First term—Whately's Logic, with practical exercises, three times a week. Second term—Whately's Rhetoric; original essays, orations, and forensic disputations, three times a week.
Senior	First term—Coppee's Rhetoric and Logic; Weekly exercises in composition and elocution throughout the year. Second term—Weekly exercises in composition and elocution throughout the year.	First term—Cleveland's English Literature; original essays, orations, and disputations, three times a week. Second term—Cleveland's English Literature; original essays, orations, and disputations, three times a week.

Source: course catalogs of Male High School and Kentucky University for the 1865–66 academic year.

we also see those texts that were in earlier circulation at the school shared by the curriculum of the university. This comparison demonstrates the consistently collegiate aspirations of Male High School's English instruction , and the ongoing overlap between the two sites of instruction.

The scholarly work of the English course at Male was advanced in this direction in 1866, when the principal, Dr. E. A. Grant, was replaced by professor R. L. Butler. One of Butler's qualifications for this position was as professor of Belles Lettres, as Grant before him had been. But Principal Butler's election also reflected the increasing professionalization of higher education at the high school, as he was elected based not only on his "sound judgment, and practical experience" within the school but also on his "thorough scholarship" in the field. This shift was in line with the professionalization of other higher schools and colleges, indicating a transformation in the education professional as a whole, one that would affect the teaching and learning of English writing and rhetoric in its course.[20]

The schools' curriculum continued to shift in the coming years as they continued to struggle with their identities, especially in their attempts to balance access with excellence in the high schools. While some critics disparaged the high schools—particularly the Male High School—insisting that they should be more challenging and advanced, it was equally problematic that the rigor of the high schools was actually *too stringent* for many students already. In particular, it was found that the examinations of 1866, "while they compare favorably with those of any previous year, suggest to the committee that perhaps too much is required of these classes. Of those who enter the High Schools but a small proportion graduate, and it cannot be denied that there are too many conditions and failures" of those entering the high school as well. In short, though more students were advancing into and through the high schools, still not enough were doing so, and school leaders sought to reconfigure the school in such a way as to both increase its prestige and ensure recruitment and retention, especially as the schools contained only 3 percent of the whole number educated in the public schools in 1867, though required 10 percent of the expenditures to maintain them.[21]

In response, the school board made changes to the curriculum. They even briefly considered a proposal to merge the Male and Female High Schools in order to reduce the inefficiency and expense of these schools. Instead of taking this measure, board president William H. Morris proposed the establishment of preparatory departments as a means to increase the success and persistence of students through the course. He found precedence for a preparatory department in the colleges of Boston, New York, Philadelphia, and Baltimore, which each justified a lengthier time to degree than the high schools because they included a year or two of preparatory work. He argued:

> It is in this particular we need to learn a lesson, both of economy and efficiency. We have been struggling along for many years trying to educate young men to a standard sustained in other institutions, while it is a known fact that the preparation required for admission to the Male High School is very far below what is required for admission to the Freshman Class of any college in the country. It is without doubt this want of an introductory course of one or two years that has heretofore rendered the High School so expensive, inefficient, and unpopular.[22]

Thus, a preparatory department was added to Male High School in 1868 in order to bridge the gap between the grammar schools and high schools (notably the very same gap complained of by college men across the country, who had not been relying on the completion of an intermediary high school course).[23]

Perhaps significantly, no instruction in rhetoric or composition was designated in the course schedule for the preparatory department that first year, although almost every other subject is covered there, including classics, math, natural science, German and French. The annual report of the following year celebrates the new preparatory course, which "has given us a Freshman Class one year in advance of the usual standard in Classics and Mathematics."[24]

But the course was altered the same year: composition and elocution were moved from the regular course of study and now listed in the preparatory year—and *only* in the preparatory year. The English language study that remained in the subsequent years of the belles lettres curriculum does include Bonnell's *Rhetoric*, notable for its emphasis on composition, as well as Kame's *Elements of Criticism*, Shakespeare and Milton, and Coppee's *Elements of Rhetoric*, which shows that students did still study composition (and perhaps elocution) throughout the course of study.[25] Nonetheless, the term "composition" itself had moved in this developing curriculum into the realm of a primarily preparatory course.

Further changes in this direction were made in 1868, when the belles lettres curriculum was pulled out and marked as its own separate school of study within the high school. The new school of belles lettres at Male was comprised of the history of Greece, Rome, and ancient Europe; philosophy; and rhetoric, composition, and literature. Within this belles lettres curriculum, students studied rhetoric and composition from the beginning, using Bonnell's *Rhetoric* in their freshman and sophomore years and adding Kame's *Elements of Criticism* in the sophomore year (the latter had formerly been used in the junior year). In their junior year, students studied Shakespeare, Milton, and Coppee's *Elements of Rhetoric*, and in their senior year no rhetoric or literature text is listed, though students were studying logic and philosophy. With these seemingly minor changes, we see the emergence of the belletristic ideal and the sidelining of composition instruction in the evolving high school curriculum.

This was a result, at least in part, of the suppression of general education in an increasingly crowded high school course of study. As the annual report of Louisville's Male High School explains in 1871, the area of belles lettres is "so large that, of necessity, to one study the rest are made subservient." The study to which the others became subservient was the history of English language and literatures. Other subjects, it is explained, were integrated into literary study: "In every class Declamation and the Art of Composition is assiduously practiced. The principles of Rhetoric and Criticism are taught theoretically, by text-books, and are also practically applied to the interpretation of Literary Art as found embodied in English Classics."[26]

A similar trend is observed elsewhere, such as in Chicago's high school, where rhetoric and writing were first relegated to less rigorous academic courses, and then displaced altogether by literature. There, students were studying English literature by at least 1866 in the upper division of the four-year general and classical programs, though not in the two-year normal program. Composition was studied throughout the whole course of all three programs, but rhetoric, on the other hand, appeared *only* in the general and normal departments (with Quackenbos's text). Thus, something of a hierarchy begins to emerge across these programs: literature is a more advanced, academic subject, while rhetoric and composition are more general and preparatory. As at Male, these changes coincide with a period of time during which school leaders were advocating for the extension of the school, via the classical course, into a full city college. Following this trend of making English literature a separate area of study, by 1872, rhetoric, composition, and declamation, were no longer mentioned in Chicago's annual reports.[27]

Emerging here is the privileging of literary and philosophical study in the higher branches. This is representative of the move to professionalize English through the study of literature at this time, in part because literature could claim a research basis for their work in the new German model of the research university. As Thomas Miller and others have argued, in their attempt to stake claim to the institutional space of the research university, English faculty played into the devaluation of composition that suggested that practice in writing was necessarily remedial. As Miller argues, "The institutional demarcation of the field of literature from the work of reading and writing can be dated from the literacy crisis that was manufactured to justify the expansion of the profession." Thus, the profession of English becomes attached to the study of literature, with rhetoric relegated to the first years of study—in both the college and the high school.[28]

As the curriculum continued to advance and change back at Male, the faculty continued to develop their own positions and their school in line with the emerging standards of collegiate faculties, extending the trend of specialization in the university model. In this way, the separation of the belles lettres courses laid the groundwork for the division of all courses at Male High School into separate schools of study, and by 1869 that division of the curriculum was made official in the rules: the classical or regular course of study became the only comprehensive degree-granting option, as the English/scientific track was merged with the partial or commercial track and subsequently reduced to a two-year course (in addition to the preparatory work of one year for all courses of study).[29] That is, while the school previously offered two full academic courses—the classical course resulting in a bachelor of arts degree and the English/scientific course resulting in a bachelor of science degree—it now recognized only the classical course as a collegiate course. The practical English course was no longer considered a collegiate option. In this way, the school was internally managing the emerging distinction between a high school and college course by differentiating the existing courses of study based on subject-area focus and time commitment.

By 1872, Male High School made the effort to internally manage the distinction between general education and advanced specialization even more explicit: it now offered what were called a high school and a university course, the latter of which built on and extended from the former in a hierarchical arrangement (fig. 4.1).[30]

The status of each program was no longer determined by content so much as duration: the studies of Male High School now embraced two graded courses, a business and a classical course, each of three years and resulting not in a degree but a diploma of graduation. "Besides these," the curricular program stated, "there shall be a University Course of two years, varying, according to the election of the student, and entitling him to Degrees." This "university course" was offered within the Male High School, comprising two additional years of study beyond the "high school" courses. As one student explained the situation, the university course was understood to comprise the junior and senior classes of the school. So, while a "high school" was still not a separate place or even a distinct curriculum in Louisville, it was now a relative designation, subordinated to the "college" or "university" above it.[31]

But confusion and conflict resulted from these institutional transformations when, during the transition to a "university" curriculum in the 1870s, it was found that some students were graduated who did not study all of the required subjects of the course.[32] This concerned commentators, who saw it as a troubling reduction in standards. As a result, charges of mismanagement were leveraged at Dr. E. A. Anderson, principal of the school. These charges were both political and personal, meaning that they involved debates about the definition of a high school and college more broadly, by way of Anderson's specific actions and inactions as an individual leader.

The charges, forwarded by one Dr. Yandell of the school board, alleged violation of the rules of the school regarding graduating students who had not completed the studies of the school. They also included habitual failure to maintain discipline and order in the schools, physical unfitness for the office of principal (due to low vision and hearing loss), and a want of scholarship. A multitude of articles deliberating the merit of these charges circulated in the local papers, authored by students, alumni, and citizens both for and against the principal. In a rather carnivalesque affair, the school board even heard the testimony

COURSE OF STUDY FOR THE MALE HIGH SCHOOL.

		BELLES LETTRES.	ANCIENT LANGUAGES.		MATHEMATICS.	APPLIED MATHEMATICS.	NATURAL SCIENCE.	MODERN LANGUAGES.	
		ENGLISH LITERATURE.	LATIN.	GREEK.		ENGINEERING.		FRENCH.	GERMAN.
FIRST YEAR.	FIRST SESSION.	Bonnell's Rhetoric, Elocut'n.	Bingham's Grammar.	German may be substituted for Latin.	Robinson's University Algebra.	Walter Smith's Drawing Series.	Hooker's Natural History.	Latin may be substituted for German.	Woodbury's New Method and Exercises.
	SECOND SESSION.	Bonnell's Rhetoric, Elocut'n.	Bingham's Grammar, " Reader.		do.	do.	Hutchinson's Physiology.		do.
SECOND YEAR.	FIRST SESSION.	Fowler's Grammar, Rawlinson's History.	Gildersleeves' Grammar, Latin Exercises, Bingham's Cæsar.		Chauvenet's Geometry.	Warren's Elementary Plain Problems.	Steele's Natural Philosophy.		Woodbury—continued.
	SECOND SESSION.	do. Elocution.	do.		Chauvenet's Plane Trigonometry.	Smith's Topographical Drawing.	Steele's Astronomy.		Woodbury, continued, Anderson's Reader, Adler's Dictionary.
THIRD YEAR.	FIRST SESSION.	Scott, Fowler's Grammar, Student's Hume.	Gildersleeves' Grammar Exercises, Virgil.		Chauvenet's Spherical Trigonometry.	Gillespie's Surveying.	Roscoe's Chemistry, (Inorganic.)		Worman's Echo, Composition Anderson's Tales.
	SECOND SESSION.	do. Elocution.	do.		do.	do.	Roscoe's Chemistry, (Organic.)		Echo contin'd, Composition.

COURSE OF STUDY FOR THE UNIVERSITY OF THE PUBLIC SCHOOLS.

		BELLES LETTRES.	ANCIENT LANGUAGES.		MATHEMATICS.	APPLIED MATHEMATICS.	NATURAL SCIENCE.	MODERN LANGUAGES.	
		ENGLISH LITERATURE.	LATIN.	GREEK.		ENGINEERING.	CHEMISTRY & TECHN'GY.	FRENCH.	GERMAN.
PREPARATORY YEAR.	FIRST SESSION.	Bonnell's Rhetoric, Elocut'n.	Bingham's Grammar.		Robinson's Algebra.	Bartholomew's Drawing Series.	Hooker's Natural History.		Woodbury's New Method and Exercises.
	SECOND SESSION.	do.	Bingham's Grammar, Bingham's Reader.		do.	do.	Hutchinson's Physiology.		do.
FRESHMAN YEAR.	FIRST SESSION.	Fowler's Grammar, Rawlinson's History.	Gildersleeve's Latin Exercises, Bingham's Cæsar.	McClintock's & Crook's First Lessons.	Chauvenet's Geometry.	Warren's Elementary Plain Problems.	Steele's Natural Philosophy.		Woodbury, continued.
	SECOND SESSION.	do.	do.	McClintock's & Crook's, continued, Reader.	do.	do.	Steele's Astronomy.		Woodbury, continued, Anderson's Reader, Adler's Dictionary.
SOPHOMORE YEAR.	FIRST SESSION.	Scott, Fowler's Grammar, Student's Hume.	Gildersleeve's Grammar, Latin Exercises, Virgil.	Hadley's Grammar, Boise's Exercises, Xenophon's Anabasis.	Chauvenet's Plane Trigonometry.	Smith's Topographical Drawing.	Roscoe's Chemistry, (Inorganic).	Fasquelle's Large French Course.	Worman's Echo, Composit'n, Anderson's Tales.
	SECOND SESSION.	do. Elocution.	do.	do.	Chauvenet's Spherical Trigonometry.	Gillespie's Surveying, Simm's Leveling.	Roscoe's Chemistry, (Organic).	do. Fasquelle's Telemaque, Spier's & Surrenne's Dictionary.	Echo, continued, Composition.
JUNIOR YEAR.	FIRST SESSION.	Shakspeare and Milton, Shaw's Literature.	Gildersleeve's Grammar, Composit'n, Cicero de Officiis.	Grammar, continued, Prose Composition, Herodotus.	Robinson's Analytical Geometry and Conic Sections.	Mahan's Industrial Drawing, Mahan's Civil Engineering.	Dana's Geology.	Fasquelle, continued, Un Philosophe, sous les Toits.	Heyse's Grammar, Composition, Maria Stewart.
	SECOND SESSION.	Coppee's Elements of Rhetoric, Shaw's Literature, Coppee's Logic (commenced).	Gildersleeve's Grammar, Composition, Livy.	Grammar, continued, Prose Composition, Homer.	do.	Gillespie's Roads and Railroads, Haupt's Bridge Construction.	Dana's Mineralogy.	do.	Grammar and Composition, continued—William Tell.
SENIOR YEAR.	FIRST SESSION.	Stewart's Philosophy of the Human Mind, Coppee's Logic (completed).	Composition, Tacitus.	Composition, Demosthenes.	Courtenay's Calculus.	Peck's Mechanics, Loomis' Practical Astronomy.	Analytical Chemistry.	Noel and Chapsal's Grammar, French Composition, French Echo.	Composition, Essays, Jean Paul's Walt & Valt.
	SECOND SESSION.	Guizot's History of Civilization, Butler's Analogy.	Composition, Juvenal.	Composition, Plato.	do.	Stevenson's Canal and River Engineering, Fenwick's Subterranean Surveying.	Technology. (Manufactures).	do. Moliere, Lectures on Literature.	Essays. Lectures on Literature.

Fig. 4.1. Schedule of course requirements for Male High School and the University of Public Schools, printed in the *Annual Report* of 1873. COURTESY OF JEFFERSON COUNTY PUBLIC SCHOOLS.

of faculty, students, and the eloquent Dr. Yandell against Dr. Anderson and his school in a public hearing.

Following the public hearing of the school board, Anderson responded to the charges, characterizing them as "puerile, feeble, vaguely worded, poorly arranged—evidently the work of a novice, stating things about which he had no personal knowledge and giv[ing] bunglingly the statements of others." He insisted, of course, that he was as capable of managing the school as ever and turned the charge that he "is no scholar; he can't spell, violates rules of grammar, uses incorrect language" against the accuser, Dr. Yandell. Unsatisfied with this reversal, the *Courier-Journal* called Anderson's a "weak, undignified, unscholarly" response, and another respondent insisted that "what the people are interested in knowing is, can Dr. Anderson write good English or preside with dignity and ability over the Male High School? They conclude from his reply to the charges published in your issue of Tuesday that he can not."[33] Thus, the conflict continued.

Telling of the institutional stakes of these seemingly personal criticisms, the professor of modern languages at Male resigned in 1873 amid this flurry, "fearing [his] ability to meet the wants of so advanced a class as [he] would be compelled to meet in that school." This is to say, the professor seems to have been coming to terms with the aspirations of the high school as a "university of public schools" through this public debate, and chose not to have his own credentials swept up in the imbroglio. Thus, while the figure of Principal Anderson became a lightning rod for debate, the controversy really centered on the status of the high schools for the city.[34]

In the course of these changes to the high school's status, the English curriculum changed in turn. In particular, composition was further established as a preparatory subject, as rhetoric and (especially) literature simultaneously became advanced subjects, removed from the first session of the freshman year in 1873 and concentrated in the more advanced years of "university" study. The English and rhetoric instruction in both the high school course and the first two years of the university course were identical, consisting of the study of rhetoric (with a textbook from Bonnell), elocution, and grammar (with a textbook from Fowler), and a reading of Scott (presumably the writings of Sir Walter Scott). Those first years of study are then followed in the university course by the study of Shakespeare and Milton, Thomas B. Shaw's *A History of English Literature*, and Coppee's *Elements of Rhetoric.*

Even when the high school and "university" were contained in the same school system, even the same building, and with the same students, composition instruction was becoming relegated to the early years of study. Prior to 1873, students practiced composition throughout all four years of their education at Male. But exercises in composition and elocution or declamation that had previously been college fare in the English curriculum were demoted by the last quarter of the century. They were now determined to be preparatory studies. That is, as the collegiate curriculum was shifting and transforming to an English curriculum or a more broadly elective curriculum, composition did not come along as a fully collegiate subject. It was replaced instead by the study of literature.

One explanation is that, as colleges determined composition to be a non-collegiate subject, a high school that aspired to a collegiate standing perforce suppressed its own composition offerings accordingly. As Connors notes, the categorization of composition and rhetoric as general rather than specialized areas of study sealed their fate as the university model increased the value of disciplinary specialization—even within the high schools. Elizabethada Wright and S. Michael Halloran similarly explain the connection between the growth of specialized knowledge and the development of English composition, as "new disciplines and professions left a smaller and smaller place in the curriculum for 'rhetoric.'" Composition became "simply a course in our sense of that term, competing for the students' time and attention with an ever growing array of other courses." In this way composition became decentralized and devalued both in the college and the high school curriculum.[35]

At the same time, in the context of the public high school, the concentration of composition in the early years of study is also more complicated. There, the change speaks also to the ongoing *value* of composition and the school's commitment to access. After all, as the justification for this preparatory department suggests, most matriculants of the high school never graduated. This was an ongoing refrain in the school board reports across the decades. The consequences were that the upper branches were underpopulated. In his report from 1873, Principal Anderson was clearly under pressure concerning the fact that so few students continued beyond the high school certificate to the university courses.[36] It meant that those upper branches were particularly expensive to operate. It also meant that most students missed out on whatever was taught in those branches. By concentrating the most general subjects into the first years, school leaders ensured that the greatest number of students were able to benefit from them.

There is also more to understand about the relations between literature, rhetoric, and writing here than meets the eye. For example, the listing of Bonnell's "Rhetoric" is particularly notable because it most assuredly refers to the *Manual of the Art of Prose Composition: For the Use of Colleges and Schools* written by John Mitchell Bonnell—the president of Wesleyan Female College. Bonnell's book is credited by Thomas Conley for the "separation of composition and delivery, with only the art of composition laying legitimate claim to the title 'Rhetoric.'"[37] The fact that this composition text is listed not by its own title, but as a "rhetoric" is significant because it marks an early shift toward what Connors calls "composition-rhetoric" in the schools, and an early beginning for the field of writing studies writ large—particularly the equation of rhetoric with composition. It also shows how composition instruction can be seen to have persisted throughout this period, even if nominally marked as rhetoric or even literature.[38]

Women's Higher Schooling: The Common School Connection

Similar developments occurred at Female High School, where they experienced their own growing pains in relation to both the writing curriculum and the larger identity and location of the high school overall. Despite frequent protestations to the contrary, this school was never supported and valued as highly as the "university of public schools." This is due both to its subordinate status as a "high school" and to the fact that its patrons were young women—two traits that are consistently intertwined.

The lack of parity is evidenced clearly in terms of school resources and facilities. While Male High School was operated from a grand facility on the university campus, Female students had long endured inadequate facilities not suited for the purposes of a high school, which affected student performance and their overall health and well-being, as the rooms were often poorly heated and ventilated. Superintendent George W. Morris even reported that so many students at Female were getting ill from the school, sometimes fatally, that "the statement has become very current in our community, that we are only educating young ladies to graduate and die." A new building was proposed and built for Female in 1864, which helped alleviate many health concerns.[39]

But that didn't resolve matters entirely. As the schools continued to grow and change—as did conceptions of who a high school girl was and what she needed in her education and life—already by 1872 it was determined that the new school was "unfitted for the purpose, the rooms separated from each other by only thin board partitions—while the increase in the number of pupils has far exceeded that of any previous year." This was certainly understood to hinder learning, and it was explained that if the examinations of students "should not be up to the usual standard we cannot complain." The school opened in 1873 in an impressive new building, which superintendent of the Boston city schools John D. Philbrick pronounced to be one of the handsomest and best equipped in the country (fig. 4.2). According to a later publication, this celebrated new building marked "a new epoch" in the school's career, which was "the beginning of increased efficiency, attractiveness, and usefulness" for the school.[40]

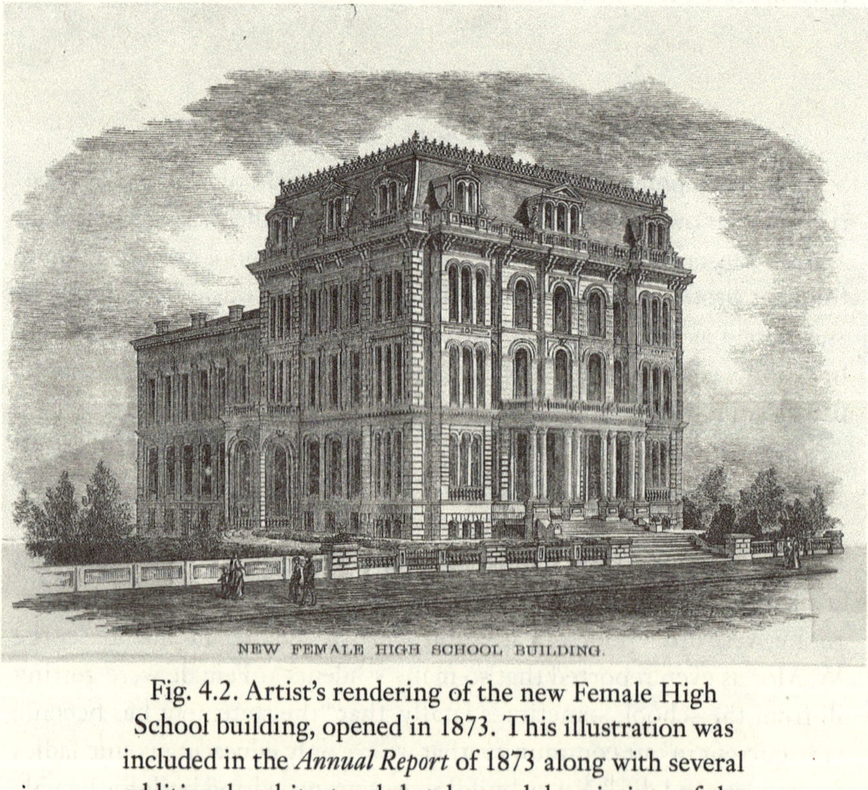

Fig. 4.2. Artist's rendering of the new Female High School building, opened in 1873. This illustration was included in the *Annual Report* of 1873 along with several additional architectural sketches and descriptions of the building. COURTESY OF LOUISVILLE FREE PUBLIC LIBRARY.

Reflecting this "new epoch," the new building was attended by changes to the curriculum as well, many of which mirrored changes to Male's curriculum, such as the impulse toward specialization in the proliferation of professional programs and courses affiliated with the high school. Calls for the establishment of a separate normal school and training school (or "lab school" attached to a public grammar school) reverberated from at least 1868, and persisted even after the establishment of a separate training school in 1871.

Controversy about the status of the Female High School emerged in relation to the Training School for teachers, as the rules of the school board privileged the graduates of the Training School (of just two years) over the "scholars" of Female for teachers of the public schools. Was the best training for teachers broad scholarship, or training in instructional methods? What was the relation between the two? These questions reflected changing notions of the high school and its status in the academic hierarchy, as well as changing notions of expertise, scholarship, and professionalism.[41]

The changing conceptions of the high school led to, among other things, a decrease in rhetoric and composition in the upper years of study. By 1867–68 English grammar and composition were taught formally only in the freshman year (fig. 4.3). Rhetoric was taught every term of the sophomore and junior years, and English and Latin etymology in senior year, while "Exercises in Elocution, Composition and Light Gymnastics shall be required of the pupils throughout the entire Course of Study; and lectures on Physiology and topics connected with History and General Literature may be delivered by the Principal or persons invited by him."[42] Thus, composition and elocution were practiced throughout the course, but only alongside these other ancillary activities that were not deemed central to the curriculum.

This trend continued. Rhetoric and composition instruction took on an increasingly extracurricular status outside of the first years of instruction. In place of the former emphasis on rhetoric and composition throughout the curriculum at Female was a belletristic emphasis on literature in the higher branches, with attention to reading over writing texts. The English curriculum in 1872 featured Boyd's *Elements of English Composition* for the first and second years; Shaw's *Outlines of English Literature* in the third year; and readings in classical literature and Graham's *English Synonyms* in the fourth or senior year. The explicit mention of

GRADED COURSE OF INSTRUCTION. 67

FEMALE HIGH SCHOOL.

FIRST YEAR CLASS.

FIRST SESSION.	SECOND SESSION.
Mental and Practical Arithmetic,	Intellectual and Written Algebra,
English Grammar and Composition,	Latin Grammar,
Hooker's Natural History,	Botany,
General History, with Geography,	History (continued),
Vocal Music.	Vocal Music.

SECOND YEAR CLASS.

FIRST SESSION.	SECOND SESSION.
Algebra,	Algebra,
Latin Grammar and Reader,	Latin Grammar and Reader,
Natural Philosophy,	Natural Philosophy,
Rhetoric,	Rhetoric,
Vocal Music.	Vocal Music.

JUNIOR CLASS.

FIRST SESSION.	SECOND SESSION.
Geometry,	Geometry,
Latin—Ovid's Metamorphoses,	Latin (continued,)
French or German,	French or German,
Chemistry,	Chemistry,
Rhetoric,	Rhetoric,
Vocal Music.	Vocal Music.

SENIOR CLASS.

FIRST SESSION.	SECOND SESSION.
Astronomy,	Astronomy,
Physical Geography,	Geology,
Mental Philosophy,	French or German,
French or German,	English and Latin Etymology,
English and Latin Etymology,	Mental Philosophy, with Theory and Practice of Teaching,
Vocal Music.	Vocal Music.

Exercises in Elocution, Composition, and Light Gymnastics shall be required of the pupils throughout the entire Course of Study; and lectures on Physiology and topics connected with History and General Literature may be delivered by the Principal or persons invited by him.

Fig. 4.3. Graded course of instruction for Female High School, printed in the *Annual Report* of 1867.
COURTESY OF LOUISVILLE FREE PUBLIC LIBRARY.

rhetoric as a course of study drops out entirely, and formal instruction in composition is confined to the first year of study, though students also completed "weekly exercise in reading, spelling, and composition" throughout every year of study. As Wright and Halloran argue, such a shift to belletrism entailed a shift from eloquence to one of taste, which "tends to make rhetoric an art of the audience more than of the speaker or writer. . . . Eloquence thus set the stage for the elevation of interpretation and reading over invention and writing that would characterize the discipline of English studies."[43]

Students evidence this increasingly belletristic conception of the value and purpose of language in their writing. An essay titled "American Footprints on the Sands of Time" by Female student Sallie Thuston dated June 17, 1872, is an example. The essay, composed when Thuston was a senior in the school, contrasts with the school writing of her peers from the previous decade (see chapter 2), suggesting a shift in the approaches to writing instruction toward a more abstract, belletristic approach.[44]

Completed in a school examination "blue book," the essay is comprised of reflections on the power of language and education. Focusing on the fate of Native Americans in the history of the United States, Thuston argues that language systems are a means of studying cultural and political history:

> The language of a people sheds light upon its history, unfolds the relations it sustains to other nations and affords a key to its character. That of the Indians, the Aborigines of America formed a true [index] to theirs. Familiar with nature in all its variety and grandeur they delighted in drawing figures from objects which she presented, representing prosperity by the glowing sun and adversity by the lowering clouds. There is something sad in the fate of this unfortunate people, much to awaken our sympathy and much in their character which betrays us into involuntary admiration.

In its argument that the language of a people reflect their history and character, Thuston's depiction ultimately argues for an understanding of the Native American people as primitive and fated to be superseded, even as they also evoke "involuntary admiration" from the colonizers. Shoring up the narrative of "manifest destiny," Thuston goes on: "This beautiful country was not intended by the Almighty always to be their [the Native Americans'] home, sometime far off heroes more destined to discover the many beauties, explore her lakes and rivers, climb the steep ascent of the mountains, pursue the chase on her plains and render useful the many precious ores hidden in her soil."[45] Thus, the Native Americans are ultimately not the "heroes" of this narrative.

Modern readers are likely to find fault in Thuston's historical interpretation and its racist and colonial overtones. At the same time, though, we would do well to attend to another compositional trend that underlies this kind of argument: that in constructing this narrative Thuston must enter into the composing task with a very different sense of authority and expertise than her peers had in their writing of a decade ago. In contrast to the commencement essays discussed in chapter 2, Thuston's essay takes as its topic something of which she herself has no direct experience, and its abstract title—"Footprints on the Sands of Time"—brings it further into the realm of the abstract. In this way, it is a clear example of the much-derided student "theme" writing. When compared to the previous examples, this trend of belletristic abstraction and potentially current-traditional writing appears to be new to the school, as the curriculum of the high schools shifted in the last quarter of the century.

But understanding the role of this seemingly current-traditional conception of writing also requires attention to the school's relationship to other schools in the system and the writing valued there. In the case of Thuston's essay, the date and an accompanying "Grammar Certificate" for "satisfactory examination in required studies" dated July 1, 1872, suggest the essay was an exam. Given that Thuston was graduating from the high school at this time, the term "Grammar Certificate" suggests that the essay and accompanying certificate were teacher certification for the grammar schools, not an academic examination for her high school course. Indeed, an aspect of Female's English curriculum for the senior year of study was the review of English branches specifically for the purposes of teaching preparation. In this way, writing such as Thuston's is linked to the values and practices of the lower schools, or at least to conceptions about how to prepare for teaching in such schools.[46]

This points to an important difference from Male's curriculum, which is visually apparent in the layout and complexity of the course of study for each school as well. In contrast to the elaborate curricular structure at Male (see fig. 4.1), Female's curriculum (see fig. 4.3) is a straightforward list of subjects, with little emphasis on details such as the textbook in use or the duration of study. This difference in the curricular tables reflects a difference in self-conception and status for each school: If Male High School's identity and function was defined by its relation to the college or university ideal, Female High School's was defined by its relationship to the public school system. Always marked as a high school and never staking claim to be a college or university, Female's curriculum aligned more straightforwardly with the emerging standards of a high school in its embrace of the English subjects and its uniform curriculum. It was also conceptualized in closer relation to the lower schools, which continued to be the primary benefactor of the Female High School throughout the century, and which interfaced richly with the work of the high schools as part of one holistic system.

Composition across the Public Schools

While the high schools decreased their explicit instruction in the area of composition, attention to composition arose more generally in the school reports for the lower schools at this time. The Committee on Examination and Control expressed concern that "the art of original composition has been to a great extent neglected" in the common schools. Making a case for the importance of composition instruction and practice, they explain that the concern about writing is not only or even primarily in relation to preparing students for the high schools, but instead in recognition of the fact that "the largest number who enter our District Schools never reach the Intermediate, and only a few comparatively enter our High Schools."[47]

Reporting on the examination of students' writing in the schools, the committee attests that "the correct writing of a few connected sentences was to all a tedious, to many an impossible task." The problem, as they figure it, was that not enough attention was paid to composition in the schools anymore. Though the high school graduates were consistently praised for their commencement essays, the students in the lower schools were not benefitting from the same attention. Complaining that "the sole instruction given in rare instances has been confined to exercises not founded on any regular system," they recommend the adoption of a proper textbook or handbook to redress this problem. But, following the New Education and its focus on student-centered learning processes, they hasten to clarify that slavish study of grammar rules is not the goal either, as "all must admit that it is only the practical application of its rules that renders the study of grammar useful,—parsing must be considered subordinate to composing, and the analysis of our language is secondary to its synthesis."[48] In short, the committee was interested in reviving the study of composition across the curriculum—at this foundational level if not the high school level.

School administrators remained conscientious of the more practical applications of writing for the majority of students who did not matriculate to high schools. Thus, on their final examinations at the culmination of their grammar school course, students were invited to compose highly practical essays directly reflecting their own experiences and real-life contexts, such as addressing a letter to the principal of the high school stating which studies you like best and in which subjects you think yourself deficient, writing a receipt for the payment of rent on a house you own, or writing a note inviting a friend to Central Park to witness the celebration of St. John's Day.[49] With their very specific sense of audience and context, these assignments were not only practical but also quite rhetorical.

Even with this increased attention to composition across the schools, though, the examination committee remained frustrated by the results. That same year, 1873, they renewed complaints about surface-oriented writing instruction in the schools, objecting that "nothing was attempted save an absurd enumeration of technicalities in punctuation, which a child is utterly unable to comprehend, and for which, in constructing his own simple sentences, he has no use."[50] And students were still found to be generally underprepared for the high schools as well.

School leaders rightly note the tremendous shifts in the system at this time as a contributing factor. The school board report of 1872 explains:

> Your attention is again called to the small proportion of the [preparatory] Class who have passed unconditionally into the Freshman. This is due to the fact, that within the last three years the standard of admission into the school has been very much lowered, while the course of study here has been made more difficult. There is a wide gap between where the Grammar School Course ends and where the High School Course begins, hence the fewness of those who manage to maintain themselves after being admitted into the school.[51]

This complaint provides renewed perspective on the perennial problem of students' writing preparation: even as school leaders tried to address the needs of a diverse and expanding cadre of students, the shifting status of these programs and institutions as they swelled put the core "democratic" mission of the high schools at risk, and raised concerns about the shared preparation of students in the spirit of the common schools. In particular, observers of the schools were concerned about access: Who was able to gain admission to the schools, and why were so few graduating? As national discourse about high school and college alignment began to circulate, local school leaders found that the joints of even their own school system were not well articulated. From this perspective, writing pedagogies and practice are revealed to be a shared concern among educators determining the appropriate role of composition instruction in a time of shifting programmatic and institutional standards. Students weren't changing; the schools were changing.

The confused relations continued, both on a national and local level, all hinging on the indeterminate language of higher learning. Presented both as an extension of common schooling and as a thing set apart, the high schools were a rich site of negotiation about the purposes of advanced language instruction and liberal education for citizens, communities, and society, which necessarily highlighted tensions around the boundaries of these terms. That is, who counts as a citizen? Whose needs represent the needs of the community? How do the needs of the individual citizen intersect with those of the community or society? What form of higher learning can address the varying needs and interests of an increasingly diverse student body? As a new form of higher learning without European models to follow, U.S. high schools had to answer these questions largely for themselves, creating a hybrid form of higher learning that drew on multiple existing forms and their values—particularly those of the common school and the traditional liberal arts college.

It is into this increasingly complex educational landscape that the Central Colored High School entered. That school may have been established many years after the first two high schools for white students, but it, too, was involved fundamentally with these same institutional transformations across the last third of the nineteenth century—in addition to the ever-evolving discourses of race and racism in the period of Reconstruction and Redemption that the country was entering.

5

"Just on the Border of the Intellectual World": Central Colored High School

> Add continually to the stock of knowledge which you have already acquired. Remember that you have just begun to learn: that you have found the sum of only a few terms of the infinite series of the mind's progression; that you stand just on the border of the intellectual world, at the base of the hill of science. Go onward and upward then, for further on and higher there are riper fruits and richer fragrance.
>
> —*Principal J. M. Maxwell, "The Colored Children,"* Courier-Journal, *June 30, 1877*

If the academic status of "higher" schools for white students in the nineteenth century was up for debate, the status of high schools for African American students at this time was, predictably, all the more complicated. Since "high" is a relative term, the educational advancements of public higher schooling for Louisville's free and freed black citizens and their children took place under a number of banners and names—and under various fronts of opposition. Some limited higher learning was available to African Americans from early in the century, often sponsored by African American communities themselves. Integrated higher education was available at predominantly white institutions like Oberlin College as early as the 1830s, and African American colleges and universities like Wilberforce and Lincoln were established as early as 1856. Interracial and historically black colleges and universities (HBCUs) accomplished important work for the higher education and empowerment of African American students, "serv[ing] as beacons of light for academic excellence and for the nurturing of talents and abilities across a full range of academic experience and potential." Studying such schools and the people who labored in and for them remains crucial for obtaining "a fuller understanding of [African Americans'] historical presence in academic arenas, and thereby in composition studies."[1]

Louisville's vibrant, free-black community had laid the groundwork for such educational advancements in their own city by organizing schools for their children in the basements of local churches around the city in the years before the Civil War. Building on these precedents, the city made initial efforts to develop public higher schooling for African Americans in Louisville just after the war, in 1868, when the Freedmen's Bureau and the American Missionary Association established the Ealy Normal School, which was staffed by northern white teachers and provided the only free education for black students in the city. Ealy came under the control of the local board of education in 1897 and continued to function until 1935, later evolving into Kentucky State University (an HBCU still in operation in Frankfort). The transformation of Ealy into a municipal school and then a state university is a story typical of many schools which underwent a series of institutional conversions as the landscape of higher education shifted at the turn of the century.[2] After the war, Louisville's Simmons University was established as the only college controlled by African Americans in the commonwealth of Kentucky, and it remained so until its incorporation with the University of Louisville in the twentieth century.[3]

But the status of these schools was never well established. Historian J. Blaine Hudson notes that African American colleges like the state land-grant institution and the private collegiate institute "functioned essentially as vocational high schools," not colleges. Other colleges in the area fare no better: interracial Berea College was one of the only true sites of higher education for African Americans, according to Hudson, until, with the passage of the Day Law officially segregating schools in 1908, school leaders established a segregated African American branch of the college that became "recognized as one of the premier *secondary* institutions for African Americans in the South." An 1889 report on a "State *High School*" for the African Methodist Episcopal Church of Kentucky in Harrodsburg, Kentucky, evidenced similar confusion around secondary and higher education in its proposal to erect a "*college* building" and assurance to supporters that the "*college* was a certainty now."[4]

At last, true higher education was provided for African Americans in Louisville with the establishment of the racially segregated Louisville Municipal College in 1931 as a branch of the University of Louisville. This college was recognized as among the first nine municipal higher education institutions established for African Americans in all of the United States by that time. The problem is that the first six of those institutions were normal schools, with the other two being part of the regular public school system "housed in the same buildings with the public schools and under the control of the local Boards of Education."[5]

These institutions did important work. What their stories illustrate, however, is the confusion surrounding these terms and designations. Indeed, like their white counterparts, black colleges and universities of Louisville don't have a clearer pedagogical claim to the status of "higher education" than their high schools. Instead, they follow the trajectory of white institutions in their confused relationship to one another and to common educational categories in use today—but with the added element of racism. In light of racist efforts to limit black rhetorical literacy and higher learning, we need to critically examine the language used to name African American education and consider the heightened stakes of excluding various institutions from a consideration of African American higher learning.

As Frank Bowles and Frank A. De Costa argue, "many other Negroes [outside of colleges and universities] obtained higher education of various types that were regarded as proper higher education during the period."[6] A primary example of an alternative site of higher learning, public high schools represent an often-overlooked tradition of formal rhetorical, academic, and professional opportunity for African Americans. Though they faced substantial public resistance and other formidable challenges, nineteenth-century African American high schools emerged as important centers of academic development and community pride in the several cities in which they were established.

Following the Civil War, African Americans quickly began seeking access to public schools across the country, and school enrollments of five- to nineteen-year-olds rose from 10 percent of the African American school-aged population in 1870 to 34 percent in 1880, compared to an enrollment of roughly half of school-aged white students across the same period. Increased enrollments in the lower schools enabled more students to go on to higher education, contributing to a push for high school and college access. While high school graduation remained low throughout the century for both white and black students, hovering around 2 to 3 percent of the school-age population until the last decade of the century, the numbers increase dramatically when you count those students who received some higher schooling without graduating, and the achievement of even a year or two of advanced education was consequential.[7]

These African American high schools taught their students advanced rhetoric and literacy skills, and in many ways they succeeded *because of* their status as high schools, not in spite of it. This is because of the seemingly humble and democratic purpose of the high school and its uncertain position in relation to the college. As in the case of women's higher education, the ambiguous political status of the high school provided an opportunity for higher learning as a subtle development rather than as a dramatic and visible social reform movement.

In this chapter, I trace the history of African American higher learning in Louisville to demonstrate the significance of municipal high schools to our histories of rhetoric and writing instruction. Acknowledging the advanced rhetorical and educational opportunity at schools like Central Colored High School challenges our reliance on standard institutional nomenclature as a guide in discussing historical schools and reveals the implicit prejudice of invoking the boundary between high school and college in this period. I argue that by not paying attention to the politics behind these institutional titles, we may be inadvertently perpetuating the political inequity they represent. So, in addition to the previous six African American normal schools and the two junior colleges housed with the public schools mentioned above, in what follows I demonstrate that we must attend to the role of institutions such as Central Colored High School (and even the "A" grade that I introduce below) in the story of "college" writing.

While sharing much in common with the other Louisville high schools, this account warrants its own chapter for several reasons. First of all, Central Colored High School's timeline is different enough from the first two high schools to intersect differently with the curricular and bureaucratic trends outlined in previous chapters. Established nearly twenty years after the high schools for white students, by the time Central was established, the American high school was a recognizable institutional form, and a national educational commissioner was working to measure and standardize it. Even as Central Colored High School evidences the continued variability of the high school form and function, the context was significantly changed.

In addition, this chapter focuses on the particular role of race and Reconstruction, pointedly illustrating the ways in which educational formations reflected not a coherent vision of the "high school" or "college" but instead an amalgamation of educational goals shaped by raced and gendered attention to the student bodies therein. As in the case of Female High School, the school's collegiate or noncollegiate status was determined as much by the demographics of the students as by the curriculum—the appropriate "higher schooling" for white middle class males being understood to be collegiate, while that of women, working class, or African American students was not. This is to say, the boundaries between high school and college education have been particularly fraught for such groups who were broadly barred access to the most privileged forms of higher learning and cultural power. Access to these schools—and the continual upgrading of their standards—was not a given, but a hard-fought achievement for the community and their supporters, and one that was increasingly under fire in the years of escalating public racism and race-based violence following Reconstruction. Thus, in this chapter, I demonstrate that the high school-college divide has been as much about *who* is learning as it has been about where or what they learning.[8]

I begin by outlining the context for African American common school education in Kentucky, particularly the legislative struggles overcome by educational advocates within the community. I then turn specifically to the development of the high school course, via the initial offering of an "A Grade" for aspiring teachers at the Central Colored School. Like women's education at Female, the high school for African Americans was initiated by a need for teachers in the lower schools. I outline the ways in which the school's identity as a normal school served as a warrant for offering increasingly advanced and collegiate subjects. From there, I trace the course offerings and student commencement themes through the last decades of the century, when the school's principal, J. M. Maxwell, came under criticism for his curriculum because it did not sufficiently prepare students to pass the teaching exam. Opponents used this fact to suggest that students weren't learning at the school, but evidence from the school board hearing suggests that students were just learning *the "wrong" things*: politics and rhetoric over rudimentary arithmetic and geography. While normal training served as a warrant for initial education advancement, then, it also served a constraining function as the purpose of the high school became more finely tuned and scrutinized in the last decade of the century, and as critics of black schools sought ways to neutralize the imagined threat of black rhetorical literacy and higher learning.

Through this account, I demonstrate that nineteenth-century black high schools like the one in Louisville had a strong and persisting tradition of academic excellence focused on civic rhetoric—a tradition important to the history of composition studies. Though access to a formally recognized public college for African Americans in Louisville would be delayed for nearly another half century, Louisville's African American students were learning (and teaching) writing in public and private institutions of higher learning since at least the 1870s, thanks to high school leaders.

Legislating Learning: The Beginning of Public Education for Louisville's Black Children

The state of Kentucky enacted its first legislation concerning the education of African Americans in 1866, which stipulated that taxes from that segment of the community be collected by local county agents, and that the funds be appropriated equally for providing education and caring for the black community's paupers. Combining the complex issue of postbellum poverty with that of education, the law led to undersupported education systems, while doing little to address the needs of the impoverished.

In 1867, that law was amended to provide for education only, not the care of paupers. The change was celebrated by the Colored Educational Convention in Lexington that year, as it showed what was to them a proper and much needed emphasis on education as a public priority. By the next year, however, the community's hopes were dashed when the law was amended yet again, this time designating that providing for paupers was not only within the purview of this fund but was indeed *the priority* for allocations, and that only residual funds from the tax could be applied to establishing schools. This was discouraging news for educational advocates, and the Colored Education Convention, this time meeting in Louisville, petitioned the legislature to return the funds to their original purpose of education.

Issues of allocation persisted, foreclosing the possibility of educational progress for at least the first four years following the war. As state superintendent of public instruction Z. F. Smith wrote in his 1870 report to the governor, these "legislative experiments" in funding black schools were "most unfortunate, and have inflicted great injury and injustice on this class." As Smith explains, it was no wonder that no educational progress had been made, given the confusion around the ever-changing law and the lack of motivation among white county officers responsible for enforcing it. And, whereas the African American community was initially reported to be enthusiastic about imposing a tax on themselves in order to support their children's schools, Smith reported that their lost faith in the system had led them to avoid contributing to a tax that they trusted would be misappropriated. Since the African American community was "ardently desirous to educate their children, and would gladly pay a reasonable tax therefor," Smith recommended, along with the Colored Education Convention, that the issue of education needed to be separated from that of pauperism. "Imagine," he mused, "the School System of Kentucky for the whites dove-tailed into and mixed up with a plan for the support of white paupers, and ill managed under provisions of legislation as confused and unintelligible as these! What would be thought of a Legislature that would propose such a policy?"[9]

Reflecting this sentiment of frustration and impatience with the state legislation, a revised Louisville Charter adopted on March 3, 1870, took up the work locally, providing for public schools for "children of the African race" in the city, to be supported by their own taxes. Interestingly, though, the charter provided for these schools almost indirectly, as an outgrowth of the Jim Crow racism of the South: one provision determined that funds raised for the city's schools must be allocated to the schools only, and another assured that the city would not "suffer children of the African race to become pupils of said schools with white children" and would therefore collect funds from this community to apply to educating the children "of said African race" only.[10]

The city remained generally stringent about separating the white and black schools of the city, including the teachers and even the administrative oversight of the schools. Accordingly, in July 1871, a Board of Visitors of the Colored Schools was appointed, comprised of nine African American leaders: Horace Morris, Marshall Woodson, Jesse Merriwether, G. W. Brown, Washington Watson, A. J. Bibb, Napoleon Bonaparte, John Morris, and J. R. Riley. Serving as a school board in miniature, it was determined that "the committee on colored schools of The City of Louisville shall have the immediate control and supervision of the colored schools, and report, from time to time, upon their condition, character and efficiency. They shall recommend to the Board suitably qualified persons as teachers for the colored schools."[11] This "separate but (un) equal" arrangement provided the African American schools with relative autonomy of operation from within the larger city school system, but also limited access to resources, including school buildings and salaries.

Initial efforts to supply public schools in the basements of local churches and the old Ealy Normal School building being unsatisfactory, African American leaders, including the Board of Visitors, petitioned the school board for better resources in the ensuing years, pointing out that some three thousand African American children between the ages of six and eighteen now resided in the city.[12] But funding and appropriation problems continued. Writing in 1872, the superintendent complained of the quality of the public schools for African Americans in the city, attesting to their desire for and right to better schools:

> The fund appropriated for the purpose of carrying out these schools is entirely inadequate, and much injury is hence sustained by this class of citizens. In the early years of their freedom it is eminently expedient that every facility should be given them for the improvement of their intellectual condition . . . Upon examination, it is found that good progress has been made by them within the last year. They manifest a laudable desire for improvement, and when we consider the difficulties under which they labor, we are encouraged to assist in alleviating their troubles as far as possible . . . It is therefore recommended that your body take this important question under advisement, and endeavor to suggest some plan that will

relieve them, thereby removing from yourselves a burden that is becoming embarrassing.

Under legislation from the state legislature and governor, passed January 31, 1873, three new schools were at last to be erected for African American students, located in the central, eastern and western sections of the city. The first of these new schools was Central Colored School, named for its central location in relation to the other proposed schools. The school met with opposition from local residents of the area, who considered it a "violence" and a "nuisance" to the white citizens of that area to build the school there. One self-described "curmudgeon" captured the racism and white supremacy at play in these complaints when he wrote to the *Courier-Journal* that "the negro's voice should not be wholly heeded in this matter; that the negroes should be very thankful to have a good school, without asking to be put too prominently before the very nose of the yet superior white population."[13]

But the school's supporters were undeterred, arguing in the Annual Report of Central Colored (1873–74): "The patience with which our colored citizens awaited the slow process of procuring them educational facilities is worthy of all praise; and the intelligence, self-denial, and perseverance with which they are seeking to improve their minds and add to their scholarship should, and no doubt will, reap their reward in the near future." Responding to the "curmudgeon" who had written to the *Courier-Journal* against the school, an "American Citizen of African Descent" further pointed out that "the colored people have rights under the law that they have never demanded. They know that under the Fourteenth amendment to the Constitution they can force their children into the white public schools, but they do not desire to do it. But," he asserted, "they want their children educated."[14]

And, through such powerful rhetorical appeals as this, they succeeded. The new school, which was to be opened October 1873, was celebrated as "probably the handsomest and best arranged building for colored children in the country," containing "ten spacious, well-lighted and well-ventilated rooms, besides a large chapel, amply supplied with furniture of the most approved character, and will comfortably accommodate six hundred children" (fig. 5.1). While it was referred to as the "Colored High School building" from early on, among the things it didn't yet have was a curriculum beyond grammar school.[15]

The "A" Grade

The public "higher" schooling of African Americans in Louisville began with the inauguration of the "A" grade at the Central Colored School, which was approved at the October 2, 1876, meeting of the school board. This class was a course of study for prospective teachers, established as a matter of some necessity. As the school board's Mr. Pope would later explain, "There was at first a great difficulty in obtaining teachers, and the graduates of the first grade who were old enough were employed" as teachers in the early years of the school.[16]

The "A" grade was an answer to this problem as well as a recognition of the advancing preparation of the city's African American students who, "having passed the examination required for admission to the High School," entered a "course of study . . . embracing the elements of some of the higher branches, to be completed in one year." It was reported that "quite a number of young ladies and gentlemen completed this course—the majority of whom were appointed to positions as teachers in the city, and are now engaged in teaching in the schools in which, a few years ago, they were pupils." In this way, access to the higher branches came about

CENTRAL COLORED HIGH SCHOOL (SIXTH AND KENTUCKY STREETS.)

Fig. 5.1. Artist's rendering of the Central Colored High School building, printed in the *Courier Journal*, September 6, 1888. COURTESY OF UNIVERSITY OF LOUISVILLE.

from the side rather than from straight on: the "colored schools," as they were called, remained both physically and ideologically segregated well into the twentieth century. As historian Hudson explains, "The state's determination to preserve the color line by staffing its segregated Black schools with Black teachers prompted the development of limited public higher educational opportunities for African Americans."[17] Although limited, these opportunities included the "A" grade (and, later, high school), where an advanced academic curriculum was offered largely for the purposes of teacher training.

The first class of students applied for admission to this class in June 1877, under the guidance of John Miller Maxwell, who was the first principal elected to Central from its erection in 1873, and is responsible for the development of the "A" grade and the eventual high school course.[18] One of the first graduates of the "A" grade in 1877, William H. Perry, would later become principal of the Eastern Colored School, and others moved into similarly responsible positions in the community, demonstrating the role of Central's "A" grade in fostering educational and professional advancements to individuals and the community from its earliest years. Reflecting this sense of progressive change, principal J. M. Maxwell's remarks upon graduation in 1877, quoted above, represent a mantra for the school itself as much as for the graduates of that class: "Add continually to the stock of knowledge which you have already acquired. Remember that you have just begun to learn . . . that you stand just on the border of the intellectual world, at the base of the hill of science. Go onward and upward then, for further on and higher there are riper fruits and richer fragrance."[19] In such a way, the school grew under Maxwell's leadership from the initial "A" grade to a three-year and eventually a full four-year course of study, raising its intellectual and rhetorical aims for both students and teachers with each passing year.[20]

The same year that the "A" grade was initiated, the Colored Teacher's State Educational Association first met in Louisville, under the guidance of state superintendent of public instruction, A. M. Henderson. Principal Maxwell spoke at the meeting about the intellectual work to be accomplished by that body on behalf of the "colored schools." In particular, he set out an intellectual mission for black education leaders, emphasizing the importance of producing local knowledge and an education theory of their own, rather than relying on the production of knowledge to come from the white community:

> While the great heart of the intellectual world is throbbing with emotion our hearts must 'responsive beat.' We should not be passive recipients, continually feasting on the thoughts of others; we should be authors of original thought, and eat of the food prepared by our own hands . . . it is in *our* power to set tables of our own, and, though they may not be spread with dainty viands, the food will be pleasant to our taste, and adapted to the growth of our minds, because of its kindred nature.

In this, Maxwell calls his colleagues to be intellectual and scholarly leaders in and for their schools. He goes on to underscore the educative process of teaching itself, arguing that "the mind does not grow strong so much by what it *receives* as by what it *gives.* It was this *out-going* of thoughts more than the *incoming* knowledge that gave to the minds of Demosthenes, Cicero, Socrates and Plato their great power, and caused them to shine as stars in the galaxy of ancient lore." He argues that these great teachers of antiquity, though they did not "possess a knowledge of so many facts of history and science in general as many of our school boys and girls at the age of twelve years," became great "by the contact of *mind with mind.*" In this way, he calls his fellow teachers forth to work together with their students and one another, to produce their own "original thought," as the ancient lyceums had done.[21]

Maxwell's remarks invite us to recognize the public school as a site of professional practice and intellectual work for students and teachers alike, dedicated to the particular educational needs and interests of the black community. Accordingly, the course of study also advanced each year under Maxwell's inspiring leadership. The "A" grade for 1880–81 included English and history, listed as being taught from Butler's *Practical and Critical Grammar*; Greene's *Analysis of English*, with exercises in composition; and reading aloud, reciting or speaking selections in prose and poetry. By the next year, changes were made across the course listings and English language work was becoming more rich and multifaceted (fig. 5.2). In particular, the combined "English and History" with Butler's text was replaced by three separate course listings: Hart's

Course of Study.

"A" GRADE, COLORED SCHOOLS.

***English and History*—Butler's Practical and Critical Grammar.**

Greene's Analysis of English, with Exercises in Composition.

Anderson's General History.

Reading aloud, reciting or speaking selections in prose and poetry.

***Mathematics*—White's Arithmetic reviewed.**

Robinson's Elementary Algebra.

Hunter's Geometry.

***Natural Science*—Guyot's Physical Geography.**

Steele's Natural Philosophy.

Fig. 5.2. Course of study for the "A" grade of Central Colored School, which predated the establishment of a high school course at the school. Printed in the *Manual of the Board*, 1881. COURTESY OF JEFFERSON COUNTY PUBLIC SCHOOLS.

A Manual of Composition and Rhetoric, English Literature, and Anderson's General History. Courses on spelling and defining were added, as well as weekly lectures on the theory and practice of teaching.[22]

The specific textbooks used in the "A" grade deserve notice, particularly Hart's *Composition and Rhetoric*, which has received widespread attention as a "first" in several histories of the field. According to Robert Connors's *Composition-Rhetoric*, Hart's is the text that introduced personal writing to composition classrooms. Though Schultz contends that other textbooks for the schools did so earlier in the century, Hart's is still noted as the earliest example of what Carr, Carr, and Schultz call (drawing on Connors) a "composition-rhetoric," a significant genre in their history of writing instruction. For Carr, Carr, and Schultz, composition-rhetoric texts "orient their account of rhetorical principles toward a direct intervention in student writing" and "selectively adopt some practices of composition books." These texts were not philosophical treatises on rhetoric but instead combined theory and practice, as Hart explains his own text does:

> This is, on the face of it, a text-book. It has been written for learners, not for the learned. Its object is, not to extend the boundaries of the science by excursions into debatable ground, but to present its admitted truths in a form easily apprehended. . . . Original investigation is felt to be out of place in a text-book for instruction in the elements.[23]

Its identification as a composition-rhetoric has made Hart's text a lightning rod for disagreement among scholars, particularly in relation to its audience. Namely, the texts considered composition-rhetorics by Carr, Carr, and Schultz were all for college audiences or a combined audience of college and high school. Since part of what defined such composition-rhetorics for Carr, Carr, and Schultz is the inclusion of practice alongside theory, they point out that their findings complicate Connors's claim that "between 1865 and 1890, the exercises of the earlier part of the century were relegated to secondary school texts, while college texts again became treatises."[24] They argue that the colleges did not so uniformly leave practice to the schools, taking on theory as their purview once again. Instead, the composition-rhetoric texts that were including a combination of rhetorical theory and composition practice, like Hart's, were according to Carr, Carr, and Schultz aimed at a combined college-high school audience.

In fact, the audience of such a text was even more complexly configured than that, but my own findings help to explain the disagreement over texts like Hart's. The attempt to distinguish between high school and college rhetorical traditions has always been confounded by the uncertain relationship between these educational sites and their audiences before the turn of the century. And these distinctions are further blurred by the introduction of a program like the "A" grade into the educational landscape, which served as a high school course in the absence of other options. The use of a textbook like Hart's in the schools invites us to unsettle these distinctions as we seek to understand the writing practice and instruction in such ambiguously positioned schools. Indeed, we may be trying to map a distinction that just wasn't there in the same way for the authors or users of these texts and institutions in their own time. Recognizing the overlap in these forms, the chairman of the Colored School Committee of the school board at the 1886 commencement even "presented certificates of graduation to forty-two persons who had passed a successful examination in the 'A' grade of the public school before the High School was established in 1882"—a move that would later be replicated by University of Louisville, which retroactively conferred university degrees on 300 graduates of Male High School.[25]

High School Beginnings, Again: Reinventing the High School for African Americans

It wasn't until 1882 that a three-year high school curriculum actually replaced the "A" grade at Central Colored School and the Central High School was officially born, becoming one of the first high schools for African Americans in the country and one among only sixty-four such schools for African Americans in the country as late as 1916.[26] To make this transformation from an "A" grade to a high school, the new course of study for the 1882–83 year confined much of the curriculum from the "A" grade to the first year and a half of study, adding coursework in American literature, analysis of words, the Constitution of the United States, trigonometry, astronomy, geology and physical geography, intellectual philosophy, botany, zoology, as well as Latin, Roman history, Caesar, and Virgil. A note asserted that weekly exercises in reading and elocution would be included throughout the course as well. Intellectual philosophy and theory and methods of teaching were listed in the final year of study. Thus, while sciences and mathematics were rising in rigor, language studies remained paramount at the school alongside teaching preparation.[27]

Though we don't know the textbooks in use at the school by this time, the curriculum tracks with the advanced subjects studied at other high schools and colleges. And, like Male and Female, the approach to these studies seems to have been infused by educational approaches of the New Education, which Maxwell and a guest lecturer each discussed at the Kentucky Colored Teacher's Association in 1885.[28]

Under whatever system of teaching, the students at Central thrived academically, and the work of the school was presented and noticed at several public events, including the New Orleans Exhibition of 1884. Contemporary observers particularly remarked on the rhetorical training students received. This training was evidenced each year by the public commencement exhibitions, at which the essays and orations were praised as "fully up to the average of such exercises, the country over; and in a few instances they have been of a decidedly superior character."[29]

Of course, some of the praise of these students was undercut by the clearly low expectations held by the writers. One report from that New Orleans Exhibition described the Central High School exhibit (with equal parts racism and admiration) as "a source of surprise and pleasure to those who had hitherto entertained honest doubts as to the negro's capacity to receive in equal measure with other races that higher culture which adorns the civilization of the present age." A *Courier-Journal* report on the graduation of Central in 1883 reflected more subtle racism and white supremacy in its report that

> there were young men who had by their own energies mastered the difficulties of a curriculum that equals in severity any used in white schools—young men who stood there with intelligence and enlightenment stamped on every feature, and young women who had written essays that would put many of those of their fairer rivals to shame, who showed proficiency in music, tastefulness in dress, modesty in deportment and an air of intellectual accomplishment that was simply surprising.[30]

Opportunities for black students to showcase their rhetorical achievements continued throughout the century, and these public exhibitions and ceremonies were considered by students and audience members alike to demonstrate not only their mastery of the subject matter but also the "steady advancement of the colored children in this city" more broadly. As an example, an address by Central pupil John T. Bell on "Kentucky," published in full in the city's newspaper, sheds light on the students' own perspectives on this educational advancement. Bell avers that the state was "rapidly coming out of the shadows which had been thrown over it, and was becoming foremost on the great question of education." Indexing the educational achievements to the broader cultural and economic progress in the black community, the author maintains that "the work accomplished by the Colored High School showed the advancement made by the colored race, which was now ahead of those in the adjoining States."[31]

In addition to showing what students thought of their own school and accomplishments, such speeches also provide insights into the writing and rhetorical instruction these students received, as each student presented their own work during the ceremony, many reading their own original pieces of prose and poetry. In the early years of the "A" grade, in particular, graduations featured a range of genres, including a narrative poem, a humorous stump speech, and historical orations and essays. Popular topics included historical figures and places, such as Frederick Douglass as "the hero of the colored race, the world over," and "Our Next Door Neighbor, Mexico." Students also wrote on more abstract themes such as "A Rolling Stone Gathers No Moss" (a theme suggested by the students' textbook), "Life Is What We Make It," and "Progress." Several students spoke directly to themes of "oratory" or "rhetoric,", showing a sort of metacognitive engagement with the subjects of their own education, while an oration on postal geography in 1888 showed students engaging with topics of practical, professional significance to their lives. That student "argued against the present system of management of the telegraph companies, and in favor of the Government taking charge of the telegraph, offering in proof of the arguments he used statistics concerning European telegraphy." Given that the post office had been opened to black workers in 1865 as one of the only white-collar careers available to African Americans (besides teaching), this essay may reflect the professional aspirations and plans of this student after graduation.[32]

In these speeches, students also drew on the humanistic traditions of the liberal arts education they were receiving, alongside religious and popular influences, to compose philosophical and deliberative arguments about controversial social and political issues. For the valedictory address of the first official graduating class of the school in 1885, for example, Charles S. Morris gave an ambitious address (which was noticed at length in the newspapers and then reprinted in full the next day) on the topic of Christianity and Western civilization. In the address, Morris asserts the existence of a divine power against "skeptics" such as evolutionary theorists, drawing on examples from history to show the progress of Christian history not as fatalism, destiny, or evolution, but as "divinity." Evidencing the internalization of racist and colonial ideologies of the time, the speech draws amply on literary and historical references to justify slavery (and the ongoing "civilizing" efforts on the African continent) as a necessary evil in the development of the "African race" that, though painful, was itself divinely inspired. In light of his rhetorical context, Morris uses an extended metaphor of schooling to comment on the experience of slavery and freedom, imbuing both graduates and the broader African American community with the responsibility to prove themselves responsive to this harsh lesson:

> While it was apparently an inspiration of the devil, it [slavery] really was a school in which the barbarian Pagans of Western Africa were to be taught the first lessons of civilization and Christianity and stern discipline, which no other state of existence, I believe, could have accomplished in the same time. It is true the teacher was rough but the pupil was rough also; he demanded heroic treatment, and as he paid rather dear for his tuition, he should accordingly value the instruction received; rejoice that he has graduated from his stern Alma Mater, and show that he has well learned his lessons, by the practice of industry, economy and virtue.

Ultimately, Morris celebrates that "American slavery is now dead" and holds up the American experiment—where "on common soil, governed by the same law, under one flag, [there are] gathered the inhabitants of the three continents, the descendants of the three sons of Noah"—as the best proof of divine providence.[33]

The speech was commended for its composition and the speaker noticed for his talent by the white men who reported on the event. One reporter remarked: "His logic was strong, his metaphors forcible, and his language elegant. His delivery was excellent and his gestures correct. It was one of the best commencement orations ever heard in the city." Another report noted that the speech was "highly commended both for its intrinsic merit and the oratorical ability of the speaker. As a specimen of what has been accomplished by his race."[34] Such comments evidence the high stakes of oratorical performance by these students, who were judged on their individual ability but also seen as representatives of their entire race and its potential. As Shirley Wilson Logan asserts, speakers and audience members would have understood "rhetorical ability as a sign of intelligence and, therefore, as deserving of all the rights of citizenship," and in this way the public demonstration of these skills had significance for the democratic self-advancement of African Americans in the city. Morris would have understood this fact. He also may have understood that his white audience would appreciate his neutralization of the violence of slavery and the perceived threat of racial integration in his speech.[35]

Whatever their motives, these speeches show the rhetorical skill of students and the liberal and intellectual self-conception of these schools, which is also evidenced in their developing curriculum. Although Southern whites are often thought to have only supported industrial education for black students, the materials from Central High School support the observation that virtually all African American high schools in the South were actually "classical or college preparatory" into the twentieth century. Louisville was no exception. By its first official high school graduation ceremony in 1885, the course of studies had been amended to include Latin in the first year, as well as a course in critical reading, and by the 1887–88 school year students were enrolling in a full three years of Latin. In this way, liberal education offered at what would become Central High School—taught by all African American teachers—came to represent a significant educational opportunity, pedagogically comparable to and at times in advance of black (and even some white) collegiate education of the time.[36]

In 1892, the Colored High School began offering a four-year course of study. That course was almost identical to the studies at Female High School.[37] The explicit alignment of Central's academic curriculum with Female's speaks of their shared identity as academic but ultimately noncollegiate high schools, each with a strong teacher-training mandate. Though their instruction was ambitious and advanced into the highest branches of study, there was no attempt to offer the same course of study as the male "university of high schools," and no suggestion that they would ever aspire to be recognized as colleges.

But, arguably, these schools could advance precisely because they were *not* marked as colleges, and therefore not perceived as a threat to existing white male supremacy. The national elaboration of the curriculum beyond the classics in the higher branches had destabilized the traditional equivalence between "academic" and "collegiate" and opened a space that high schools like these filled. As much as schools were disadvantaged by this distinction and their relative position in relation to the college, they also leveraged it strategically. It is thus that the course of study at Central and Female extended and progressed, while each remained committed to teacher training.

As at Female, the teacher-training mandate of Central was in some tension with its academic aspirations. Tension became controversy when a resolution was advanced to provide teaching certificates to graduates of Colored High School. Ironically, given the school's ostensible emphasis on teaching, the resolution failed when the school board report from 1885 showed that eighteen of the twenty-one African American applicants (mostly graduates of the high school) had failed the teacher certification exam. Specifically, "Many of the colored applicants failed on geography, which they have not studied recently, and in which they were asked such important questions as 'What European country covers the same area as California?' etc."

While evidencing advanced knowledge and practice in other areas, the inability of graduates to answer such "important questions" pointed to persisting uncertainty about the purpose imagined for the high school for African Americans: Was the school to focus on the provision of more rudimentary knowledge, deemed necessary to teach in the lower schools, or to provide the same advanced academic education of the white high schools? This question came to a head in the 1890s, coalescing around the figure of the principal, J. M. Maxwell, just as a similar controversy had circulated around Professor Anderson of Male High School in the previous decade. While a reporter in 1886 had, seemingly unsolicited, seen fit to attest that "Mr. Maxwell is a Christian gentleman and eminently fitted to have charge of our intermediate and high schools, as there has never been a breath of reproach against him," the shifting status of the high school unsettled the status of its leader as well, and the controversy over his leadership points to these important questions of institutional status for the high school in the final decades of the century.[38]

"Incapable of Teaching High-School Classes": Another Principal Up for Removal

Due to the extension of the high school course into a four-year course of study, no commencement was held at Central Colored High School in 1893. Nonetheless, there was much attention to the school that summer, revolving specifically around the figure of principal J. M. Maxwell (fig. 5.3) and his high school course. That summer, the school board was ensconced in debate about the fitness of Maxwell for the principalship; Maxwell was up for removal from the school on charges of "gross inefficiency, neglect of duty, and insubordination," and the board was fairly split on the issue.[39] As in the controversy over Male's Principal Anderson, each of these charges was directly inflected by negotiations of the purpose and status of the high school—though Maxwell's charges differed in that they were also particularly shaped by white concerns about African Americans in an increasingly segregated, Southern-identified city following the era of Reconstruction.

Fig. 5.3. Sketch of principal J. M. Maxwell, of Central Colored School, printed in the *Courier Journal*, September 6, 1888. COURTESY OF UNIVERSITY OF LOUISVILLE.

Maxwell had been principal of the Central Colored School since its inception and, as such, he was also principal of the Colored High School when that program was initiated at his school. He had overseen the students in their ever-advancing studies, presided over school activities and commencements each year, and was actively involved in (and at several times president of) the State Teacher's Institute as well. Though he had completed only a high school (and not a college) degree program and therefore "didn't consider himself fully educated" in an era of increasing administrative structure and professional standards, his status had long gone unquestioned in light of his active professional agenda. Nonetheless, members of the school board had now decided that "Prof. Maxwell was incapable of teaching High-school classes."[40]

The charges were precipitated by the extension of the high school course into a four-year course the previous academic year, which brought increased attention and scrutiny to the school (exacerbated, again, by heightened racial tensions following Reconstruction). Board members had gone to the school to examine the operations of this new course. What they found, they said, was that students were inept. Students in the lower grades were unable to identify the boundaries of Kentucky. Students in upper grades, too, were not adept with physical geography upon impromptu examination. In addition to these impromptu examinations of geography at the school, Maxwell's opponents charged that his ineptitude to teach high school was evidenced by the fact that his graduates did not fare well on the annual teachers' examination used to certify teachers for the public schools. More specifically, it had for some time been observed that students often couldn't pass the preparatory subjects taught in the lower schools. According to the charges, all eighteen graduates of 1888, each of whom sat for the teachers' examination, failed to pass, "though the examinations were the same as are passed every year by the children of the First and Second grades in the [white] ward schools," or what we would now call seventh and eighth grades. With 65 of 100 points required to pass, the highest student scores from this class were reported to be in the 40s and 50s across the subjects of spelling, grammar, written arithmetic, mental arithmetic, geography and history. Their highest scores were in mental philosophy (50) and algebra (65), which are subjects not taught in the ward schools—and therefore considered of little value to a cadre of future teachers. According to reports, only one graduate out of seven passed the teachers' examination in

1890, and four out of twelve in 1892. Thus, "those who oppose Maxwell say that this is sufficient proof that he is an incompetent principal, else High School graduates would not make such a miserable showing when confronted with a simple examination."[41]

Of course, the problem just might have been that it was, indeed, a "simple" examination. That is, while students routinely failed in physical geography and other primary subjects, they succeeded in other studies—studies that might be considered more advanced rather than preparatory, and wouldn't be found on the teachers' examination. In fact, Maxwell readily admitted during an interrogation at the school board meeting that, though the teachers' examination includes spelling, history, grammar, arithmetic, and geography, these subjects were not taught in the high school. When pressed later in the meeting on the subjects of grammar and spelling, Maxwell answered that these subjects were "incidentally taught by correcting errors when made."[42]

Thus, Maxwell's students were certainly learning—but some were of the mind that they were learning the wrong things for a black public high school. The case of the political economy course illustrates well the tensions that accrued around the pedagogical and political aims of a black high school at the turn of the century. Of this subject, Maxwell's detractors reported that "last year he had to teach political economy, which eminent authorities recommend as a fine study for colored schools. It was a small English hand-book like a primer, only teaching fundamental principles. One day we decided to go out and see how the class in economy under Prof. Maxwell was progressing."

What they found was that, though this little, simple primer "of course, contained no reference to 'Democratic' and 'Republican' parties, each one of those colored boys repl[ied] to the questions on free trade and protection by saying that the Republican party advocated protection, and it was right, while free trade and Democracy would bring only ruin." Because there was no reference to American political parties in the textbook, the committee pressed Maxwell to explain his methods, persisting at a later meeting:

> "Did not your boys, when we asked them about political economy, answer questions not in the book?" they asked. "Yes," Maxwell replied, "When we had a debate, following Harvard and Yale, on free trade and protection." Then there was much

> explaining of political economy, in which Prof. Maxwell did most of the talking, answering questions put to him. Next he explained how he taught the subject. His answers were very intelligent and he created a favorable impression.[43]

This tension between Maxwell's collegiate model—"following Harvard and Yale"—and the board's interest in faculty "only teaching fundamental principles" from a textbook brings into focus the fact that the notion of the "colored high school" was, to some citizens, not about providing higher education and opportunities to develop as citizens and scholars, but instead specifically aimed at an impoverished definition of teacher preparation pointedly detached from political engagement. That is, the problem was about the very purpose and definition of a "high school" for African Americans.

As the reports of this event suggest, this issue was certainly political—not just about the charge of teaching politics, but also about the charge of engaging politics, and doing so as a black man. The implicit policing of Maxwell's political activities is brought out by the mention in this same report of Maxwell's own active opposition to a bill to segregate train cars in the state—a seemingly unrelated topic. Although ostensibly irrelevant, Maxwell's own politics and those of the school board each certainly shaped the definition of high schooling in this context.

The definition of the high school and its proper oversight was already clearly on the minds of board members, as the motion had just gone forward to discharge the Committee on Colored Schools in favor of merging oversight of the Central Colored High School with that of the white high schools. This suggests that school operations were regularized enough that "high school" was becoming a more useful category for the school administrators than the previous category of "colored school" (which saw race as the most salient criteria for thinking about the school, and thus merged the work of all grade levels).[44]

Because the high school was becoming more distinct as a type, and increasingly reflected the values of professionalization and academic credentials, Maxwell's removal from the position of principal may have also had to do with his lack of formal credentials in an increasingly formalized professional market. Though Maxwell was educated at a high school in Xenia and studied eighteen months at Howard University, he did not graduate from Howard. Not persisting to graduation was once the norm for many who received advanced education, but that was changing by the end of the century. By 1888—the time when Maxwell's credentials and teaching came under question—all high school faculty of Louisville, including at Central Colored High School, had studied at a college or university.

Of course, the decision was also about power and control, which is particularly evident in thè attendant charge of insubordination against Maxwell. The charge seems to have originated nearly a year earlier, when Maxwell had gone against the directions of the chairman of the Committee on Colored Schools, George F. Simpson, and refused to discipline two of his female students for ostensibly bullying a white boy in the neighborhood. In response to the bullying, Simpson had lectured the teachers for how they conducted the school, "saying that they must do better." He was greeted at his office the next day by a reprimand of his own, with Maxwell telling him that "your talk to my teachers yesterday was not such as should be directed to ladies and gentlemen." During a later visit, too, Maxwell is said to have treated Simpson "disdainfully, and told him that he cared more for the intelligent colored people, whose support he had, than for the committee." The sense of impropriety in these interactions has everything to do with race, of course; thus, another trustee is reported to have said that "if Maxwell had so spoken to him he would have knocked the negro teacher down a spot."[45]

Even if he was at odds with the board, though, Maxwell wasn't wrong about the support he had in the community, evidenced by the appearance by his side of all the teachers in his school, three hundred other African American citizens, and "every colored minister in the city." But that, of course, was never the point among the white school board members who opposed him. To them, the issue of his behavior and qualifications ultimately had little to do with his ability to teach the students or lead the community. Instead, as Maxwell said of the quarrel between the white and black students, it seems that with his own case "there were two sides to the story—a white side and a black side."[46]

Maxwell was removed from the principalship that month. The increased scrutiny of the academic course and emphasis on normal training persisted. Shortly thereafter, the school began to transform from "exclusively an academic institution" to a school "geared toward academics and useful skills in a large number of fields," particularly manual education, under the prodding of Booker T. Washington. In their graduation speeches, too, students more frequently discussed the need for what they call industrial education as "an opportunity to secure the proper equipment" to make a living.[47]

The transformation toward manual education was a trend across the city and the country, signaled by the establishment of a Manual Training High School for white male students in Louisville in 1892 and the establishment of similar schools in cities across the Midwest. These schools provided a general and applied scientific curriculum similar to (and in some ways preparatory to) that of technical and land-grant universities. They used "hand-training" as a means to practice mental discipline and attention and avidly distinguished themselves from vocational training schools. Notably, these schools provided a valued education that led many students on to further study at the college and university by the end of the century.

But where manual training was forcefully distinguished from vocational specialization at such white training high schools, it overlapped much more with career applications at Central by the first decades of the twentieth century. Thus, the longer history of this high school, segregated until 1958, serves to index the ways educational terms and trends have continued to be differentially applied to different student bodies—"college" and "high school" being only two among many terms that have served to both sponsor and undercut educational opportunity for people of color.[48] While Central High School continued to serve as an important site of opportunity and community in Louisville, its history demonstrates how the idea of a high school was clearly variable and context-specific—which is to say, audience-specific. It was also continuing to transform by the end of the century.

6

Inventing the High School, Inventing Composition

> Doubtless the secondary teacher will be roundly criticized by his collegiate superiors, just when he has, through the suppression of the student's individuality, succeeded in perfecting the preparatory machinery warranted to turn out the qualities and accomplishments demanded. . . . Indeed, for a college life, offering at the outstart liberal election in the whole field of knowledge and experience, what adequate training can be supposed to reside in the mechanical and uniform drill demanded by the entrance requirements? The articulation that seemed from superficial inspection so neat and complete turns out a delusion. . . . I urge the colleges to emphasize the vital, not the mechanical, side of preparatory teaching.
>
> —*Abraham Flexner, "College Entrance Examinations"*

As we have seen, the nineteenth-century high school—as a public nexus of debates about the very purposes of higher learning—was always contested, shaped by its relation to other educational and social institutions. The practices, pedagogies, and status of individual high schools were also reflective of the racism, sexism, and classism of the time (and our own). Though many educational histories—not to mention histories in rhetoric and composition—gloss over the story of high schools during this messy period of development, the period from around midcentury leading up to the 1880s is revealing and significant for our understanding of the complex interface between high schools and colleges in the nineteenth century and beyond.

By the 1880s, things were changing. With the end of Reconstruction, the backlash against African American achievement during that period was in full swing, constraining educational opportunity along with voting access and other foundations of citizenship. The Progressive Era was about to begin, with its emphasis on practicality and efficiency across municipal, industrial, economic, and educational arenas. At the same time, the American high school outpaced the academy in providing the multipurpose higher learning that would become what we now call secondary schooling and, according to many historians, came on the scene as a meaningful school form.[1]

In Louisville, this was a period of striking expansion for the public schools. While graduation rates remained low throughout the century, the last two decades of the nineteenth century saw exponential growth across Louisville's four high schools, with enrollment at Male rising steadily, at Female and Central nearly doubling, and at Manual High School and across other specialized programs in manual education, business, and teaching more than doubling (fig. 6.1). These trends did not abate in the twentieth century, and the cohort of high school graduates became increasingly diverse as a result.[2]

As the high school became more popular and more diverse, national efforts were made to determine its role in American education, particularly in relation to the college. A U.S. commissioner was appointed in 1867 to study and recommend changes to the growing national education system, and myriad committees were constituted to deliberate the status of the high school in the emerging academic hierarchy, particularly by the last decade of the century. Landmark committees included the National Education Association's Committee of Ten on the Teaching of Secondary English in 1892, chaired by Charles Eliot of Harvard; the 1895 Committee of Twelve by the American Philological Association; the 1897 Committee on College-Entrance Requirements; and regional organizations like the Southern Association of Colleges and Schools.

A point that has been underemphasized by many who write about this period of development is that much of what these seemingly innumerable committees and reports at the turn of the century determined was, of course, prescriptive rather than descriptive, responding centrally

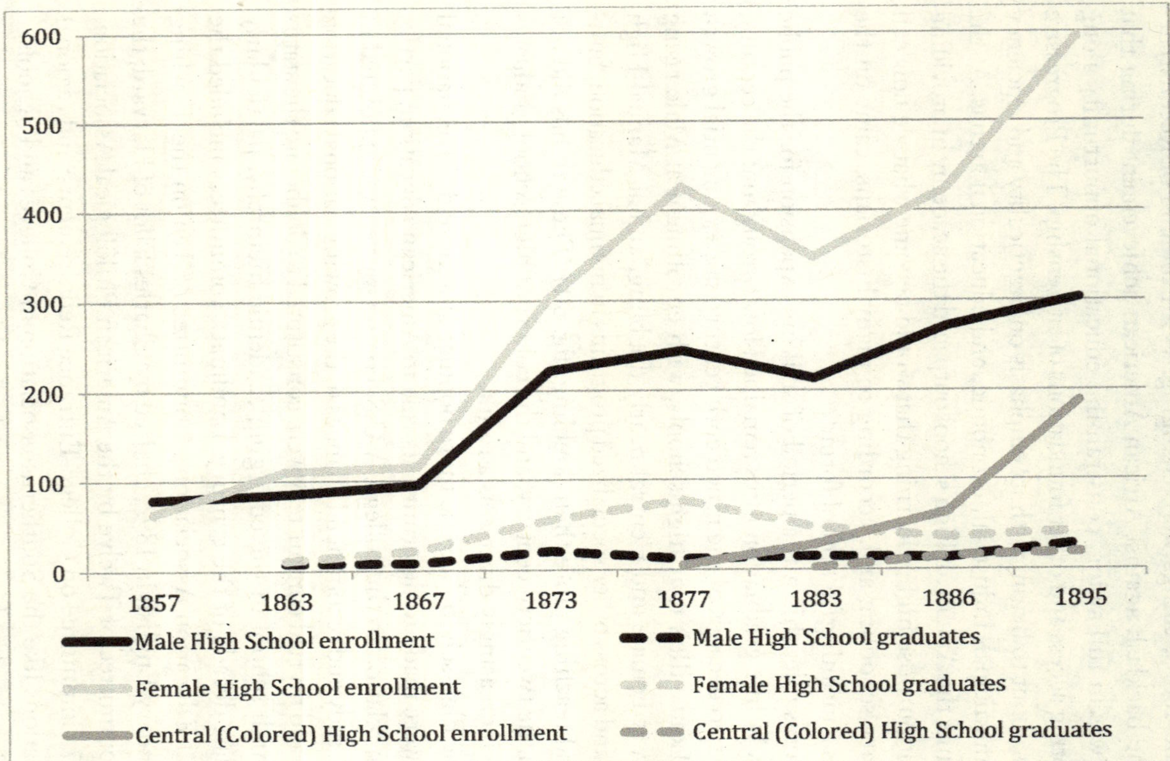

Fig. 6.1. Enrollment and graduation trends for all Louisville high schools, 1857–95. Graduation numbers were approximated from school board reports and newspaper articles.

to the reality of institutional and programmatic overlap. The committees described what they *hoped* would become the relations between schools over time. On the one hand, they hoped that more students would graduate and enter college, that they would graduate at a later age and with more preparation. On the other hand, they also hoped that the high schools (having overtaken the popularity of academies and Latin grammar schools) would begin to take on their preparatory role, aligning their curricula in hierarchical relation to that of the colleges and universities. This was a dual movement: ostensibly elevating and also, in turn, suppressing high schools, keeping them (and their increasingly diverse student bodies) in their place.

Though the influence of their specific curricular recommendations was minor, the indirect influence of these "authoritative" statements about what high schools should be and do profoundly shaped the idea of the high school, affecting privileged and under-privileged high schools alike as the distinction between high schools and colleges was increasingly scrutinized.[3] In the same way, when the citizens of Louisville had begun to criticize the "absurd effort" the high school had been making to be a college over the years, they not only named but participated in the creation of a distinction between the two.

Through the symbolic action of such committees and public discourse, though, real change occurred. Namely, the conception of high school as a distinctly preparatory experience subordinated to colleges became an accepted truth, if still not a lived reality. Controversy around the status of the high school in Louisville was sparked when the course of study at Male was once again reconsidered and was characterized by the *Courier-Journal* as an "inflated and impossible university foreign to every principle of education, justice, economy and true progress" and beyond the "legitimate scope within which municipal education should confine itself." As this critic elaborates, "Its high-sounding programme of studies and its pretentious character dazzled, at first, the eyes of the people, but they see now that it has been an institution that has cultivated superficiality and conceit, and they mean to have it changed."[4]

When a long-delayed debt was called in by the trustees of the university, giving notice that they would require rent of the Male High School property, the school's collegiate status was brought into further question. Having tried again to get rent for the Male High School building, the university trustees served notice to the Male High School to vacate the building in 1876, but the city won possession of the building in the dispute, as the court decided the building was being used for its intended purposes as an academical department of the university. A "Willing School-Tax Payer" wrote in 1881 to defend high schools, reminding readers of the history of voter support for them in their present collegiate form and asking,

> Then why tamper with our High Schools and attempt to emasculate and degrade them? Why try to cut out any or all of the dead languages, when the experience of the educated world is that there is no system of mental training equal to a proper study of those languages, and that they are necessary to a well-balanced education? And why try to dispense with them when the people have twice expressed themselves at the polls in favor of continuing their High School as a college, "with the rights, privileges and immunities" of colleges, "and of conferring degrees?"[5]

The concern about the schools being "emasculated" is significant, gesturing to the increasingly gendered associations of the high school in relation to the college, and the alignment of that gendering with a sense of degradation.

Against such protests, the university began to take more active steps to claim the Male High School building as part of the university property (rather than city property) in 1883, proposing an addition to the building that would be used as a teaching hospital. The property dispute worked as much as any other means to encourage the distinction between the university and the Male High School. The contest was continuing in 1886, around which time the first mention of the high school as Boys' High School (rather than Male High School) seems to appear, further gesturing toward the fulfillment of the "emasculated" and "degraded" stature of the school that the "Willing School-Tax Payer" had feared.[6]

The academic hierarchy, with the university as its pinnacle, fundamentally changed the landscape of higher learning in Louisville. As a result, the Male High School became distinguished from the University—initially, as we have seen, as two separate course offerings reflecting the extended degree of university study (see illustration 4.1), but eventually as separate and distinct institutions by the turn of the century. Both advanced study and specialization were reserved for the university, as the high school confined itself to a subordinate and preparatory role. In a related move, Female and Central were both officially detached from the normal school function they once encompassed, each now focusing exclusively on academic and preparatory (as well as increasingly vocational) programming.

Meanwhile, the establishment of Louisville's DuPont Manual Training High School in 1892 and similar schools in other cities further established the idea that these proliferating programs that were once encompassed in the "multipurpose" high school belonged in separate institutions with more precise missions and differentiated audiences in the academic hierarchy. Following the lead of Calvin M. Woodward's Manual Training School of Washington University in St. Louis, these schools extended the interest in manual training found in the early high schools (via the philosophies of Pestalozzi, Froebel, and Louisville's William Hailmann), elaborating it into a distinct educational philosophy and institutional form of its own by the last quarter of the century. While adamantly not vocational in aim, such manual training programs did conceive of themselves as markedly distinct from the tradition of mental training of the high school and college, which was criticized as "impractical." In doing so, they brought further scrutiny to the traditional collegiate high school, questioning whether all classes and professions were in actuality served by an educational program designed for the learned professions.[7] The high school, it was increasingly argued, needed to cater to a broader range of outcomes than the traditional college was seen to do—it should prepare both for college and for a range of careers and professions. Of course, this was also an implicit argument that certain students were not fitted for a collegiate curriculum, an idea we already saw circulating in previous chapters, though one that was now enforced via curricular and institutional policies. It is thus that, from an indeterminate and catholic form of higher learning, the high school was becoming established as a particular institutional type of its own in the emerging academic hierarchy.

Nonetheless, high schools continued to overlap significantly with the work of colleges. This is especially true insofar as the college and the university themselves were transforming, incorporating new subjects, areas of specialization, and overall student choices. They continued to grapple with their own role in the provision of general education or specialized training, their own goals in relation to access and exclusivity. Thus, the operational differences between colleges and universities and the high schools that were now supposed to be preparatory for them continued to be elusive.

A memorial biography of Louisville published in 1896 still identified the high school as the "people's college" and praised the "college course" offered at Male, even as it framed the school as preparatory to "a more thorough course of studies" to be found at Yale, Harvard, University of Virginia and other universities.[8] Still, some students from the Louisville high schools—like Atherton High School principal Emma Woerner—were able to enter universities with advanced standing as sophomores and even juniors well into the twentieth century. Though this fact—if acknowledged at all—is generally thought to speak of the low standards of colleges, it also speaks of the high standards of at least some high schools and academies, and the overall variability of educational practices in all schools. It also reflects persistent uncertainty about the role of each of these school types, particularly in relation to general education and specialized study. As late as 1903, Edwin Cornelius Broome of Columbia University explained,

> There are numerous overlappings. The first two years in most of our colleges belong to the period of secondary education; also certain studies, distinctly secondary in character, have filtered down into the upper grade of the elementary school. In other words, the joints in our educational system, because of the unique position of the college and the public high school, have become dove-tailed.

Broome goes on to argue that "secondary education, per se, however, stops the moment specialization begins; and that time may be, as it usually is, about the middle of the college course; or it may be, as it really should, at the close of the high school course," but his distinction between what "may be" and "usually is" versus what "should" be the difference is telling, revealing that the strict divide between high school and college was still a proposal rather than a widely accepted reality.[9]

In 1905, when the Carnegie Foundation for the Advancement of Teaching was established, the movement for defining a four-year high school program in relation to college was still flummoxed by the fact that, as its director Henry Pritchett explained, the terms *college* and *university* had "no fixed meaning on this continent" and it was "not uncommon to find flourishing high schools" that bore "one or the other of these titles."[10] This was materially significant to the Carnegie Foundation in relation to their plan to provide pensions to qualifying college and university faculty—that is, allowing these high schools to continue to "flourish" as such would cost money.

To add to the confusion inherent in the system, the "joints" at the upper end of higher learning were just as confounding as those between the high school and college. As discussed in chapter four (and reflected also in Broome's comments above), the confounding intersections between institutions was not confined to the high school and college but instead were quite pronounced in relation to professional education and the issue of specialization at the upper end of the system as well. The definition of the liberal arts was very much at issue.

The new model of the research university had implications for liberal arts education at both colleges and high schools, as "Champions of 'the German model' returned [to the United States from Germany] with visions of a new academic order, not merely wishing to graft graduate schools onto existing colleges, but questioning the colleges' intermediary role between secondary and specialized and professional studies."[11] That is to say, some reformers were considering offloading general liberal education to the secondary school altogether, after which students could choose to go on to specialized, professional study. Again, professional schools (including law and medical schools) still did not often require an undergraduate degree for admission in the nineteenth century, demonstrating the profound lack of distinction between high schools and colleges in relation to their role of providing general education. The overlaps meant that some professional schools were criticized for having graduated students lacking a liberal background altogether, and thus woefully underprepared to be professionals.

The concern about professional schools, particularly schools of medicine, led the Carnegie Foundation to commission a report on the status of medical schools in the United States. The man in charge of that research and report was Louisville's own Abraham Flexner, who would go on to produce a famously scathing indictment of the medical education system that lead to massive reforms in the twentieth century. But Flexner's work was not limited to a critique of professional education. Instead, it comprised a critique of the whole education system. His ideas, based in his experience teaching and learning in the Louisville schools, would influence the national discourse on higher learning for decades.

But, most importantly for our purposes here, his ideas—captured in publications into the 1930s—also highlight how intransigent many of the concerns about the complex system of higher learning would prove to be over the coming decades, and how the secondary schools often lost out in the process of sorting it out.[12]

"They Have Tightened the Screws on the Secondary Schools": Louisville's Abraham Flexner and Progressive Era Educational Reform

A Louisville native, Abraham Flexner had attended Louisville's Male High School for six years in the 1880s—two in the preparatory department and four in the high school course—after which he continued to Johns Hopkins University, graduating after just two years.[13] Upon graduating from Hopkins in 1886, Flexner returned to Louisville and took an assistantship teaching classics at his alma mater, at just nineteen years old. Flexner taught at Male for six years, during which time he was celebrated for introducing several "new ideas" to the school, including the introduction of child development and education ideas from Pestalozzi, Herbart, and Froebel.[14] He wanted students to learn more flexibly in high school so they could learn more deeply in college and across their professional lives. He called this, drawing on the European theorists, the "kindergarten idea."

This "kindergarten idea"—which would have also been known as the "New Education" a few years prior—was the subject of one of Flexner's first educational publications. He writes, "the Kindergarten idea, it seems to me, is so valuable as an educational factor, not only in early childhood, but throughout the educational period, that we should not be content until it is exhibited in this light." Specifically, the "ideal of the imaginative reason"—represented by the kindergarten idea—

> should be speedily pursued throughout the common school, the high school, and the college, where the appeal must be continually and equally made to both sides of the pupil's nature. . . . We can understand, then, that there is no inherent incompatibility between science and poetry, between utility and beauty.

In these comments, Flexner echoed his predecessor William Hailmann to a remarkable degree. But, where the comments of Hailmann and his colleague Principal Holyoke could earlier be seen to reflect something of the educational atmosphere of the school in which they worked (see chapter 3), Flexner found his reform efforts in this direction ultimately constrained by the public high school context. [15] In an increasingly bureaucratized, hierarchicalized, and stabilized schooling system—the resemblance of Flexner's recommendations to Hailmann's represents the changed educational context by the 1890s. Though growing out of many of the same "high-minded philosophies" earlier in the century, the schools by the 1890s had become what Lawrence Cremin calls a "depressing study in contrast": overcrowded and underfunded schools in which "rote efficiency reigned supreme" as a matter of survival. Despite early successes and ideals, it is to these conditions that progressive educational reform of the late nineteenth century responded. The idea of the public high school had changed, and Flexner no longer saw it as a place where the kindergarten idea could thrive.[16]

Consequently, Flexner left after just a few years teaching at Male to start his own private college preparatory school in 1890. In his own school, he "abolished all purely 'artificial tasks' such as looking up lists of words in the dictionary, assigning long compositions on unfamiliar topics, and drilling in abstract English grammar."[17] In addition, he cut down the course of study, particularly grammar, and "did away with English 'readers' wholly, substituting for them real literature, based upon which was a daily written composition." He averred that "tho the greatest diversity, in point of aptness for various studies was at once disclosed, I discovered that practically all children could be interested in and taught the subjects required for college admission."[18] Thus, although he himself was focused on preparing students for college entrance, in tacit acceptance of the academic hierarchy, he sought to do so not through relentless preparatory drill but by fostering their curiosity and interest in the present.

His approach seems to have worked. Flexner's school was hailed by Harvard's Charles Eliot as preparing students for his college better than any other school. Eliot observed that boys from the school were "coming to Harvard younger and graduating in a shorter period of time than students from any other school." In explanation, Flexner "told him it was all very simple, that [he] treated these boys as individuals, and that [he] let each go at his own pace. [He] took hold of pupils where they were strong, not where they were weak, and having whetted their appetite by success in one field, usually succeeded in arousing interest in another." He elaborated this plan in an article published in the *Educational Review* titled

"A Freshman at Nineteen"—a critique especially of the graded system of instruction that typically led students to enter college at a late age.[19]

In these changes, he was received as revolutionary, presaging the innovations of Dewey's laboratory school in the next decade. And these innovations resurfaced, to much public recognition, in his own laboratory school, the Lincoln School of Columbia University's Teacher's College. As Cremin points out in regard to that school, though Flexner later attributed the source of his ideas there to the influence of Dewey and Harvard's Charles Eliot, "a close examination of his autobiography locates the principal source in his own teaching experience in the school he organized and conducted as a young man in Louisville, Kentucky."[20] Thus, while the Lincoln School became one of the most famous experiments in progressive education, it was little more than a return to practices from earlier in the century, drawn from his alma mater and his own experimental school in Louisville.[21]

But Flexner's desire for authentic learning opportunities continued to come up against constraints in the developing education system, which he had come to characterize as a "human staircase."[22] His frustrations reflect the changing structure and function of higher learning by the century's end, and highlight the future-directed, progressive system as a key cause of struggle for the high school teacher and student alike. Though certainly not all students went on to study at college, the attempts to align the high schools and colleges into one system and the idea that college was the higher goal in this arrangement powerfully and fundamentally changed the idea of writing in both high schools and colleges. With this structure, Flexner argues, came dominance by the college, its interests, and its pedagogical philosophies.

As colleges came to assert their position above high schools in the academic hierarchy, Flexner laments that the colleges had "tightened the screws on the secondary schools." The problem was the progressive or hierarchical conception of education and the external pressure thus exerted on the high school from the college, such that "the definite collegiate formulations of what is wanted in each subject have reacted on these schools, practically determining for them the spirit, method and contents of their instruction." Of course, these determinations were never uniformly adopted. How could they be? But the ostensible goal of college admissions (and the particular requirements thereof) exerted pressure on high schools: not only the pressure we typically assume, to elevate their standards, but also a downward pressure to stay in their place in the hierarchy. According to Flexner, the system simply "requires the secondary school teacher to be a drill master, without responsibility for the liberation or definition of the pupil's significant tendencies."[23] As a result, "in the high school there is less and less room for pedagogical initiative; there has never been much in the college."[24]

The mechanism by which secondary teachers were forced into position of "drill master" was the college entrance examination. The examination, Flexner argues in an article on the subject, was "fit for little more than to measure superficial knowledge." As a result, "its influence on previous education tends to develop the external, mechanical and insincerely imitative at the sacrifice of the internal and spontaneous."[25]

Writing instruction was no exception. As Flexner explains in the epigraph to this chapter, the effect of examinations on writing instruction was to emphasize surface correction and all manner of details that he and many of his fellow educators found peripheral to true learning. They also emphasized content and memorization in areas that he deemed laughable for determining college readiness. See, for instance, Flexner's account of the famous English A examination, which uses questions on classic literature as the topic for judging student expression:

> In one and a quarter hours a boy is to read and choose three out of twelve such problems, get his ideas into shape and set them down "correct," without the chance to reconsider, readjust, rewrite or recopy, which the most practiced writer demands, and which every good teacher tries to get the pupil to require of himself!

He concludes with disgust that "a process better calculated to torture the teacher and to divorce expression from experience in the pupil could hardly be devised" and argues that "the closer the apparent articulation thus secured between secondary school and college, the more certain becomes the internal educational hiatus." In abstracting the labor of the high school to serve the "system," such an exam does not attend to the complex work of teaching and learning in actual schools and sets up students for failure as intellectuals and engaging writers.[26]

Thus, across Flexner's publications we get an alternative vision of high school and college articulation efforts. We have tended to accept that college reforms such as the admissions exams instituted at Harvard were attempts "to upgrade secondary school education," as John Brereton put it. But Flexner's perspective suggests that just the opposite may have happened: The logic of articulating one continuous school system entailed a suppression of the high school and its writing practices as much as an elevation of the college. As Flexner and others have observed, part of what was at issue in these developments is what some called "college dominance": the shaping of high school curricula by college men not involved in their daily operations. With little educational philosophy beyond the establishment of the hierarchy itself, "the terms of admission to college are prescribed from above, and are more or less meekly accepted below. . . . Neither institution has properly conceived its relation to the other; neither institution has yet learned to subordinate itself to a large and inclusive conception of education."[27]

The local nuance of individual schools, classrooms, and students was thus generalized and flattened into an abstraction, and managed as part of this system. That abstraction of the high school could hardly represent the variety of practices across the more privileged (white, male) high schools, leave aside the different experience, methods, and needs of segregated, differently resourced, and increasingly vocational schools like Louisville's Female and Central. In each case, articulation of the system rendered deviation from an established norm—including audience-specific adaptation or innovation—as a liability.

Composing First-Year Writing in the College

As preparatory institutions in this "articulated" educational system, high schools were tasked with attending to the surface features of writing and responsible for assigning reading lists that would prepare students for exams. This situation will sound familiar to many writing educators across institutional levels today: that what students are tested on in order to certify preparation for future learning is at odds with the habits and mindsets needed to succeed in that future context. This conundrum is commonly acknowledged. Yet our general lack of attention to the tradition of writing instruction in high schools has led us to misunderstand this development.

Thus, Connors finds it "ironic" that "just as the teaching of 'error-based' grammar was accelerating in college rhetoric," the Committee of Ten on the teaching of Secondary English was proposing that grammar instruction be limited to the final year of instruction, in recognition of the fact that formal instruction in grammar does not serve writing. He identifies this as the "first major questioning of the use of grammar," asserting that grammar instruction had been the dominant tradition for teaching writing in high and grammar schools as well as colleges. But, as we have seen, the focus on grammar was questioned in many schools from at least midcentury. The real irony that Connors is tapping into is that the pedagogies of the college had long lagged behind the practices and pedagogies of the high schools, though high schools increasingly had to attend to surface features and grammar puzzles by the end of the century as the colleges valued these features on entrance examinations.[28]

In a similar vein, scholars of rhetoric and composition have done much to make sense of what the "required freshman English" class meant in the changing college context of this time. The role of the Harvard entrance requirements and English A have loomed large in these accounts, even as later scholars have worked to decenter Harvard's role. But both those who have celebrated Harvard's role and those who have critiqued it have missed a key point in assuming "that secondary schools had previously based their curriculum on college preparation." As Hobbs and Berlin explain it, it is this fact, along with Harvard's prestige and "the absence of any new curricular model for the new high school" that "all conspired to make the new entrance policy decisive in shaping secondary English courses." The result, as Berlin explains the situation elsewhere, was "that English instruction received more attention in secondary schools, fixing it permanently in the curriculum."[29] Much of this discussion presupposes a more established curriculum for the college and a more preparatory role for the high school than actually existed. By contrast, Flexner reminds readers that "the independent high schools...originally influenced the colleges powerfully. They first created the 'modern side'; in a measure their popularity forced the colleges to accept modern subjects on a par with the classics and mathematics." The "modern subjects" that high schools pressured colleges to accept included English and writing as prominent examples.

Instead of being preparatory or rudimentary, writing instruction in historical high schools (and academies) was part of a practical curriculum preparing students for civic life. In the words of Hailmann and other followers of the New Education, learning was not to prepare for life, but was itself characteristic of living. But as the high school became rendered as preparatory and subordinate to the college, the long and rich tradition of teaching writing in the higher branches of those schools became a deficit—composition, the story goes, is the work of the high schools, and if the high school is no longer considered the site of intellectual and collegiate work, then composition is not a truly intellectual, collegiate subject. Because the tradition of teaching writing in the high school had not previously been predicated on high school being more rudimentary than college, the assertion that composition should be "taken care of" in the high school relied on the diminishing status of high school, which had become merely preparatory to college by the end of the century. In this way, the devaluing of composition as a preparatory subject goes hand in hand with the devaluing of the high school that was being accomplished at this time.

From one perspective, then, the articulation of high schools with colleges played a role not in addressing but in *producing* the uninspiring writing instruction that college-level compositionists have subsequently worked against for more than a hundred years. That is, in asserting the difference between high school and college writing, we may have done "little more than create a daemon for the sake of expelling it."[30] The numerous organizations and committees on writing at the turn of the century created distinctions between these institutions—or created, at least, the ideal of such distinctions. They sought systemization and consistency across institutions. But they did not do so without cost.

Unfortunately, it is at this point of transition that most histories in rhetoric and composition tend to pick up the story, providing us with the sense that "college was fairly easy to define . . . college was defined through *difference*" from the high school.[31] But as we have seen in the Louisville case, the high school, college, and university grew up not in separate spaces or with clearly defined distinctions, but instead in intimate conversation with one another—sometimes as one-and-the-same thing. This relationship, then, has not been characterized by the clear institutional distinctions we may have assumed, and also not by a shared pedagogical goal or commitment, but instead by overlap and even competition. Indeed, while much of the educational atmosphere had changed across Flexner's career, the situation by the end of the century was in one key way similar to that at midcentury: the boundaries of high school and college remained blurred. As late as 1930, Flexner argued in *Universities: American, English, German* that high schools and colleges alike provided secondary instruction, or general education—to be contrasted with the advanced education of the university. The battle over general education—or, in some cases, the desire *not* to be answerable for providing general education—was of central importance in this equation. And, as part of general education, the status of writing instruction was always centrally involved as well.

Actual practices remained highly variable and confounding to administrators, but the lack of clear institutional boundaries was not only the nuisance college advocates determined it to be by the end of the century; it has also represented an internal flexibility and locus of control that enabled citizens and school leaders to determine the contours of higher learning for their own communities. For a time at least, high schools had been a rich site of educational experimentation with implications for the teaching of writing and rhetoric, and the disregard of the practices of the high schools has obscured that tradition and also served to degrade the achievements in higher learning and teaching by women and African Americans in that context.

As should be clear by this point, bringing first-year composition, as a course, into the college in the last quarter of the century had to do with the changing relations at all levels of the educational progression: high school, college, and university studies. The classical curriculum was on the wane, and the location of general education and the status of preparatory studies was shifting. The modern subjects and the elective system were in ascendance, and college admissions examinations sought to gauge preparation in these new areas among diverse students. Thus, while other historians have seen Harvard's English A or other such college courses as the beginning of composition as a disciplinary area, we might also recognize courses like English A "produc[ing] difference where difference was not apparent before" and ascribing composition instruction to an officially preparatory status, not to be integrated throughout higher learning but to be "taken care of" at the outset of college course of instruction before students continued on to more advanced studies.[32]

Looking at the histories of nineteenth-century high schools, then, we start to see the contours of a different narrative for composition's history, a narrative that challenges some of our assumptions and invites us to interrogate our own values and our own tacit role in the constitution of the educational institutions in which we work.

So what can we do with this alternate history?

CONCLUSION

Blurring the Boundaries

> Reform movements are notoriously ahistorical in outlook. They look forward rather than back; and when they do need a history, they frequently prefer the fashioning of ideal ancestors to the acknowledgement of mortals.
>
> —*Lawrence Cremin*

Ultimately, in directing our attention to the Louisville high schools, I am not arguing that they are exemplary and worth celebrating on their own terms (though I believe they are). I am not establishing the need to examine other high schools and their rhetorical practices (though that may well be useful). I am not suggesting we use such high schools to elaborate a more nuanced history of college writing (though they certainly help us to do that). Further, this project does not uncover any "new" data or previously overlooked facts about American education. Quite significantly, these exceptions and slippages have been noted all along, particularly by educational historians. What I want to accomplish with this history is to question the categories of "high school" and "college" altogether.

Moving beyond a paradigm of "rescue, recovery, and reinscription," I follow Gesa Kirsch and Jacqueline Jones Royster in their invitation to compose histories in the field of rhetoric and composition that move toward a more critical and imaginative engagement with historical subjects and their stories, "to critique our analytical assumptions and frames, to critique guiding questions reflectively and reflexively."[1] In this way,

I want to use the history of high schools like Louisville's as an historiographic lens—a tool that allows us to ask: What happens when we not only acknowledge but for the moment *focus on* these overlaps and "exceptional normal" cases at the intersection of high schools and colleges? What does the history of "higher schooling" help us to think? How does it help us to think differently?

My own provisional answer is that, by bringing under scrutiny the very categories of college and high school on which we have come to rely, we usefully unsettle our historical and contemporary confidence in their internal coherence and distinctiveness. I hope that my research demonstrates the variety, fluidity, intermingling, and changeability of U.S. higher schooling that insists that we rethink our discursive frameworks and standards of assessment. The illusion of institutional stability—with parity among peers, and distinction between levels—has been just that: an illusion.

Rather than ever stable or discrete, reliable or neutral in their form, high schools and colleges in the United States are ideological constructs influenced by a range of traditions and changing conceptions of knowledge and labor in a given historical moment and locale. As such, they are open to (re)negotiation and continual change, always intersecting with other educational institutions and forms, and in constant translation and transformation. This lack of stability is particularly characteristic of the nineteenth century, when current educational–institutional forms were just emerging, and were actively and publicly negotiated. But it has persisted meaningfully into the present as well. Thus, these categories need seriously to be reconsidered, interrogated as political rather than solely pedagogical or administrative constructs that enable certain kinds of action and constrain others, with implications for teachers and learners today.

In this final chapter, I will shift our gaze away from Louisville and the nineteenth century and toward applications to the contemporary context of higher learning in the United States today. Namely, I want to shift our gaze toward one of our own ostensible reform movements: dual-credit and concurrent enrollment, or what is called more generally "accelerated learning" models, which have circulated widely in the disciplinary discourse, but thus far largely without a discernible history.[2] Here, I want to connect the foregoing history of "higher schooling" to the present, outlining some theoretical shifts suggested by this account as well as some more practical considerations it makes available.

Dual Enrollment: Defining "College-Level" without the College

In broadening the scope of inquiry to encompass all of "higher learning," this history troubles any easy definition of "college." And, needless to say, our conception of *college* will, perforce, affect our perspective on "college level" and the writing practices and values it entails. It is imperative for rhetoric and composition scholars to know, then, what we have meant by *college level* and how those definitions have shaped programs, practices, and policies. This question has taken on renewed urgency in light of accelerated learning programs (concurrent-enrollment, dual-credit, AP, and the like) that are blurring the divide between high school and college in the United States.

According to the National Alliance of Concurrent Enrollment Partnerships (NACEP), 10 percent of high school students—or more than 1.4 million students—take college courses from postsecondary institutions each year, and this rate has been growing by some 7 percent each year since 2002. Indeed, Louisville's Male High School, Central High School, and DuPont Manual High School (which merged with and absorbed Female High School in 1950) each boasts robust accelerated learning programs today, including dual-credit, early-college, advanced placement, and concurrent-enrollment courses.[3]

Concurrent enrollment, which typically uses high school instructors to teach college courses, remains the most prevalent delivery model. It is also the most controversial model. Particularly controversial to some has been the suggestion that college writing need not occur at the site of the college—that "college . . . is no longer a specific place, if indeed it ever was" as Kathleen Blake Yancey put it.[4]

From this perspective, our fear (and, perhaps, confidence) in relation to these programs has been grounded in our (over-)reliance on the location of a course at the "college" as a defining feature of "college writing." As Brice Nordquist observes in his book on the enactment of the contemporary nexus between high school and college (fortuitously located in Louisville), "We tend to approach classrooms, schools, and colleges as places that exist rather than places that occur or become." This approach to classrooms, schools, and colleges flattens our sense of the internal complexity within institutional categories and shifts our attention to the ostensible differences *between* them rather than *within* or *among* them: "Rather than the places themselves existing in states of internal complexity, flux, and consequent friction, the only frictions in the figuration reside *between* places and frames of time; the meritocratic and mechanical nature of high school is in tension with the exploratory and generative nature of college."[5] This flattened, internally consistent conception of high schools—differentiated from one another primarily by categorizations of high-performing, struggling, or even failing schools, with their own trajectories of performance over time, but without complex internal frictions—effectively serves as a foil for the college, an other against which it can define its work. This sense of the fundamental distinction between high school and college writing contexts poses serious problems for conceptualizing writing pedagogies and programs that will cross this institutional and ideological divide.

Organizations with a stake in this work, such as the Two Year College Association (TYCA), have already begun moving the conversation from a focus on the location of instruction in order to begin to operationalize the meaning of college-level writing. They locate concerns about concurrent enrollment programs in issues of quality and oversight. According to TYCA, "College courses taught by high school faculty at the high school often have minimal oversight by the sponsoring colleges because of limited budgets. The lack of sufficient release time for collaboration between college faculty and high school faculty makes the quality of instruction difficult to guarantee." As Eva Payne, former TYCA chair, argues, well-designed dual-enrollment programs *can* prepare students to be ready for college-level work if and when they matriculate to college, but we need to adhere to the standards set by NACEP. Payne emphasizes, "Supporting the high school teachers who do this difficult work and ensuring that students have truly transferable credits that benefit them as they move forward is a common goal for everyone who supports dual enrollment. This requires thoughtful, thorough guidelines at the state level and stable, adequate funding for oversight to ensure that high standards are met."[6]

This perspective helps us move away from a reliance on the site of the college toward a focus on the teaching and learning that occurs in the writing classroom, and the resources that support that work. But, I argue, it still retains a sense of stability and a sense of distinction between high school and college writing goals that is less than productive. In place of the imagined location is a set of standards that can be reliably articulated and administered across contexts. Those standards rely for their very definition on the difference between high school and college writing practices, in a hierarchical arrangement, and posit success in other college and career writing as the unequivocal goal. And they rely, in their course, on a language of futurity and a conception of education as credentialing that serves to undercut the value of writing as a living practice in and for itself and the present. That is, education here (and elsewhere across U.S. educational discourse) is structured in terms of what Nordquist calls "the relentless future orientation of formal education and its models of vertically integrated knowledge"—education as credits to *transfer* as students *move forward*—rather than a "pedagogy of the present" that focuses on the work students are doing with language today. The language of futurity undergirds the discourse of college- and career readiness that permeates U.S. education today. That language of college- and career readiness, in turn, reifies differences between these ostensible contexts, and supports a conception of education as credentialing that, as demonstrated in the previous chapter, has attended many of the problems of flattened instruction for articulation and standardization in U.S. writing instruction since the Progressive Era.[7]

All of this administrative language relies on an underinterrogated acceptance of the academic hierarchy, comprised of clearly defined and articulated steps:

> By focusing on how to best prepare students for self-evident futures—the next grade level, the first year of college, an academic discipline, a job—policies, pedagogies, and assessment often disregard the ways in which imagined futures and embodied histories shape needs, desires, perceptions, practices, and places in the present. . . . Fixations on progress towards, transition into, and transfer for the future often prevent us from recognizing education as a process of placemaking . . . in the present.[8]

Thus, the focus on "standards" for defining college-level writing is inadequate insofar as it perpetuates notions of writing as acontextual, institutional types as stable, and education as equivalent to credentialing for future opportunities, to the neglect of students' complex present experiences, needs, and desires.

Translanguaging Higher Learning

Drawing on a mobility framework, Nordquist asserts that we might approach our writing courses not as stable locations but "as movements along overlapping and diverging paths" in order to "understand ourselves, students, and materials as co-creators of emergent rather than predetermined places."[9] Both the high school and college writing classroom—and, indeed, the concurrent enrollment writing classroom—are such emergent places. In this light, we might reconsider how we think about college writing not just in the past, but also today.

Building on this perspective, I draw on another theoretical framework to help represent the historical fact of institutional fluidity and change outlined above, and consider how it affects our conception of institutions, classrooms, and practices today. Namely, I'd like to rethink this history as an attempt to "translanguage" the institutions of higher learning. This notion draws on work in rhetoric and composition that has attended to the interaction between and among language varieties. As articulated in a 2011 translingual statement from Bruce Horner, Min Zhan Lu, John Trimbur, and Jacqueline Jones Royster, a translingual approach questions "myths of unchanging, universal standards for language [that] have often been invoked to simplify the teaching and learning of language" and instead

> takes the variety, fluidity, intermingling, and changeability of languages as statistically demonstrable norms around the globe. It confronts, as well, the practice of invoking standards not to improve communication and assist language learners, but to exclude voices and perspectives at odds with those in power. It treats standardized rules as historical codifications of language that inevitably change through dynamic processes of use.[10]

Thus, a translingual approach encourages us to examine not only apparent difference but also apparent sameness, asking what interests these distinctions serve.

Although it may seem like a surprising left turn to take in a historical study of rhetorical education such as this, a translingual perspective offers a vocabulary and theoretical framework for understanding constant change and overlap as it occurs in all aspects of teaching, learning, and language events of interest to compositionists. To translanguage educational institutions is to understand them as emergent sites of social interaction that constitute institutions through educational, rhetorical, and political practice; it refers to the ways in which the philosophies of educational institutions "can be continually reconstituted." Our schools are ideological, cultural, and discursive constructions in their own right. They are always already "multi" and "trans," and this difference and fluidity is both a reality and a resource.[11]

Thus, as resistant as our educational systems often are to widespread change and reform, they are simultaneously bubbling with local changes and revisions. They are, like languages, porous and "in constant revision."[12] Recognizing the fluid and emergent nature of institution types in this way reminds us to attend to the sociopolitical and cultural field in which these questions of status are (provisionally) settled—and unsettles our histories in the process. Thus, instead of seeking a definition of "college," we might seek an understanding of the processes by which "college" has been defined, continually, over time, and to what rhetorical ends.

Christie Anne Farnham makes a similar point in her defense of southern women's colleges. Recognizing that many women's colleges have been excluded by historians from the category of college because they also offered preparatory work, Farnham highlights the implicit hypocrisy in the fact that the status of male colleges that also introduced partial or parallel courses (including many of the most elite and long-standing institutions) is not impugned as a result. Thus, the female college is actually held to a *higher* standard than the male college for inclusion in the same category—they are asked to meet the rigor of the "best" men's colleges. By contrast, though, Farnham contends that "if they met the standards of the 'worst' institutions to be considered colleges, that should suffice to establish their claim to the category." In a similar vein, I contend that the fact that high schools were not equivalent to the "best" colleges does not mean that they weren't the pedagogical and even political equivalent of a great number of other colleges. The status of these schools was not, after all, determined by rigor and curricula alone.[13]

But I want to take Farnham's point one step further, using her important observations to argue against the utility and reliability of these categories altogether. Instead, the categories and status of institutions have been fluid and unstable, shaping and informing one another, drawing on the status of kindred institutions and suppressing the status of others in accordance with shifting educational and socio-political values across the decades. At times, this has entailed the preservation of tradition, amounting to what Charles Francis Adams in a 1907 speech to the Harvard alumni characterized as "A College Fetich" [sic] for classics over modern languages, as supporters of English and modern languages had long been perceived as "a vulgar and contemptible majority" against which the college supporters must hold strong. But at other times, as Ryan Skinnell contends in *Conceding Composition*, cultural capital came to accrue to schools based not only on prestige but also based on democratic values of access. Countering the common presumption of composition as a liability to the status of college learning, Skinnell contends that composition has actually been a "boon" to the status of the college, "routinely . . . used to evince postsecondary institutions' credentials as providers of mass education."[14] If this is so, then it is at least in part due to composition's affiliation with and history of practice in the "people's college," the U.S. high school. Thus, the college and high school have long traded on one another's cultural and political capital, continually shifting and renegotiating boundaries not based on what should be preparatory or advanced so much as what subjects and pedagogies belong with a given matrix of values for "higher education" at a given time and in a given place.

Our histories have similarly traded on the value of elite and democratic origins. As Fitzgerald puts it, we are ever trying to "recuperate a tradition capable of legitimizing the field as a university discipline, yet also capable of grounding a contemporary democratic ethic radically different from the ethic of its elitist institutional origins." I argue that our definition of "college" has remained an underinterrogated condition at the core of those efforts. Against our common assumptions and even some of our early scholarship, I have argued that college has never been as easy to define as we have believed—not as different from the high school in expectations, attitudes, or even location.[15] Consider, to this point, the uneasy status of the community college in the academic hierarchy, which, Mary McMullen-Light characterizes as "sandwiched between high schools and four-year colleges." Though a full examination of the community college and two-year college is outside the scope of this project, the alignment of its history with the confounding institutional status issues explored here deserves more attention.[16]

This is not to say that these various educational institutions *shouldn't* be different, just that they never really have been. My point here, then, is not about acknowledging local differences—that "not all colleges are the same"—or simply recognizing the nineteenth century as an aberration in relation to higher learning morphology. Rather, my emphasis is on the always-emergent intra-group differences that confound the very categories themselves. Thus, the ideology challenged here is not the idea that high schools should be different from community colleges, liberal arts colleges, or universities, or that different institutions do or should have different missions. At issue is the ideology that prohibits high school and college from having contact with each other, associating overlap "with contamination and lack of proficiency." In light of dual-credit and concurrent-enrollment programs, we can no longer afford to conceptualize the high school and college in this way. This conception of the attendant high school and college, of their relationship, and, particularly, of the "meritocratic and mechanical nature" of the high school, has a history, and that history is linked to the college and its penchant to construct an educational system to suit its own credentialing needs. Along with Horner et al., in their translingual statement, we might then ask, "What produces the appearance of conformity" or coherence with a category like "college," and "what . . . might and might not [that appearance] do, for whom, and how."[17] While eroding our confidence in institutional locations and categories within higher education, I suggest that collapsing our traditional distinction between secondary and college writing might, paradoxically, enable us to erect more robust and useful definitions of writing in its place.

What College-Level Writers *Do*

In asking us to attend to differences between and among institutions and recognizing that the formation and definition of institution types are fluid, this research invites us to reimagine institutional categories in ways that promote access, collaboration, generative cross-pollination and local, operational definitions of writing in and for higher learning. Our definition of "college-level writing" should not, I contend, replicate the sense of stability and uniformity that previously accrued to the institutions themselves. Instead of the official designation of institutional categories, the pragmatic, goal-based strategies of school leaders, teachers, and students determines the work of teaching and learning, the status, the form, and the meaning of the educational institution and its writing practices for participants.[18]

While understanding the challenges posed by lack of standardization, I contend that emphasizing this fluidity as a resource and not only as an aberration to be corrected refocuses our attention on the local work of teaching and learning writing. From this perspective, we can reframe students' differential writing performances and goals as a desirable facet of the educational scene. As Nordquist argues, "By presenting scenes of literacy and scales of education as multiple, heterogeneous, and emergent rather than determined by the single scale of education that circulates preconceived standards and conventions, we might help these students recognize themselves as placemakers, actively making the environments in which they participate."[19] This will not help us to address issues of access that circulate around differential allocation of school resources, but neither will proceeding as though those conditions and their results are simply foreordained and unchangeable or, worse, that they are neutral, to which I fear the language of standards can lend itself. Instead of using assumptions about institutional classifications as our starting point, both our histories and our future plans for writing can be—with students—a response to and construction of events on the ground.

From this perspective, students in dual-credit or concurrent-enrollment courses are not receiving an established or standardized college-level curriculum to prepare for future college practice but are instead creating the connections and language experiences to support their varied literacy goals in and for the present as well. They are participants in the construction of their classrooms and their learning experiences.

We might eschew "standards" for a focus on experiences and habits of mind like those articulated in the *Framework for Success in Post-Secondary Writing* and the *CWPA Outcomes Statement for First Year Writing.* In their attempts to provide guidance to writing instructors and students engaged in "college-level writing," both documents avoid the language of standards that has dominated educational discourse at the K–12 level (most notably in relation to the Common Core State Standards). They focus instead on the experiences and habits of mind that students should engage to develop as writers and citizens, reserving the question of standards for local determination.[20]

The language around these documents remains limiting insofar as terms like "college-level" and "college readiness" presuppose the college to be hierarchically above and temporally sequential to the high school, and to be the aspirational goal of all students. In so doing, it necessarily suppresses the value and potential of the high school writing classroom, continuing to position it as a subordinate other against which "college-level" may be defined. And, while it may well be desirable for more students to matriculate into college, we would do well to question the presumption that the college is the best or only place where advanced rhetorical literacies are developed and practiced.

While still relying on the future-oriented language of "college readiness," such articulations of rhetorically productive habits of mind and experiences can actually help us de-emphasize the college-ready or preparatory versus college-level distinction in favor of seeing writing development as an ongoing process that, as the *Framework for Success* itself asserts, "takes place over time as students encounter different contexts, tasks, audiences, and purposes." That is, documents like the *Framework* may help us to combat the public and administrative discourse that has framed writing development as containable within a single course or two and that has taken the college composition course to be little more than a mark of our high schools' failures—a one-off course requirement that would go away if the high schools did their jobs better. These documents also help us challenge the idea that college writing is something that only happens at and for college, contained from both high school writing and writing in the world.[21] Instead, if what we mean by college-level involves experiences and habits of mind such as those outlined in the *Framework*, what would it look like for all of our high school writing courses to be "college-level"? What would it look like for all of our high school writing courses to represent dual enrollment, even conferring college credit, depending on the work and goals of students and teachers? How do the stakes of the former question—about college-level pedagogies—differ from the latter, about college credit? Those questions *should* differ. Too often, from the perspective of the colleges and the organizations certifying dual-credit and concurrent-enrollment equivalency, I am afraid they get collapsed.

A History for the Present

If we follow these recent documents in defining college level by the practices and mindsets fostered in a classroom, then the nineteenth century contexts explored here represent a powerful example of just that. Of course, things have changed since then. But while the local nuances of academic socialization and education policy standards today create complex rhetorical and institutional contexts that are different for high school and college students today than they were for students in the nineteenth century, the complex and messy overlaps between categories persists. A document like the *Framework for Success* may help us to focus on those contexts themselves, and to draw on them in developing students' sense of rhetorical situations, rather than proceeding as though these contexts are neutral or that even the most robustly regulated dual-credit or concurrent-enrollment program can erase the effects of local, contextual differences in teaching and learning—or, that such erasure is desirable.

This history, then, helps us to see that many dual-enrollment programs *are* a threat to writing, but not necessarily because of the challenge they pose to the high school–college divide. That divide has never been reliable. Instead, such programs have been a threat to writing because of the suggestion that writing is little more than a requirement that can be simply completed—and the earlier the better. Thus, our gripe here is not with high school writing teachers or teaching, of course, but with an impoverished view of writing as a "one-off" kind of course—a box that can be checked off. Instead, the field of rhetoric and composition sees writing as integrated in learning, *as* learning. We understand writing as rhetorical, and therefore as changing fundamentally with the rhetorical context not only of high school and college but also of disciplines and workplace cultures. What we know about writing suggests that students not only benefit from instruction and practice in their first year, but throughout a vertical writing curriculum. And we might more insistently frame that vertical curriculum as extending into the high school as well, connecting us with the work done there. That is, we should encourage students to take advanced writing courses of all kinds, including in the high school, as we work locally to extend writing practice vertically through our programs and across the curriculum on our own campuses.

If we are to stem the tide of commodification of writing, we can't hold the front line at the boundary of the college. Not only is that boundary historically and intellectually unstable, it keeps out as many allies as insurgents. Protecting the sanctity of our own discipline and insisting on the separateness of institutions and their pedagogical values serves as a means (however inadvertent) of marginalizing the work of K–12 teachers and schools of education. Further, that boundary serves to devalue writing insofar as, from the point of distance across this divide, we cannot properly defend *all* writing from accountability assessment, timed testing, and other policies and practices that contradict our disciplinary knowledge about the teaching, learning, and practice of writing.

When it comes to dual and concurrent enrollment programs, we must acknowledge that "a prime factor for the proliferation of such programs has more to do with the perception that something is wrong with US high schools," thus inviting colleges to intervene to reduce the amount of time students have to spend there through these programs. However, as Howard Tinberg and Jean Paul Nadeau argue, "If genuine reform of secondary education is to occur, surely it must involve educational authorities and legislators working with the high schools for genuine transformation of those schools, rather than abandoning them for the greener pastures of higher education."[22]

To this end, this history supports what Jonathan Bush calls "the teaching of writing as a global proposition—one that doesn't make distinctions between the values that guide the teaching of writing in the elementary school and those that guide teaching in colleges and universities." Recognizing the "two schools of exclusive scholarship" or "worlds of teaching" with "minimal interaction, both physically and theoretically," Bush calls us "not to create a cohesive theory that guides all teachers of writing, but to create an ideal of understanding and ethos that allows composition practitioners to learn from others who teach and write about writing. The goal, then, is to make the developmental-level borders permeable and pliable by helping others in recognizing their shared goals and common practices."[23]

Such calls have resounded across the pages of our disciplinary journals for years now. In this same way, Keith Gilyard argued some years ago for the importance of connecting K–12 and college-writing teachers in our policy discussions. Heidi Estrem has similarly advocated stronger ties between English education and rhetoric and composition in graduate education. Bronwyn Williams has drawn our attention to the ways our scholarship circulates (or not) outside of our own field, among other literacy-related fields. And documents such as the 2013 Mt. Oread Manifesto—by proposing "an integrated curriculum in rhetorical education to replace separate introductory courses in communication and first-year composition in order to develop citizen participants, not simply future employees or literate students" along with an affirmation of pedagogy as "a respected area of scholarship"—remind us of the other allies we have around rhetorical education in the academy as well.[24]

The case of the nineteenth-century high school provides a long, rich, and shared tradition of permeable and pliable writing and rhetorical instruction across academic levels to draw on in this effort—a history for what Bush calls the "big tent" of composition professionals across academic levels. As Connors argued some years ago, "We need shared stories because our self-definition is tenuous at best . . . we need each other to provide a larger meaning for all our work. We need the communality provided by historical knowledge because of both the peculiarly troubled nature and the unequaled moral power of composition studies as a college discipline."[25] We might add the unequaled moral power of composition as a practice, as a process, as a fundamental civic and human activity both inside our schools and out. In the process, these shared stories invite us to ask whether first-year composition is a "thing" that "began" at some point—a course that emerged due to this or that labor pressure or demographic shift—or whether "college-level writing" has been a shifting set of practices and values that has nonetheless *always* had a place in (and throughout) higher schooling.

Through this history, I hope to have made the distinctions between these institutional and course "types" less obvious once again, and invite the field to see where this perspective might lead us as we continue to compose a shared history and future for the American high school and college.

NOTES

BIBLIOGRAPHY

INDEX

NOTES

Preface

1. I use the term "American" throughout to refer specifically to the United States of America, though many of the observations contained here apply to the context of North America more broadly.
2. I only discuss briefly the fourth public school, DuPont Manual Training High School, opened in 1892. While that school's history reflects the trends and themes discussed in this volume, its establishment is also tied to the manual education movement that is itself deserving of a book-length study. Because it was opened much later—after significant changes to high schools and higher learning outlined in the second part of the book—and serves the same population as Male High School, I have not addressed it at length here.
3. See, for example, foundational work on high schools in Philadelphia (Labaree), Boston (Reese), Illinois (Gutowski; Walker), St. Louis (Graves), New York (Beadie), and Massachusetts (Katz; Ueda; Vinovskis).
4. L'Eplattenier, "An Argument for Archival Research Methods: Thinking beyond Methodology," 67–79.
5. Male High School does have a lovely alumni room with several historically valuable volumes and yearbooks, particularly from the twentieth century. The alumni there generously gave me a copy of *The First Hundred Years*, a thoughtful commemorative history authored by two of the school's alumni that proved to be a valuable resource for this research and a treasured item on my shelf. I was unable to get in touch with someone from Central High School or DuPont Manual High School to ascertain whether they have similar historical resources. My impression from speaking to various administrative assistants at each school is that their own rich histories have not been a major part of their present identities, and they have generally not been in the practice of preserving or exploring their past in the ways Male has done.

6. Louisville Girls High School Alumnae Club collection finding aid, University of Louisville, https://nyx.uky.edu/fa/findingaid/?id=xt7vt43hxs9d.
7. William DeGenaro discusses the value of rare published material like this as "archival" evidence as well. See DeGenaro, "William Rainey Harper," 183.
8. For more on school yearbooks and memory books in the twentieth century, with archival material from the Louisville schools, see Lueck, "'Classbook Sense,'" 381–406.

Introduction: High Schools, Higher Learning, and Our Histories

1. Cited in Draper, "New York," 148.
2. Thelin, *History*, 97; Reese, *Origins*, 34, 17. On the relativity of high schools, see also Tyack, *Turning Points*, 354; Krug, *Shaping*, 7. Indeed, the blurred lines between institutions of higher learning are considered common knowledge to many educational historians. See, for example, a recent article by educational historian Hampel, "Long View," 8–12.
3. Gelber, "City Blood," 279; Herbst, "Diversification," 198.
4. Fitzgerald, "Rediscovered Tradition," 224–50; Skinnell, "Institutionalizing Normal," 13; Lindblom, Banks, and Quay, "Mid-Nineteenth-Century Writing Instruction," 94–115.
5. Angelo, "Social Transformation," 267; Geiger, "Era of Multipurpose Colleges," 128. As educational historian W. Bruce Leslie explains of his own research on academies and colleges, "My anachronist [*sic*] categories blinded me to the colleges' financial dependence on those [preparatory] branches (whose enrollments often dwarfed those of the college) and to the fact that these were multi-purpose campuses. After all, I was 'doing' the history of *higher education*." Leslie ends up with the same recognition of overlap, opting for the term "higher schooling" to discuss academies in order to break from the anachronism of existing categories. (Leslie, "Where?," 263, n. 2–3). While Leslie posits that high schools have had a clearer position in the academic hierarchies and are perhaps the reason the academy's role is misunderstood, the arguments of this book complicate that claim.
6. See Fleming, *From Form to Meaning*; Rose, "Language of Exclusion, 341–59; Stanley, *Rhetoric of Remediation*; and VanOverbeke, *Standardization of American Schooling*.
7. Ogren, *American State Normal School*, 1.
8. For examples of the expansive tendency in the field, see historical work on rhetorical education at small rural colleges (Gold, *Rhetoric at the*

Margins), women's colleges (Gold, *Rhetoric at the Margins*; Gold and Hobbs, *Educating*; Mastrangelo, "Learning from the Past," *Writing a Progressive Past*), HBCUs (Gold, *Rhetoric at the Margins;* Hoogeveen, "Progressive Faculty"; Jarratt, "Classics and Counterpublics"), Indian schools (Myers, "Raise Your Right Arm"; Katanski, *Learning to Write "Indian"*; Enoch, *Refiguring*), land-grant colleges (Mendenhall, "Joseph V. Denney"), junior colleges (DeGenaro, "William Rainey Harper"), normal schools (Fitzgerald, "Rediscovered Tradition"; Donahue and Moon, *Local Histories*; Ostergaard and Wood, *In the Archives*), academies (Eldred and Mortenson, *Imagining Rhetoric*; Buchanan, *Regendering Delivery*), and spaces and practices outside the classroom (Enoch, *Refiguring*; Gere, "Kitchen Tables,"; Logan, *Liberating Language;* McComiskey, *Microhistories;* Royster, *Traces of a Stream*).

For work in rhetoric and composition on textbooks and pedagogies in the schools, see Buchanan, *Regendering Delivery*; Carr, Carr, and Schultz, *Archives of Instruction*; Schultz, "Elaborating Our History"; Schultz, "Pestalozzi's Mark"; Schultz, *Young Composers*; Eldred and Mortenson, *Imagining Rhetoric.*

For evidence of the general neglect of high schools in our conception of the field, see the lists of institution types in collections such as McComiskey, *Microhistories*, 25; Glenn, Lyday, and Sharer, *Rhetorical Imagination*; and Gold, *Rhetoric at the Margins*, 4.

An interesting wrinkle in this discussion is the role of English education programs for teaching writing in the high schools, as explored by Lane, "A 'Forgotten' Location" and Stock, *Composition's Roots.* See also Williams, "Seeking New Worlds," 127–46 for examples of scholars challenging this divide and an argument for more rich conversation between what he calls "literacy-related fields."

9. Ritter, *In the Archives*, xi. Also see Ostergaard, *Composition;* Wood, *Praising Girls* and "Rhetorical Praxis."
10. Ostergaard and Wood, "Adding Stories," 3.
11. Crowley, "Material of Rhetoric," 363.
12. Graves, *Girls' Schooling*, 107. Also see Krug, *Shaping*, 3; VanOverbeke, *Standardization of American Schooling*, 18, 27; Farnham, *Education*; Gordon, *Gender and Higher Education*; Brown, *American High School*, 30; Gidney and Millar, *Inventing Secondary Education*, 254; and Leslie, *Gentlemen and Scholars*, 8.
13. Angelo, "Social Transformation," 267.
14. Salvatori, *Pedagogy*, 6; Donahue, "Disciplinary Histories," 225. Also see Labaree, *Trouble with Ed Schools*, 22.

15. Katz, *Reconstructing*, 167.
16. Adams, Godkin, and Nutter, "Report of the Committee," 123.
17. Strickland, *Managerial Unconscious*, 26–30, 34. For more on our disciplinary beginnings, see Berlin, *Rhetoric and Reality*; Brereton, *Origins of Composition Studies*; Connors, *Composition-Rhetoric*; Crowley, *Methodical Memory*.
18. Donahue, "Disciplinary Histories," 225.
19. Royster and Williams. "History," 581.
20. Fitzgerald, "Rediscovered Tradition," 224–50.
21. Skinnell, "Institutionalizing Normal," 13.
22. Thelin, *History*, xv–xvi.
23. Federal Writers' Project, *Centennial History*, 19; Hackensmith, *Out of Time and Tide*, 171; Yater, *Two Hundred Years*, 53. Master's degrees were conferred on graduates who engaged in professional practice (including teaching) for three years after graduation. The first master of arts degrees were honorary degrees conferred in 1862 upon James S. Pirtle and Lewis D. Kastenbine, who had been the first graduates of Male in 1859 (the only graduates that year).

    While Veysey uses undergraduate and graduate instruction in the liberal arts as the primary criteria for discussing universities, Angelo references schools like Temple and the University of Pennsylvania—and, we might add here, University of Louisville—that were "only peripherally in the undergraduate business" as providing an alternative tradition for the development U.S. universities (Angelo, "Social Transformation," 267).
24. *Public School Laws of the City of Louisville*, 20–21; "History," on Atherton High School's official website, Jefferson County Public Schools, accessed March 15, 2015, http://schools.jefferson.kyschools.us/high/atherton/history.html; "History of the Louisville Normal School," Anniversary Number, 1871–1931, University of Louisville Archives and Special Collections, LGHS, folder 3, 13.
25. Farnham, *Education*, 18, 67.
26. In fact, Maris Vinovskis's research suggests that high school, academy, and even college attendance may be even higher than previous scholars had supposed, if we were to better account for high turnover in the aggregate attendance data usually referenced and thereby identify the students who, even if briefly, experienced some high school (Vinovskis, "Have We Underestimated?" 552).

    Women's attendance at colleges also rose substantially across the last quarter of the nineteenth century, even if they were underrepresented as graduates. At both colleges and high schools, enrollments often far outpaced graduation rates. But as women remained underrepresented in colleges until 1978, they have constituted the majority of high school graduates from at least 1870 (Davies, *Woman's Place*, 57; Graves, *Girls' Schooling*, xvii).

27. Gold, "Remapping Revisionist Historiography," 17.
28. McComiskey, *Microhistories*, 24; Lepore, "Historians," 133, accessed August 1, 2016, http://www.jstor.org.libproxy.scu.edu/stable/2674921.
29. Katz, *Reconstructing*, 164.

1. The Idea(l) of the High School

1. This is to say nothing of these schools' relationship to "university" work, which, by the last quarter of the century, was coming to be understood as entailing the upper levels of specialized education, which will be discussed in chapters 4 and 6.
2. As John Elbert Stout explains, "The word 'English' as applied to departments or courses was used in the broad sense to indicate all subjects except Latin and Greek and retained this general meaning even after a multiplication of titles became an established practice. The more restricted use of the term, as now employed, was very rare prior to 1880, and even after this use became well established, English courses did not necessarily offer any more work in English than did the courses having other titles" (Stout, *Development*, 53).
3. "From Tampa Bay," *Louisville Morning Courier*, September 7, 1849, 2, Proquest; "Classified Ad 5," *Daily Courier*, August 27, 1855, 5, Proquest; Leslie, "Where," 265. See Mattingly, *Secret Habits* for more on the tradition of Catholic schools, including those in Louisville. For work on Kentucky's Science Hill Academy, see Eldred and Mortenson, *Imagining Rhetoric*.
4. Walker, "Development," 264–79. "Annual Report on the Public Schools," *Daily Courier*, August 5, 1854, 2, Proquest.
5. Cited in Cox and Morison, *University of Louisville*, 9.
6. Cox and Morison, 14; Johnston, *Memorial History of Louisville*, 236. In 1846 by act of the General Assembly the Louisville College and the Louisville Medical Institute were combined, and a law school was added, to form the University of Louisville (Cox and Morison, *University of Louisville*, 14). University historians Cox and Morison use this trajectory to tie the much-contested lineage of the University of Louisville to the founding of the Jefferson Seminary in 1798 (a claim that was not made on behalf of the university until 1948).

7. Cox and Morison, *University of Louisville*, 7.
8. "University of Louisville—Academical Department," *Louisville Morning Courier*, April 29, 1850, 2, Proquest.
9. "Louisville University—Academical Department," *Louisville Morning Courier*, April 13, 1850, 2, Proquest.
10. "Louisville University—Academical Department," *Louisville Morning Courier*, April 23, 1850, 2, Proquest; "University of Louisville—Academical Department," April 13, 1850, 2. *Louisville Journal* is quoted within the above citation.
11. Johnston, *Memorial History of Louisville*, 239.
12. *Public School Laws*, 20–21; "Proceedings," *Daily Courier*, May 15, 1851, 2, Proquest; Johnston, *Memorial History of Louisville*, 238.
13. *Annual Report of the Board of Trustees of the University and Public Schools to the General Council of the City of Louisville, for the Year Ending July 1, 1855*, 22; "The School Ordinance Election To-day," *Daily Courier*, August 14, 1854, 2, Proquest.
14. Adkins and Holtzman, *First Hundred Years*, 2–3. On the "literacy myth," see Graff, *Literacy Myth*. For more on the political and class-based tensions in establishing nineteenth-century high schools, see the research on and subsequent debate about Massachusetts schools represented in Katz, *Irony of Early School Reform*; Vinovskis, *Origins*; and Katz, Stevens, and Vinovskis, "Origins," 241–58.
15. *Annual Report* 1855, 23.
16. *Annual Report of the Board of Trustees of the Male High School, Female High School, and Public Schools of Louisville, to the General Council of the City of Louisville, for the Scholastic Year of 1859-'60* (Louisville: Bradley & Gilbert), 31–32.
17. Johnston, *Memorial History of Louisville*, 235–37.
18. *Twenty-fifth Annual Report of the Board of Education of the City and County of New York*; *Eighteenth Annual Report of the Board of Education*, 84; *Twelfth Annual Report of the Board of Education*, 6; *Thirteenth Annual Report of the Board of Directors of the Saint Louis Public Schools*. The pattern of withholding collegiate education from women students, offering them first normal schools and then high schools, is consistent across many cities in the East and Midwest.
19. *Annual Report* 1860, 16.
20. "Annual Report on the Public Schools," 2.
21. Matthews, "History of Education," 85. Also see Gold, *Rhetoric at the Margins;* Ostergaard and Wood, *In the Archives*.

22. Matthews, *History of Education*, 84.
23. While teacher training is work that has been attributed almost exclusively to academies and normal schools in some educational histories, Louisville demonstrates the early impact of normal departments in high schools as well. For an example of this argument, see Sizer, "Academies: An Interpretation," 10.
24. "Popery and the United States," 397.
25. "Domestic Summary," 235. For a critique of the tacit Protestant bias in histories of literacy, see Mattingly, *Secret Habits.*
26. Geiger, "Era of Multipurpose Colleges"; Leslie, "Where?"
27. Keeling, *History of Public Education*, 20.
28. Harney, "W. W. Harney and the Board of School Trustees," *Daily Courier*, July 14, 1856, 1, Proquest.
29. The controversy over Harney's appointment also raised questions of politicization in the schools, which the *Daily Courier* hoped to highlight for its readership at the time. Seeing this as a personal and political issue, they write in regard to Harney's case: "Men are now paid for party zeal; for unscrupulous devotion to party interests; for maligning the opposition; not for anything that is worthy in themselves, or for any act that has subserved the public welfare." In short, the *Courier* asserts that Harney was rejected because of his political affiliation as a Democrat. This complaint was not based on Harney's case alone, as the school board—which the *Daily Courier* characterizes as "a body composed entirely of Know-Nothings"—had also removed a Mr. Heywood from their ranks recently, supposedly for the same political reasons ("More Know-Nothing Proscription," *Daily Courier*, July 10, 1856, 2, ProQuest). The Know-Nothing Party, or the American Party, was an anti-Catholic and anti-immigrant party composed of primarily Protestants that was popular in the 1840s and 1850s, particularly in the North. They got the popular moniker "know nothings" because of the secrecy around their party positions, candidates, and membership—specifically, when asked about their political positions, Know- Nothings were supposed to respond, "I know nothing." Of course, then, the *Daily Courier* wouldn't have actually known whether members of the school board were all Know Nothings, since their membership logs were kept secret. However, his point draws attention to the significance of party politics in the establishment of public schools and education at all levels—enterprises which are, of course, never politically neutral.

30. "The High School—Mr. Harney's Case," *Daily Courier*, July 11, 1856, 2, Proquest.
31. "Town Brevities," *Daily Courier*, June 23, 1856, 2; Meeting Minutes of the Louisville School Board, 1856–1878, JCPS Archives, Louisville, Kentucky, 414.
32. "Declined," *Daily Courier*, October 22, 1856, 3; "Freedom of Speech in Kentucky," *National Era* 10, no. 474 (January 31, 1856), 19.
33. *Annual Report* 1860, 2; *Annual Report* 1861, 49; *Report of the Board of Trustees of the Public Schools of Louisville, for the Year Ending June 30, 1872*, 63. The issue of low pay for teachers—particularly female teachers—reverberated across school board reports for years. As the superintendent noted in 1868, "Many of these [female] teachers fill their position in the most satisfactory manner; better, in many instances, than men could. A large number have families depending solely on them for support; they must always dress respectably to present a proper appearance before their pupils, and they seldom have any time or ability to do other work besides the business of teaching. . . . Those who are competent deserve better pay than they now receive" (*Annual Report* 1868, 19).
34. *Thirty-Fourth Annual Report of the Board of Commissioners of Public Schools to the Mayor and City Council of Baltimore*, 21–22; *Thirty-Ninth Annual Report of the Controllers of the Public Schools of the First School District of Pennsylvania*, 162; *Twenty-Fifth Annual Report*, 32.

    The pattern at co-educational high schools differed necessarily, but does not escape entirely this observation of gendered differences. Instead, these distinctions were managed more often through different programs within the school. For example, Chicago's co-educational high school offered a general, classical, and normal department within its school. Recognizing that "the course of study in the High School already covers as much ground as is usually reached in the Colleges of the West by the Sophomore year, and the instruction given, we believe, is superior to that furnished in a majority of the Colleges and so-called Universities," they sought to extend their system to offer a full collegiate course of study (*Twelfth Annual Report*, 39). But that course of study is expressly to be "in connection with the Classical Department of the High School, extending its advantages especially to *young men*" (75, emphasis added). A similar pattern exists elsewhere as well.
35. Farnham, *Education*, 32. See also Geiger, "Era of Multipurpose Colleges."

2. A Polished, Practical, or Profound Education: Collegiate Curricula in the First Ten Years

1. Sizer, *Academies: An Interpretation*, 15; Beadie, "Academy Students," 262.

   The shared curriculum of high schools and academies might seem to reinforce the impression that these were both secondary schools, distinct from colleges. But, while they have retroactively been identified as secondary schools, the reality is that both academies and high schools were more indeterminate in status than the term "secondary" allows today. Some students did go to college from high schools or academies (and some schools advocated that move more than others), but neither one had any necessary relation to the college or college preparation (as Latin grammar schools did). A secondary course was not a requirement for college admission, and high school students might be in their twenties, while nineteenth-century colleges often enrolled students as young as fourteen. According to a report of the Association of American Universities, the average age at matriculation of eighteen years reflects the fact that students into their thirties were entering college alongside those in their very early teens. See Leslie, "Where." For a discussion of average college admission and graduation ages, see Association of American Universities, 35–36.
2. Eliot, "New Education."
3. *Annual Report* 1861, 22.
4. Beadie, "Academy Students," 262.
5. *Annual Report* 1857, 18; Meeting Minutes of the Louisville School Board 1856–1878, JCPS Archives, Louisville, Kentucky, page.
6. Carr, Carr, and Schultz, *Archives of Instruction*, 21; VanOverbeke, *Standardization of American Schooling*, 33.
7. Connors, "Textbooks," 12.
8. Latham, *Handbook of English Language*, title page, Project Gutenberg; Carr, Carr, and Schultz, *Archives of Instruction*, 21.
9. According to Carr, Carr, and Schultz, "Rhetorics increasingly have a more stratified intended use" after the war, specifying a high school audience, only college juniors or seniors, or collegiate underclassmen. This makes sense, as it was after the war that high schools overtook the academies in the provision of "higher schooling" and national efforts to develop what Marc VanOverbeke calls a more "stratified and standardized educational system" gained traction (33). Even then, though, the format of rhetorics used in high schools and colleges did not markedly

differ, as most rhetorics for either audience were expository textbooks. See chapters 4 and 5 for more on these transformations.

10. Crowley, *Methodical Memory*, 56–57.
11. *Annual Report of the Board of Trustees of the Male High School, Female High School, and Public Schools of Louisville, to the General Council of the City of Louisville, for the Scholastic Year of 1862–'63*, 85; *Annual Report of the Board of Trustees of the Male High School, Female High School, and Public Schools of Louisville, to the General Council of the City of Louisville, for the Scholastic Year of 1863–'64*, 62–66; Crowley, *Methodical Memory*, 178 n 10; Hewett, "Samuel P. Newman's"; Connors, "Textbooks," 182.
12. *Annual Report* 1860, 13.
13. 1860 is the only year when the published school board report included student writing. Two commencement addresses were included from Male students and three from Female students, along with addresses from the superintendent and high school principals, which were more commonly included in such annual reports.
14. See chapter 1 for more on the common tropes in support of public high schools.
15. Seymour, "Address," in *Annual Report* 1860, 17.
16. Seventh Census of the United States, 1850; "The Scholastic Year: Commencement Exercises of the University of the Public Schools," *Louisville Daily Express*, July 1, 1869, 4. Kentucky Digital Library; Grivas, "History," 211; "Deaths," 1037.

    Seymour would later draw on his epideictic rhetoric practice to compose a reminiscence about one of his medical professors for *Southern California Practitioner*. There, he relates a charming story about a cat jumping from inside a medical manikin, which the professor pronounced a "remarkable instance of spontaneous delivery," and which Seymour effectively marshaled as evidence in celebration of the "witty yet dignified" professor (Seymour, "Catastrophe," 378).
17. Holland, "Peculiar Motives," 19.
18. Holland, 25.
19. "Lecture by Rev. R. A. Holland," *Daily Courier*, September 12, 1867, 1, ProQuest; "Rev. R. A. Holland's Lecture," *Daily Courier*, September 13, 1867, 1. ProQuest; "From the State Capital: Rev. R. A. Holland's Lecture," *Daily Courier*, January 19, 1868, 1, ProQuest.
20. "Rev. Robert A. Holland: What His Venerable Father Thinks of His Defection from the Methodist Church," *Courier-Journal*, March 21, 1871, 4, ProQuest.
21. 1860 U.S. census.

22. See Labaree, *Making*, for more on changes to the exchange value of the high school credential across the course of the century. See Vinovskis for more on graduation rates relative to attendance.
23. Johnson, *Gender*, 29.
24. *Annual Report* 1860, 11, 3–4.
25. Briggs, "Formal," 255.
26. Farnham, *Education*; Gold, *Rhetoric at the Margins*; Solomon, *In the Company*, 28–29.
27. Schultz, *Young Composers*, 127–28. For an extended discussion of these three speeches and the ways that notions of adolescence and gender function to provide access to the academic platform, see Lueck, "Maturity of Thought."
28. Burke, "Letters," in *Annual Report* 1860, 31.
29. "The Howard Family." Howard Steamboat Museum. http://www.steamboatmuseum.org/thehowardsaga/thehowardfamily.html, Accessed June 1, 2014; *Annual Report* 1864, 72.
30. Gibbons, "Disunion," in *Annual Report* 1860, 33–34.
31. Emphasis original, Gibbons, "Disunion," 33–34.
32. Gibbons, "Disunion," 34.
33. Ibid.
34. Schultz, *Young Composers*, 108–9; Gibbons, "Disunion," 35. Though reprints of this piece circulated elsewhere, Gibbons's reference to the "amorous swain of six years," suggests that her source is the 1854 edition of *Yankee Notions*. Despite the fact that the term "swain" refers to a male suitor, Gibbons is referring to the fictional author "Kathrun." *Yankee Notions*, July 1854: 199. Accessed September 15, 2014. Google Books.
35. Radcliffe, "Women and Dreams," 26; Farnham, *Education*, 13; Robbins, "Future," 562–91.
36. Radcliffe, "Women and Dreams," 27–29.
37. "Commencement Exercises of the Female High School." *Daily Democrat*, June 28, 1860. Microfilm; Quoted in Butler, *Poetry and Prose*, ix.
38. Butler, *Poetry and Prose*, xiii–ix.
39. *Annual Report* 1863, 99.
40. *Annual Report* 1855, 23; *Annual Report* 1860, 2–5; *Annual Report* 1868, 18. See chapter 1 for more on the appeal of teacher training in establishing the high schools.
41. *Report of the Board of Trustees of the Public Schools of Louisville*, 70; "History of the Louisville Normal School," Louisville Girls High School collection, folder 3, University of Louisville Archives and Special Collections, Louisville, Ky.

Principal Grant noted in 1860 that "nearly all" Female's graduates to date had been hired as teachers (*Annual Report* 1860, 10). In the 1864 annual report, Principal Chase noted that ten of twelve students had expressed interest in teaching, and four had already secured positions in the public schools by the time of his writing (*Annual Report of the Board of Trustees of the University and Public Schools to the General Council of the City of Louisville*, 1864, 72). In 1865, he noted that fourteen of nineteen expected to engage in teaching (*Annual Report of the Board of Trustees of the University and Public Schools to the General Council of the City of Louisville*, 1865, 68), and superintendent George Tingley used the fact that "three-fourths of those who graduate desire to engage in teaching" to argue for the establishment of a distinct normal class in 1866, as well as a training school (*Annual Report of the Board of Trustees of the University and Public Schools to the General Council of the City of Louisville*, 1866, 19).

42. Ibid.; *Annual Report* 1860, 10; *Annual Report* 1863, 99; *Annual Report* 1868, 18.
43. *Annual Report* 1863, 108.
44. *Annual Report* 1863, 98, 101.
45. *Louisville Journal*, January 12, 1864, quoted in *Annual Report* 1864, 76.

3. Practical Rhetoric and Progressive Pedagogies in the High Schools

1. *Annual Report* 1861, 22; *Annual Report of the Board of Trustees of the University and Public Schools of the City of Louisville, to the Mayor and General Council, and also, to the Tax-Payers, the People of the City of Louisville, for the Year Ending June 30, 1859*, 36; *Annual Report* 1860, 3; *Annual Report* 1864, 52. See Labaree's 1988 study for discussion of class categories in relation to these occupations. See Beadie's "Academy Students" for limitations of these categories in relation to understanding the status of farmers (255).
2. Berlin, *Writing Instruction*, 4. Also see Cremin, *Transformation of the School*.
3. See Katz, *Reconstructing American Education*; Ueda, *Avenues to Adulthood*, 40. For more on practical education's link to democratic and civic participation, see Berlin, *Writing Instruction*. For the effect of these changes on the developing U.S. universities, see Veysey, *Emergence*, 11.
4. Morris, "An Address, Delivered at the Annual Commencement Exercises of the Male High School, June 28th, 1860" in *Annual Report* 1860, 4–5.
5. Berlin, *Writing Instruction*, 41; *Annual Report* 1863, 101. For more on changes to the high school curriculum in response to students' desires as "consumers," see Reese, *Origins*.

6. Mendenhall, "Joseph V. Denney," 131–56; *Annual Report* 1857, 18.
7. See Skinnell, "Harvard, Again," 95–112; VanOverbeke, *Standardization of American Schooling.*
8. Kitzhaber, *Rhetoric in American Colleges*, 219.
9. Kitzhaber, 220.
10. Johnson, *Nineteenth-Century Rhetoric*, 227, 246.
11. Kitzhaber, *Rhetoric in American Colleges*, 220.
12. Schultz, "Pestalozzi's Mark," 23; Fitzgerald, "A Rediscovered Tradition," 225. For more on European pedagogies in the schools, see also Schultz's "Elaborating Our History" and *Young Composers.* For a counterpoint to Fitzgerald's claims about normal schools, see Lindblom, Banks, and Quay, "Mid-Nineteenth-Century Writing," 94–115.
13. For more on Hailmann, see Hewes, *W. N. Hailmann*; Roberts, *Man Who Pioneered.* Entries on him appear in several educational dictionaries and databases, usually in relation to the kindergarten movement, Froebel, or Indian education. His papers are currently held in the Department of Special Collections, University of California, Los Angeles.

    As examples of his published work, see Hailmann, *Twelve Lectures*; Froebel, *Education of Man*; Hailmann's *New Education*, merged with Elizabeth Peabody's *Kindergarten Messenger*, was first published in 1877. Hailmann wrote some twelve other books as well.
14. Hailmann, *Outlines*, 21; Hailmann, "Outlines," 20–21, emphasis in original. Telling of the interconnectedness of the "modern subjects," Hailmann was originally hired to teach modern languages at the high schools, but moved very soon into the science faculty.
15. Crowley, *Methodical Memory*, 75
16. Hailmann, *Outlines*, 62.
17. Johnson, *Nineteenth-Century Rhetoric*, 227.
18. Hailmann, *Outlines*, 38.
19. Hailmann, *Outlines*, 44, 79, emphasis in original.
20. Crowley, *Methodical Memory*, 45; Hailmann, *Outlines*, 92–93.
21. Hailmann, *Outlines*, 113.
22. Hailmann, *Outlines*, 109, 105, 87–88, emphasis in original.
23. "Superintendent's Report" in *Annual Report* 1861, 18–19, emphasis in original. Spencer's *Education* was quoted here for his critique of earlier theories of object lessons such as those of "M. Marcel" that claim students should be shown the qualities of objects rather than discover them for themselves. Louisville educators sought to distinguish their use from faulty versions of the object teaching system in circulation at the time.

24. Harvard University, *Memorial.*
25. *Annual Report* 1864, 75; Woodbury, "Class of 1858."
26. Kendall, "Educational Conventions," 355–56.
27. Woodbury, "Class of 1858."
28. *Annual Report* 1860, 10–11, emphasis added.
29. Hailmann's particular influence in promoting these theories is evidenced by the fact that he was invited by the board of trustees to compose and publish his "Outlines," which was published in the *Annual Report* of 1861 and distributed to the teachers.
30. *Annual Report* 1860, 12; Hailmann, *Outlines*, 35.
31. See Gere; Johnson; Logan; Royster. See chapter 4 for a discussion of three commencement speeches, as well as the ongoing publishing and speaking practice of one student, Marie Butler Radcliffe.
32. "Educational," *Daily Courier*, 1.
33. Jay, "Educational," *Daily Courier*, 1.
34. "Are Girls As Smart As Boys," *Daily Courier*, 1; "Are Boys Smarter than Girls?," *Daily Courier*, 1; "Are Girls As Smart As Boys—Reconsidered," *Daily Courier*, 1.
35. George W. Morris, "Reports of the Examinations of the Public Schools," in *Annual Report* 1860, 28.
36. Mastrangelo, "Learning from the Past, 57.
37. Schultz, *Young Composers*, 187n8.
38. Crowley, *Methodical Memory*, 64, 63, 59.
39. Connors, "Textbooks," 185.
40. *Annual Report* 1864, 22; *Annual Report of the Board of Trustees of the Male High School, Female High School, and Public Schools of Louisville, to the General Council of the City of Louisville, for the Scholastic Year of 1864–'65*, 1865, 14.
41. The outcomes of this division between academic and manual education and the emergence of vocationalism are discussed in the fourth chapter.
42. *Annual Report of the Board of Trustees of the University and Public Schools to the General Council of the City of Louisville*, 1867, 13.

Interchapter: The Civil War Years

1. Bush, *Louisville*, 110; "Colored Troop Regiments."
2. Adkins and Holtzman, *First Hundred Years*, 50; *Annual Report* 1862, 49; *Annual Report* 1862, 49.
3. *Annual Report* 1862, 49; Adkins and Holtzman, *First Hundred Years*, 64; Bush, *Louisville*, 76, 108; *Annual Report* 1864, 6; Thomas Clark quoted in Bush, *Louisville*, 110.

4. *Annual Report* 1862, 20.
5. *Annual Report* 1863, 11, 54; *Annual Report* 1865, 50.
6. *Annual Report* 1865, 50–51.
7. *Annual Report* 1861, 23; *Annual Report* 1859, 36.

4. The "Absurd Effort": The University Idea and the Changing High School

1. Adams, "The New Education." For more on the lack of definition of "university," see Veysey, *Emergence*, 11.
2. Turner and Bernard, "German Model," 224. See also Veysey, *Emergence*. For an alternative perspective on the origin of the university in the liberal arts curriculum, see Angelo, "Social Transformation."
3. Krug, *Shaping*, 163. It is from this perspective that Princeton's Andrew F. West defined secondary education as the period between the common school and the university in 1885, clarifying that he meant the term "university" to indicate "the period of 'self-directed activity' where the object was 'the advancement of knowledge.'" Secondary education, here and elsewhere, was conceptualized as coterminous with the liberal arts college curriculum, in whatever institution it might be taught (Andrew F. West, "The Relation of Secondary Education to the American University Problem," [1885], cited in Krug, *Shaping*, 163).
4. DeGenaro, "William Rainey Harper," 189. For more on community colleges and their relation to both secondary and university study, see Hutcheson, "Reconsidering the Community College."
5. "Our High Schools," *Louisville Daily Journal*, August 6, 1867, 2, Proquest.
6. Adams, "New Education," n.p.; "Male High School Again," *Courier-Journal*, July 3, 1871, 2, Proquest.
7. "Historical Sketch of the University of Louisville, Showing that It Is Dwarfed In Its Fundamental Parts, Owing to an Arrest of its Development by the System of Public Schools," *Daily Courier*, September 5, 1868, 2, Proquest; "Our Public School," *Daily Courier*, September 7, 1868, 1, Proquest.
8. *Annual Report* 1869, 7–8.
9. *Annual Report* 1869, 52–53.
10. *Annual Report* 1869, 58, 40; Annual Report 1869, 45. See Rose's *Mind at Work* for more on the histories of manual instruction and labor in the United States. See chapter 4 for a discussion of the New Education as a pedagogical approach in the high schools. For more on the development of universities in the United States, see Veysey, *Emergence of the American University*.

Colin Burke points out that "the record expansion in various curricula and types of schools requires an explanation more complex than 'industrialization.' Male attendance trends suggest that growth was due to more general social and economic changes" (Burke, "Expansion," 113).

11. *Annual Report* 1863, 61.
12. Cremin identifies 1910 as a "turning point" in the vocational education movement, when the increasingly expansive array of manual education offerings from the last decades of the nineteenth century was transformed into "outright trade instruction," which was officially sanctioned with the passage of the Smith-Hughes Act in 1917 (*Transformation of the School*, 50).
13. *Annual Report* 1863, 64.
14. Ibid.
15. Indeed, only a very small percentage of students persisted into these upper classes and received their degrees, many more opting to leave the school after having completed the first years of general education and receiving their diploma or certificate. Leaving after two years' study was at several points a formally recognized option at each school.
16. Hobbs and Berlin, "Century." For more on the emergence of literary study and the broader history of English instruction, see Applebee, *Tradition*.

    By the last quarter of the century, high schools and universities in several states established certification programs whereby university faculty visited state high schools to certify the qualifications of their graduates in lieu of admission examinations. For work on high school inspection programs, see Beadie; Gough; VanOverbeke.
17. Schultz, *Young Composers*, 34.
18. *Annual Report* 1864, 63–66.
19. Manolescu, "Traditions," 226.
20. By at least 1869, the rules governing the Male High School expressly determine that the principal will also be the professor of Belles Lettres and Intellectual and Moral Science, suggesting the central value of these subjects (*Annual Report* 1869, 17). *Annual Report of the Board of Trustees of the University and Public Schools to the General Council of the City of Louisville*, 1866, 8. For changes to the teaching profession, see Salvatori, *Pedagogy* and Bledstein, *Culture of Professionalism*.
21. *Annual Report* 1866, 32; *Annual Report* 1867, 17. For a similar negotiation of access and exclusivity, see Labaree, *Making*.
22. "Educational Matters," *Louisville Daily Journal*, June 2, 1868, 4.

23. School leaders in St. Louis made a similar argument when they established their Intermediate Department in 1869 to "supply a necessary link" in the school system and address overcrowding issues without prohibitively raising admission standards. (*Fifteenth Annual Report of the Board of Directors of the St. Louis Public Schools* 1870, 53).
24. *Annual Report of the Board of Trustees of the Male High School, Female High School, and Public Schools of Louisville, for the Year Ending June 30, 1868*, 1868, 39. *Annual Report* 1869, 74–75.
25. *Annual Report* 1869, 113–14.
26. *Annual Report* 1871, 46.
27. *Twelfth Annual Report* 1866, 24–28; *Eighteenth Annual Report* 1872, 65.
28. Miller, "Lest," 23–26.
29. *Annual Report of the Board of Trustees of the University and Public Schools to the General Council of the City of Louisville*, 1869, 85.
30. The image, drawn from an old microfilm copy of the report, is not legible here at the level of individual courses, but it shows the general structure of the school, including years of study along the left margin and some subjects of study along the top. The image is included here as an illustration rather than a table, to visually demonstrate how the high school was being conceptualized spatially in relation to the university in the school's curriculum.
31. *Annual Report* 1869, 17; *Annual Report* 1872, 15; "Male High School: What a Student Has to Say," *Courier-Journal*, July 27, 1873, 3, Proquest.
32. "School Board: Interesting Proceedings of the Regular Meeting Last Night," *Courier-Journal*, July 8, 1873, 4, Proquest.
33. "School Board: Exciting Discussion of the Male High School Difficulty," *Courier-Journal*, September 2, 1873, 4, Proquest; "Male High School Scandal," *Courier-Journal*, 7 Sept 1873, 1, Proquest; "Dr. Anderson's Reply," *Courier-Journal*, September 4, 1873, 1, Proquest.
34. "School Board: Special Meeting Last Night," *Courier-Journal*, August 12, 1873, 4, Proquest.
35. Connors, *Composition-Rhetoric*, 180–81; Wright and Halloran, "From Rhetoric to Composition," 241.
36. Report 1873, 121.
37. Conley, *Rhetoric*, 248.
38. Published in Louisville in 1867, Bonnell's *Manual* gives credit (in the preface) to Male's principal, Dr. E. A. Grant, for suggested revisions. In this way and others, the faculty of high schools like Male and Female were active in professional networks and activities that shaped

the teaching of writing beyond their own schools, playing a role in significant scholarly milestones for rhetoric and composition as a field.

39. *Annual Report of the Board of Trustees of the University and Public Schools to the General Council of the City of Louisville*, 1862, 17–18.
40. *Annual Report* 1862, 17–18; "Louisville Girls High School—50th Anniversary," Pamphlet, Filson Historical Society, Louisville, Kentucky, 8.
41. *Annual Report* 1868, 16–19. Central Colored High School (discussed in the next chapter) was begun as a normal program as well, but developed an increasingly academic and traditional curriculum by the end of the century—which became a point of contention for the school, particularly in the context of this emerging value of specialization. Male High School similarly offered business and commercial courses in the 1870s, and began to develop separate manual and industrial programs by the 1880s. A separate Manual Training High School was established by 1892. The normal, business, and commercial programs had a continually changing relationship to the regular academic course at each school over the century—sometimes being posited as a postgraduate extension of the academic courses of study and other times serving as an alternative to those courses.

    For more on the relationship between high schools, normal schools, and universities in the preparation of teachers, see Herbst, *And Sadly Teach*.
42. *Annual Report* 1867, 49; *Annual Report* 1869, 115.
43. *Report* 1872, 51; Wright and Halloran, "From Rhetoric to Composition," 224.
44. Though one cannot generalize from such a small sample, the differences in content and tone between this essay and the previous examples are so striking that it is worth noting and discussing, particularly insofar as those differences appear to coincide with other evidence of the changing culture of composition instruction in the school.
45. Thustin, "American Footprints."
46. The interest in the teaching of writing may have even mitigated against the students' own learning and practice of writing in the high school, as we will later see happened at the Central Colored High School. In any case, teaching retains its central role in the self-conception of the high school through these years, even as a separate "training department" for teaching is established in 1871. That school, designed for the better training and education of teachers, accepted for admission only graduates from Female High School, and nearly half the graduates of

Female were accepted to this program in its first years of operation. Thus, the teacher-training function of this school continued to play a role in shaping the curriculum there.

47. *Annual Report* 1869, 36.
48. Ibid.
49. *Annual Report* 1873, 89.
50. Ibid., 74.
51. *Report* 1872, 105.

5. *"Just on the Border of the Intellectual World": Central Colored High School*

1. Royster and Williams, "History in the Spaces Left," 575.
2. For example, see Hayden, "Gifts' of the Archives," 402–26; Gold, *Rhetoric at the Margins*; Gold and Hobbs, *Educating*; Ritter, *To Know Her Own*.
3. Simmons College now functions as an HBCU dedicated to biblical higher education in Louisville. Hudson, "'Upon This Rock,'" 295–326; Ellis, *History*, 236; McAfee, *Race, Religion, and Reconstruction*, 13.
4. Hudson, "Establishment," 114, emphasis added; "Colored High School," *Courier-Journal*, November 15, 1889, 3, Proquest, emphasis added.
5. Wilson quoted in Hudson, "Establishment," 120.
6. Bowles and De Costa, *Between Two Worlds*, 25. Also see Logan, *Liberating Language* and Royster, *Traces of a Stream*.
7. Snyder, *120 Years*, 6, 55; Vinovskis, "Have We Underestimated," 552. Bowles and De Costa make a similar point about college graduation rates among African Americans. While college graduation rates among African Americans also remained low, they remind readers that there were not many white *or* black college graduates across the nineteenth century. Attention to the relatively small number of twenty eight black graduates in 1870, they argue, detracts from the accomplishments of the nearly twenty-five thousand black seniors studying in American colleges that same year—a trend that tracks with low graduation rates relative to the overall enrollment of white college students as well. Thus, it is misleading to suppose that African Americans weren't engaging in advanced, formalized higher education—including rhetorical education— from an early date, even as their college graduation numbers remained low (Bowles and De Costa, *Between Two Worlds*, 14).
8. For more on the trend of increased racism and white supremacy in the era of "Redemption" following Reconstruction, see Henry Louis Gates, Jr., *Stony the Road*.
9. Doyle, *Recalling the Record*, 66, 70.

10. This provision would become a point of contention by the next year, as the Mayor interpreted the charter to allow for taxes from white citizens also to be used to contribute to black schools, while the school board insisted that the white and black school funds were intended to remain separate. The issue was resolved to the benefit of the African American community at the school board meeting of December 11, 1871. *Charter of the City*, 40; Doyle, *Recalling the Record*, 63; *Acts of the General Assembly of the Commonwealth of Kentucky*, 1870, 30.
11. Doyle, *Recalling the Record*, 78; *Louisville City Code*, 650, Google Books.
12. Doyle, *Recalling the Record*, 83.
13. *Report* 1872, 65; Doyle, *Recalling the Record*, 86, 198; "The Colored School Question," *Courier-Journal* April 13, 1873, 1.
14. *Report* 1873, 70; American Citizen of African Descent, "Colored Man's Views," *Courier-Journal*, April 13, 1873, 1, Proquest.
15. *Report* 1873, 102; "Public Work," *Courier-Journal*, May 21, 1873, 4, Proquest.
16. "Colored Children," *Courier-Journal* June 15, 1884.
17. Doyle, *Recalling the Record*, 193; "Colored Children," *Courier-Journal*, June 15, 1884, 5, Proquest; "Out of the Depths," *Courier-Journal*, September 6, 1888, 23, Proquest; Hudson, "Establishment," 113. Segregation had been made state law in 1891 with the passage of the Day Law, which enforced segregation in the state's public schools. Lincoln Institute in Simpsonville, which opened in 1912, was primarily a high school, though it offered college courses as well (Kleber, *Encyclopedia of Louisville*, 13). Though University of Louisville was desegregated in 1951 under pressure from the NAACP, public schools were not desegregated until 1956, after *Brown v. Board of Education of Topeka* in 1954. State Normal School (later Kentucky State University) in Frankfort was the first state-supported college for black students in Kentucky.
18. Maxwell was elected and gave a speech at the school's opening, but in that speech he announces that, due to salary considerations, he would be resigning the post and taking another job. At some point, he returned; Mr. Middleton was briefly the principal in the interim. Maxwell was principal by at least 1876.
19. "Colored Children," *Courier-Journal*, June 30, 1877, 4, Proquest.
20. Louisville was not alone in its limited provision of public higher schooling for African Americans. June O. Patton describes a similar situation in Augusta, Georgia, where the new "Colored High School" (later called Ware High School) that opened in 1880 consisted solely of the eighth grade, and later a ninth. Though the white schools in that city consisted

of eighth, ninth, and tenth grades, Ware could never add these higher grades because of the school board's refusal to hire sufficient teachers, and even the white high schools there seem not to have advanced to a full four-year high school course of study. Central Colored High School seems to have enjoyed a better fate than schools like Ware, able to progress over the years under the limited allocations of the city (Patton, "Black," 51).

21. "Another Step Forward," *Courier-Journal*, 23 August 1877, 3, Proquest.
22. Butler's text is produced by the city's own notable educator, Noble Butler, by a printing press in the city, while Greene's is recognizable as one of the texts in use at Female in the 1860 school year. *Manual of the Board of Trustees of the Public Schools of Louisville*, 1880; *Manual of the Board of Trustees of the Public Schools of Louisville*, 1881.
23. Connors, *Composition-Rhetoric*, 156; Schultz, *Young Composers*, 156; Carr, Ferguson, Carr, and Schultz, *Archives of Instruction*, 68, 66.
24. Carr, Ferguson, Carr, and Schultz, *Archives of Instruction*, 68; Hart, *Manual*, iii; Connors quoted in Carr, Ferguson, Carr, and Schultz, *Archives of Instruction*, 68n33.
25. "Commencement Day: A Brilliant Audience," *Courier-Journal*, June 11, 1886, 6, Proquest; "300 Male High Grads," *Alumni Bulletin*, July 1998.
26. The high school course still comprised only three years in contrast to the four-year course of study at the all-white Male and Female High Schools, but that was not uncommon among high schools. Because of its connection to the Central Colored School serving grades one through eight, this school was initially referred to as Colored High School, marking it as the only high school for African Americans and distinguishing it from the work of the lower grades of the Central Colored School. The name was officially changed from Central Colored High School to Central High School in 1945, though students, teachers, and the African American community had known it by the latter name for some years preceding the official change.
27. U.S. Office of Education, quoted in Bowles and De Costa, *Between Two Worlds*, 37; *Manual of the Board of Trustees of the Public Schools of Louisville*, 1882. For more on the relation between rhetorical instruction and science instruction for African Americans, see Logan, "'To Get an Education.'"
28. Maxwell focused on the notion of natural learning processes, arguing against Rousseau's idea that schooling should be delayed until the age of twelve, but he was also unconvinced by Froebel's idea that it should be started with kindergarten. The guest lecturer demonstrated object

teaching. "Kentucky's Colored Teachers," *Courier-Journal*, July 9, 1885, 2, Proquest. For more on the New Education, see chapter 3.

29. "Out of the Depths," *Courier-Journal*, September 6, 1888, 23, Proquest.
30. *Manual of the Board of Trustees of the Public Schools of Louisville*, 1885, 64; *Manual of the Board of Trustees of the Public Schools of Louisville*, 1888, 64; "Commencements: The Graduating Exercises of the Colored High School," *Courier-Journal*, June 16, 1883, 6, Proquest.
31. "Colored Children," *Courier-Journal*, June 30, 1877, 5, Proquest.
32. "Commencements," *Courier-Journal*, June 16, 1883, 6, Proquest; "Gifted Young Orator," *Courier-Journal*, August, 13, 1885, 6, Proquest; "Prepared to Teach," *Courier-Journal*, June 19, 1888, 6, Proquest.
33. "Gifted Young Orator," *Courier-Journal*, August, 13, 1885, 6, Proquest.
34. "Delivering the Diplomas," *Courier-Journal*, June 12, 1885, 6, Proquest; "A Gifted Young Orator," *Courier-Journal*, August 13, 1885, 6, Proquest.
35. Logan, *Liberating Language*, 63.
36. Anderson, *Education*, 199. Also see Jarratt, "Classics and Counterpublics," 136–140.
37. The differences between the two courses of study were as follows: "In the first year's course the only change is that physics is substituted for botany. In the second year the Delsarte system of physical culture is dispensed with. The course in botany is also eradicated from the list. German will not be studied. In the third year's course botany and German are scratched, and the Delsarte system of Gesture is removed and Political Economy substituted. In the fourth year English and American classics are substituted for Carey's Translation of Dante's Divine Comedy. Tacitus in the Latin course is adopted in place of Ovid, and German is abolished" ("Four-Years' Course," *Courier-Journal*, September 6, 1892, 8, Proquest).
38. "School Trustees," *Courier-Journal*, June 3, 1884, 6, Proquest; "They Are Fitted to Teach," *Courier-Journal*, July 5, 1885, 12, Proquest; "Our Colored Citizens," *Courier-Journal*, June 27, 1886, 9, Proquest.
39. "Testing the Charges," *Courier-Journal*, July 6, 1893, 4, Proquest.
40. Ibid.
41. "A Merry Time Ahead," *Courier-Journal*, July 3, 1893, 2, Proquest.
42. Ibid.
43. "Merry Time Ahead," *Courier-Journal*, July 3, 1893, 2, Proquest; "Testing the Charges," *Courier-Journal*, July 6, 1893, 4, Proquest.
44. "Storming Trustees," *Courier-Journal*, July 4, 1893, 2, Proquest.
45. "Merry Time Ahead," *Courier-Journal*, July 3, 1893, 2, Proquest; "Maxwell in a Muddle," *Courier-Journal*, July 2, 1893, 12, Proquest.

46. "Storming Trustees," *Courier-Journal*, July 4, 1893, 2, Proquest.
47. Kleber, *Encyclopedia of Louisville*, 13; "This Is the Last," *Courier-Journal*, June 20, 1895, 5, Proquest.
48. To that list we might add manual education, vocational education, and career training, among others, though a full discussion of manual and industrial education remains outside the scope of the present work

6. Inventing the High School, Inventing Composition

1. See Graves, *Girls' Schooling*, 107.
2. For more on enrollment and student culture at Female in the early twentieth century, see Lueck, "Classbook Sense."
3. Sizer, *Secondary Schools*, 189. For more on the history of educational reforms during the Progressive Era, see Cremin, *Transformation of the School.*
4. "Concerning Our 'University,'" *Courier-Journal*, August 9, 1874, 2, Proquest.
5. *Report* 1872, 62–63; Willing Tax Payer, "Our High School System," *Courier-Journal*, September 2, 1881, 6, Proquest.
6. "University," *Courier-Journal*, December 1, 1883, 6, Proquest; "School Board: The University Trustees Give Notice That They Want the Boys High-school Building," *Courier- Journal*, June 8, 1886, 6, Proquest.
7. Cremin, *Transformation of the School*, 26–27.
8. Johnson, *Memorial History*, 239.
9. "History," on Atherton High School's official website; Broome, *Historical*, 111. For a similar argument as late as 1936, see Hutchins, *Higher Learning in America*.
10. Carnegie Foundation for the Advancement of Teaching, *Annual Report.* Also see Labaree, "2013 Dewey Lecture," 6–7.
11. Leslie, "Curious Tale," 86.
12. Leslie, "Curious Tale," 90. There is some question about how influential Flexner's report actually was: Did it effect or reflect change? Either way, the report and his other publications are indicative of pervasive critiques circulating at the time, and those critiques provide useful insights into the state of higher learning at the end of the nineteenth century.
13. Though his university course was markedly accelerated, Flexner's experience represents a common reality for students of well-developed high schools and, indeed, the aspiration of many a reformer: that students would spend more time in general education in the high school and would come to college ready to specialize, if not to finish early.

14. Bonner, *Iconoclast*, 29. Of course, Flexner did not actually introduce these ideas to the schools, but rather renewed attention to them (see chapter 3 for more on the early circulation of New Education in the Louisville schools). But the ideas continued to be controversial. Numerous articles and books, such as Paul Shorey's *Assault on Humanism* (Boston: Atlantic Monthly Company, 1917), criticized Flexner and others for their adherence to the ideas of the New Education and criticisms of classical learning, which continued to have its defenders among scholars and critics into the twentieth century.
15. Flexner himself dates the beginnings of the kindergarten movement in Louisville to just 1887, to the efforts of a Miss Bryan. It is unclear whether he knew of his sometime colleague Hailmann and his efforts in the same direction in the public schools, at the German and English Academy in the 1860s and 70s, and in his writings on kindergartens in the 1880s and beyond. Flexner, "Ultimate Importance," 199, 202.
16. Cremin, *Transformation of the School*, 20–21.
17. Bonner, *Iconoclast*, 39–40.
18. Flexner, "A Freshman at Nineteen," 360–61.
19. Flexner, *Abraham Flexner*, 50.
20. Cremin, *Transformation of the School*, 280, n7.
21. Cremin, *Transformation of the School*, 280–91.
22. Flexner, "A Freshman at Nineteen," 355.
23. Flexner, *American College*, 70, 72.
24. Flexner, "Preparatory School," 368; Flexner, *American College*, 64–65.
25. Flexner, "College Entrance Examinations," 53; Flexner, *American College*, 77.
26. Flexner, "College Entrance Examinations," 58–60. These superficial examinations were linked also to the innovation of the "credit hour," which attempted to determine educational leveling by counting hours of instruction. According to Flexner, this allowed students to approach learning as a checklist of "time served" in potentially vapid courses. He wanted studies to build on one another and become increasingly challenging, which the credit-hour system and elective system did not guarantee. Flexner also brought the reader's attention to the tradition of "correspondence courses" in this regard. These courses, offered by the University of Chicago and others, allowed students to complete these "hours" from afar, with no guarantee of their value or rigor (Flexner, *Universities*, 55).
27. Flexner, "Preparatory School," 368.
28. Connors, *Composition-Rhetoric*, 133.

29. Hobbs and Berlin, *Century*, 252; Berlin, *Writing Instruction*, 61.
30. George Pullman quoted in Matsuda, "Process and Post-Process," 70.
31. Yancey, "Delivering College Composition," 1–2.
32. Donahue, "Disciplinary Histories," 225.

Conclusion: Blurring the Boundaries

1. Kirsch and Royster, *Feminist Rhetorical Practices*, 14.
2. For interesting work historicizing dual-credit and concurrent-enrollment programs, see Jones, "The Beginnings" and Moreland, "White Resistance."
3. Thus, these schools continue to challenge the high school–college divide into the present. Though it is outside the scope of this book to address the fate of these schools, suffice it to say that they have continued to grapple with the balance between general education and specialized study. They have continued to adhere to, and even exceed, the national standards for their preparatory work while trying to provide enriching educational opportunities, and have continually navigated their relationship to college coursework and credit through a variety of dual-enrollment and other special programs. While neither the political and pedagogical context today nor the nature of the organizations sponsoring these programs is what it was in the nineteenth century, knowledge of this history might provide a different perspective on this trend and how we might best address it. The schools also provide a fascinating case study of segregation and desegregation. See, for example, Garland, *Divided We Fail.*
4. Yancey, "Delivering College Composition," 4.
5. Nordquist, *Literacy and Mobility*, 40.
6. Two Year College English Association, "TYCA Executive Committee Statement on Concurrent Enrollment," March 24, 2012; Payne, "Dual Enrollment."
7. Jarausch, *Transformation*, 7.
8. Nordquist, *Literacy and Mobility*, 11.
9. Nordquist, *Literacy and Mobility*, 11.
10. Horner et al., "Language Difference," 305.
11. Such a perspective has been effectively applied beyond considerations of language(s) per se. In this way, Horner, Tim Lockridge, Cindy Selfe, and Jody Shipka have each applied this perspective to considerations of modality, calling for a greater awareness of the multimodal (or transmodal) nature of texts (Horner, Lockridge, and Selfe, *Translinguality, Transmodality, and Difference*; Shipka, "Transmodality"). In addition to resisting

a conception of the "standard language and modal norm" critiqued by Horner et al., Shipka asks us to commit fully to altering our pedagogical and research practices in accordance with this perspective—to consider how this perspective "impacts both what and how we come to know, and perhaps most importantly, how it might provide us with still other options for knowing and being, and for being known" (Shipka, 251). Jay Jordan extends this inquiry further into the "setting" of language learning and use in his attention to the "material ecologies" that shape memory and association. Critiquing what he sees as a sense of individual rhetorical agency in negotiating meaning in translingual scholarship, he calls us to attend also to "the fertile material surrounds that cannot but inform, influence, and permeate daily language activity" (Jordan, "Material Translingual Ecologies," 366, 372). And Jerry Won Lee, in his translanguaging of assessment, invites us to "translanguage" our understanding of other practices and institutions as well. "Languaging," Lee explains, "represents an emergent process of social interaction that does not merely draw from 'language' but constitutes the 'language' through ways in which it is practiced by individuals" (Lee, "Beyond Translingual Writing," 181). Drawing on this notion, the nineteenth-century high school invites us to translanguage our institutional morphologies as well.

12. Horner, NeCamp, and Donahue, "Toward," 287.
13. Farnham, *Education*, 27, 67. Skinnell excludes normal schools from the category of colleges for the same reason ("Institutionalizing Normal," 11). According to VanOverbeke, "over half of the students in colleges and universities in the Midwest and nearly half of those in the South were taking preparatory courses" in 1878 (*Standardization*, 19).
14. Charles Francis Adams, "A College Fetich," 39; Skinnell, *Conceding Composition*, xi.
15. Fitzgerald, "Rediscovered Tradition," 224. See Yancey, "Delivering College Composition," 1–2.
16. McMullen-Light, "In Our Own Backyard, 89. See DeGenaro ("William Rainey Harper") on the history of the "junior college," first established in 1901, and the subsequently developed community college.
17. Lee, "Beyond Translingual Writing," 177; Horner et al., "Language Difference," 304.
18. Recent volumes on college-level writing such as those from Patrick Sullivan and Howard Tinberg have begun the work of cross-institutional collaboration and conversation so necessary to this work. While the argument of these volumes does not fully escape the charge of "normativity" leveraged in a review by Peter Elbow—that the writers "seemed

merely to assume that the goal is a search for a Platonic essence or small constellation of essences" in their attempt to "define" first-year composition—I found that the volume's inclusion of a range of perspectives from both sides of the ostensible high school–college divide actually worked against this tendency, grounding the discussion of writing within what Jeanne Gunner calls, in the same volume, the "human social context" in which it occurs. It is to those human social contexts—in whatever variously construed institutions—and the "pedagogies of the present" that might attend to them that this history encourages us to look. Sullivan and Tinberg, *What Is "College-Level" Writing?* Elbow, "What Is Real College Writing?, 153–61.

19. Nordquist, *Literacy and Mobility*, 87.
20. CWPA, 1; CWPA, NCTE, and NWP, *Framework for Success.*
21. See also Fleming, *From Form to Meaning*; Rose, "Language of Exclusion."
22. Tinberg and Nadeau, "What," 35, 40–41.
23. Bush, "Finding Connections, Seeking Reciprocity," 340, 342.
24. Gilyard, "Getting It Together," 539–49; Estrem, "Making Pedagogy Our Business," 221–34; Williams, "Mt. Oread Manifesto, 3.
25. Connors, *Composition-Rhetoric*, 18.

BIBLIOGRAPHY

Primary Sources

Acts of the General Assembly of the Commonwealth of Kentucky. Frankfort, KY: The Kentucky Yeoman Office, 1870. Google Books.

Adams, Charles Francis. "A College Fetich." In *Three Phi Beta Kappa Addresses,* 3–46. Boston: Houghton, Mifflin, and Company, 1907. Internet Archive. https://archive.org/stream/threephibetakap02adamgoog#page/n16/mode/2up.

———. "The New Education." *Atlantic Monthly,* February 1869, https://www.theatlantic.com/magazine/archive/1869/02/the-new-education/309049/.

Adams, Charles Francis, Edwin Lawrence Godkin, and George R. Nutter. "Report of the Committee on Composition and Rhetoric." In *The Origins of Composition Studies,* edited by John C. Brereton, 101–26. Pittsburgh: University of Pittsburgh Press, 1995.

American Citizen of African Descent. "A Colored Man's Views on the Subject." *Courier Journal,* April 13, 1873, 1, Proquest Historical Newspapers.

Annual Report of the Board of Trustees of the Male High School, Female High School, and Public Schools of Louisville, for the Year Ending June 30, 1868. Louisville, KY: Bradley and Gilbert, 1868.

Annual Report of the Board of Trustees of the Male High School, Female High School, and Public Schools of Louisville, to the General Council of the City of Louisville, for the Scholastic Year of 1859–'60. Louisville: Bradley and Gilbert, 1860.

Annual Report of the Board of Trustees of the Male High School, Female High School, and Public Schools of Louisville to the General Council of the City of Louisville for the Scholastic Year of 1860–'61. Louisville: Bradley and Gilbert, 1861.

*Annual Report of the Board of Trustees of the Male High School, Female High School, and Public Schools of Louisville, to the General Council of the City *of Louisville, for the Scholastic Year of 1861-62.* Louisville: Bradley and Gilbert, 1862.

Annual Report of the Board of Trustees of the Male High School, Female High School, and Public Schools of Louisville, to the General Council of the City of Louisville, for the Scholastic Year of 1862–'63. Louisville: Bradley and Gilbert, 1863.

Annual Report of the Board of Trustees of the Male High School, Female High School, and Public Schools of Louisville, to the General Council of the City of Louisville, for the Scholastic Year of 1863–'64. Louisville: Hull and Brother, 1864.

Annual Report of the Board of Trustees of the Male High School, Female High School, and Public Schools of Louisville, to the General Council of the City of Louisville, for the Scholastic Year of 1864–'65. Louisville: Bradley and Gilbert, 1865.

Annual Report of the Board of Trustees of the University and Public Schools to the General Council of the City of Louisville, for the Year Ending July 1, 1857. Louisville: Morton and Griswold, 1857.

Annual Report of the Board of Trustees of the University and Public Schools of the City of Louisville, to the Mayor and General Council, and also, to the Tax-Payers, the People of the City of Louisville, for the Year Ending June 30, 1859. Louisville: Munger, Settle, and Co., 1859.

Annual Report of the Board of Trustees of the University and Public Schools to the General Council of the City of Louisville, for the Year Ending July 1, 1855. Louisville: Hull and Brother, 1855.

Annual Report of the Board of Trustees of the University and Public Schools to the General Council of the City of Louisville. Louisville, KY: Bradley and Gilbert, 1866.

Annual Report of the Board of Trustees of the University and Public Schools to the General Council of the City of Louisville. Louisville, KY: Bradley and Gilbert, 1867.

Annual Report of the Board of Trustees of the University and Public Schools to the General Council of the City of Louisville. Louisville, KY: Bradley and Gilbert, 1869.

"Annual Report on the Public Schools." *Daily Courier*, August 5, 1854, 2. Proquest Historical Newspapers.

"Another Step Forward." *Courier-Journal*, August 23, 1877, 3. Proquest Historical Newspapers.

"Are Boys Smarter Than Girls?" *Daily Courier*, February 2, 1867, 1. Proquest Historical Newspapers.

"Are Girls as Smart as Boys." *Daily Courier*, January 26, 1867, 1. Proquest Historical Newspapers.

"Are Girls As Smart As Boys—Reconsidered." *Daily Courier*, March 9, 1867, 1. Proquest Historical Newspapers.

"Blue Monday," September 1, 1873. *Courier-Journal (1869–1922)*. https://search.proquest.com/docview/1119067939?accountid=3730.

Burke, Laura Alice. "Letters," in *Annual Report* 1860, 30–32.

Butler, Marie Radcliffe. *Poetry and Prose by Marie Radcliffe Butler*. Cincinnati: Standard Publishing Company, 1884.

Carnegie Foundation for the Advancement of Teaching. *Annual Report*. New York: The Foundation, 1906. Digital Archive. https://archive.org/stream/annualrepor1905a06carnuoft/annualrepor1905a06carnuoft_djvu.txt.

Catalogue of the Officers and Students of Kentucky University, for the Academical Year 1865–66. Lexington: Gazette Printing Company, 1866.

Charter of the City of Louisville. Louisville, KY: John P. Morton, 1873. https://books.google.com/books/about/Charter_of_the_City_of_Louisville_Adopte.html?id=0epzq70URPgC.

"Classified Ad 5." *Daily Courier*, August 27, 1855, 5. Proquest Historical Newspapers.

"The Colored Children." *Courier-Journal*, June 30, 1877, 4. Proquest Historical Newspapers.

"Colored Children." *Courier-Journal*, June 15, 1884, 5. Proquest Historical Newspapers.

"The Colored High School." *Courier-Journal*, November 15, 1889, 3. Proquest Historical Newspapers.

"The Colored School Question." *Courier-Journal*, April 13, 1873, 1. Proquest Historical Newspapers.

"Commencement Day: A Brilliant Audience." *Courier-Journal*, June 11, 1886, 6. Proquest Historical Newspapers.

"Commencement Exercises of the Female High School." *Daily Democrat*, June 28, 1860. Microfilm.

"Commencements: The Graduating Exercises of the Colored High School." *Courier-Journal*, June 16, 1883, 6. Proquest Historical Newspapers.

"Concerning Our 'University." *Courier-Journal*, August 9, 1874, 2. Proquest Historical Newspapers.

"Deaths," *Journal of the American Medical Association* 74, no. 2 (1920), 1037.

"Declined." *Daily Courier*, October 22, 1856, 3. Proquest Historical Newspapers.

"Delivering the Diplomas." *Courier-Journal*, June 12, 1885, 6. Proquest Historical Newspapers.

"The Doctors and the Schools." *Courier-Journal*, September 14, 1873, 2. Proquest Historical Newspapers.

"Domestic Summary." *The Independent . . . Devoted to the Consideration of Politics, Social and Economics* 7, no. 347 (July 26, 1855), 235. American Periodicals Series Online.

"Dr. Anderson's Reply: In What It Failed of Proving Dr. Anderson a Scholar." *Courier-Journal*, September 4, 1873, 1. Proquest Historical Newspapers.

"Educational." *Daily Courier*, February 16, 1867, 1. Proquest Historical Newspapers.

"Educational Matters." *Louisville Daily Journal*, June 2, 1868, 4. Proquest Historical Newspapers.

"Edward Augustus Holyoke III," Holyoke Family Genealogy—Person Sheet, *Larry Holyoke's Web Site*, February 12, 2017. http://ynotamac.org/geneaolgy/database/ps02/ps02_415.html.

1860 U.S. Census, population schedule. NARA microfilm publication M653, 1,438 rolls. Washington, D.C.: National Archives and Records Administration, n.d. Accessed via Ancestry.com.

Eighteenth Annual Report of the Board of Education. Chicago: Bryant, Walker and Craig, 1872.

Eliot, Charles W. "The New Education," *Atlantic Monthly*, February 1869. https://www.theatlantic.com/magazine/archive/1869/02/the-new-education/309049/.

Fifteenth Annual Report of the Board of Directors of the St. Louis Public Schools. St. Louis: Missouri Democrat Book and Job Printing House, 1870.

Flexner, Abraham. *Abraham Flexner: An Autobiography: A Revision, Brought Up-to-Date, of the Author's* I Remember. Introduction by Allan Nevins. New York: Simon and Schuster, 1960.

———. *The American College: A Criticism*. New York: Century, 1908. Reprinted by Arno Press and the *New York Times*, 1969.

———. "College Entrance Examinations." *Popular Science Monthly* 63 (1903): 53–60. Internet Archive.

———. "A Freshman at Nineteen," Education Review 18 (1899), 353–62.

———. "A Modern School," *American Review of Reviews* 53 (1916): 465–74. http://historymatters.gmu.edu/d/4995/.

———. "The Preparatory School." *Atlantic Monthly*, September 1904: 368–77.

———. "The Ultimate Importance of the Kindergarten Idea." Kindergarten 3 (1889): 199–201.

———. *Universities: American, English, German.* New York: Oxford University Press, 1930.

"A Four-Years' Course." *Courier-Journal,* September 6, 1892, 8. Proquest Historical Newspapers.

"Freedom of Speech in Kentucky," *National Era* 10, no. 474 (January 31, 1856), 19.

Froebel, Friedrich. *The Education of Man.* Translated and annotated by William Hailmann. New York: D. Appleton and Company, 1887.

"From Tampa Bay." *Louisville Morning Courier,* September 7, 1849, 2. Proquest Historical Newspapers.

"From the State Capital: Rev. R. A. Holland's Lecture," *Daily Courier,* January 19, 1868, 1. Proquest Historical Newspapers.

Gibbons, Rachel H. "Disunion," in *Annual Report* 1860, 33–36.

"A Gifted Young Orator." *Courier-Journal,* August 13, 1885, 6. Proquest Historical Newspapers.

Hailmann, William N. "Outlines of a System of Object Teaching, Prepared at the Request of the Board of Trustees of the Public Schools of the City of Louisville by William N. Hailman, Professor of Natural Science." In *Annual Report* 1861.

———. *Outlines of a System of Object Teaching: Prepared for Teachers and Parents.* New York: Ivison, Philley, Blakeman and Co., 1867.

———. *Twelve Lectures on the History of Pedagogy.* New York: American Book Company, 1874.

Harney, W. W. "W. W. Harney and the Board of School Trustees." *Daily Courier,* July 14, 1856, 1. Proquest Historical Newspapers.

Hart, John S. *A Manual of Composition and Rhetoric: A Text-book for Schools and Colleges.* Philadelphia: Eldredge and Brother, 1881.

Harvard University, *Memorial of the Harvard Class of 1856.* Boston: George H. Ellis Co, 1906.

"The High School—Mr. Harney's Case." *Daily Courier,* July 11, 1856, 2. Proquest Historical Newspapers.

"Historical Sketch of the University of Louisville, Showing That It Is Dwarfed in Its Fundamental Parts, Owing to an Arrest of Its Development by the System of Public Schools." *Daily Courier,* September 5, 1868, 2. Proquest Historical Newspapers.

"History of the Louisville Normal School," Anniversary Number, 1871–1931, University of Louisville Archives and Special Collections, LGHS, folder 3.

Holland, Robert Afton. "Peculiar Motives to Intellectual Exertion in America," in *Annual Report* 1860, 19–25.

Jay. "Educational." *Daily Courier*, December 22, 1866, 1, Proquest Historical Newspapers.

Johnson, Josiah Stoddard. Memorial History of Louisville from Its First Settlement to the Year 1896. Vol. 1. Chicago: American Biographical Pub. Co., 1896. Hathi Trust. https://babel.hathitrust.org/cgi/pt?id=c00.31924092219215;view=1up;seq=315.

Kendall, Amos. "Educational Conventions and Associations. Kentucky." *American Journal of Education* 16 (1866):355–56.

"Kentucky's Colored Teachers." *Courier-Journal*, July 9, 1885, 2. Proquest Historical Newspapers.

Latham, Robert Gordon. *A Handbook of English Language*. New York: D. Appleton and Co., 1852. Project Gutenberg.

"Lecture by Rev. R. A. Holland," *Daily Courier*, September 12, 1867, 1. ProQuest Historical Newspapers.

The Louisville City Code. Louisville, KY: Courier Journal Job Printing Company, 1884. Google Books.

"Louisville Girls High School—50th Anniversary." Pamphlet, Filson Historical Society. Louisville, Kentucky.

"Louisville University—Academical Department." *Louisville Morning Courier*, April 13, 1850, 2. Proquest Historical Newspapers.

"Louisville University—Academical Department." *Louisville Morning Courier*, April 23, 1850, 2. Proquest Historical Newspapers.

"The Male High School: What a Student Has to Say in Defense of the Institution and Prof. Anderson." *Courier-Journal*, July 27, 1873, 3. Proquest Historical Newspapers.

"The Male High School Again." *Courier-Journal*, July 3, 1871, 2. Proquest Historical Newspapers.

"The Male High School Scandal." *Courier-Journal*, September 7, 1873, 1. Proquest Historical Newspapers.

Manual of the Board of Trustees of the Public Schools of Louisville. Louisville, KY: J. C. Webb, 1880.

Manual of the Board of Trustees of the Public Schools of Louisville. Louisville, KY: J. C. Webb, 1881.

Manual of the Board of Trustees of the Public Schools of Louisville. Louisville, KY: J. C. Webb, 1882.

Manual of the Board of Trustees of the Public Schools of Louisville. Louisville, KY: J. C. Webb, 1885.

Manual of the Board of Trustees of the Public Schools of Louisville. Louisville, KY: F. A. Crump, 1888.

Matthews, J. D. "History of Education in Kentucky." *Bulletin of Kentucky Department of Education* 7, no. 4, July 1914.

Maxwell, J. M. "The Colored Children." *Courier-Journal*, June 30, 1877, 4. Proquest Historical Newspapers.

"Maxwell in a Muddle." *Courier-Journal*, July 2, 1893, 12. Proquest Historical Newspapers.

"A Merry Time Ahead." *Courier-Journal*, July 3, 1893, 2. Proquest Historical Newspapers.

"More Know-Nothing Proscription." *Daily Courier*, July 10, 1856, 2. Proquest Historical Newspapers.

Morris, George W. "An Address, Delivered at the Annual Commencement Exercises of the Male High School, June 28th, 1860." In *Annual Report* 1860, 4–5.

"Our Colored Citizens." *Courier-Journal*, June 27, 1886, 9. Proquest Historical Newspapers.

"Our High Schools." *Daily Courier*, April 5, 1856, 2. Proquest Historical Newspapers.

"Our High Schools." *The Louisville Daily Journal*, August 6, 1867, 2. Proquest Historical Newspapers.

"Our Public School." *Daily Courier*, September 7, 1868, 1. Proquest Historical Newspapers.

"Out of the Depths." *Courier-Journal*, September 6, 1888, 23. Proquest Historical Newspapers.

"Popery and the United States." *Christian Observatory: A Religious and Literary Magazine* 1, no. 9 (September 1847), 397. American Periodicals Series Online.

"Public Work: The Bids of the Colored High School Building." *Courier-Journal*, May 21, 1873, 4. Proquest Historical Newspapers.

"Prepared to Teach." *Courier-Journal*, June 19, 1888, 6. Proquest Historical Newspapers.

"Proceedings of the Board of Trustees." *Daily Courier*, May 15, 1851, 2. Proquest Historical Newspapers.

Public School Laws of the City of Louisville, A Compilation of the Acts of the Legislature and Laws Establishing and Governing the Male High School, the Female High School and the Public Schools of the City of Louisville, Ky. from the Year 1828 to the Year 1882, prepared by Randolph H. Blain (1882). Archives and Records Center, Jefferson County Public Schools, Louisville, KY.

Radcliffe (Butler), Marie B. "Women and Dreams." In *Annual Report* 1860, 26–30.

Report of the Board of Trustees of the Public Schools of Louisville, for the Year Ending June 30, 1872. Louisville: Bradley and Gilbert, 1872.

Report of the Board of Trustees of the Public Schools of Louisville, for the Year Ending June 30, 1873. Louisville: Bradley and Gilbert, 1873.

"Rev. R. A. Holland's Lecture," *Daily Courier*, September 13, 1867, 1. ProQuest Historical Newspapers.

"Rev. Robert A. Holland: What His Venerable Father Thinks of His Defection from the Methodist Church," *Courier-Journal*, March 21, 1871, 4. ProQuest Historical Newspapers.

"The Scholastic Year: Commencement Exercises of the University of the Public Schools." *Louisville Daily Express*, July 1, 1869, 4. Kentucky Digital Library.

"The School Board: Exciting Discussion of the Male High School Difficulty." *Courier-Journal*, September 2, 1873, 4. Proquest Historical Newspapers.

"The School Board: Interesting Proceedings of the Regular Meeting Last Night." *Courier-Journal*, July 8, 1873, 4. Proquest Historical Newspapers.

"The School Board: Special Meeting Last Night." *Courier-Journal*, August 12, 1873, 4. Proquest Historical Newspapers.

"The School Board: The University Trustees Give Notice That They Want the Boys High-school Building." *Courier-Journal*, June 8, 1886, 6. Proquest Historical Newspapers.

"The School Ordinance Election To-day." *Daily Courier*, August 14, 1854, 2. Proquest Historical Newspapers.

"The School Trustees." *Courier-Journal*, June 3, 1884, 6. Proquest Historical Newspapers.

Seventh Census of the United States, 1850 (National Archives Microfilm Publication M432, 1009 rolls). Records of the Bureau of the Census, Record Group 29. National Archives, Washington, D.C. Accessed via Ancestry.com.

Seymour, Francis A. "Address of Frank A. Seymour." In *Annual Report* 1860, 15–18.

———. "A Catastrophe in the Lecture Room," *Southern California Practitioner* 13, no. 10, October 1898. Google Books.

"Storming Trustees." *Courier-Journal*, July 4, 1893, 2. Proquest Historical Newspapers.

"Testing the Charges." *Courier-Journal*, July 6, 1893, 4. Proquest Historical Newspapers.

"They Are Fitted to Teach." *Courier-Journal*, July 5, 1885, 12. Proquest Historical Newspapers.

Thirteenth Annual Report of the Board of Directors of the Saint Louis Public Schools. St. Louis: Missouri Democrat Book and Job Printing House, 1867.

Thirty-Fourth Annual Report of the Board of Commissioners of Public Schools to the Mayor and City Council of Baltimore. Baltimore: James Young, 1863.

Thirty-Ninth Annual Report of the Controllers of the Public Schools of the First School District of Pennsylvania. Philadelphia: Board of Controllers, 1858.

"This Is the Last." *Courier-Journal*, June 20, 1895, 5. Proquest Historical Newspapers.

"300 Male High Grads Become U. of L. Alumni." *Alumni Bulletin* (July 1998). University of Louisville Archives and Special Collections, Louisville, KY.

Thustin, Sallie. "American Footprints on the Sands of Time." Mss. C at Filson Historical Society.

"Town Brevities." *Daily Courier*, June 23, 1856, 2. Proquest Historical Newspapers.

Twelfth Annual Report of the Board of Education. Chicago: Rounds and James, 1866.

Twenty-fifth Annual Report of the Board of Education of the City and County of New York. New York: Wm. C. Bryant and Co., 1866.

"The University." *Courier-Journal*, December 1, 1883, 6, Proquest Historical Newspapers.

"University of Louisville—Academical Department." *Louisville Morning Courier*, April 29, 1850, 2, Proquest Historical Newspapers.

Voegtle, Anna. "The Louisville Girls High School, Kentucky," *Louisville Girls High School*, February 4, 1938. Reprinted from *Southern Association Quarterly*, November 1937. Filson Historical Society.

A Willing Tax Payer. "Our High School System." *Courier Journal*, September 2, 1881, 6, Proquest Historical Newspapers.

Woodbury, Elizabeth H. "The Class of 1858," *Record* (school yearbook), n.p., Filson Historical Society Library, Louisville, KY.

Yankee Notions. July 1854: 199. Google Books.

Secondary Sources

Adkins, Sam, and M. R. Holtzman. *The First Hundred Years: The History of Louisville Male High School*. Louisville, KY: Administration and Alumni of Louisville Male High School, 1991.

Bibliography

Anderson, James D. *The Education of Blacks in the South, 1860–1935.* Chapel Hill: University of North Carolina Press, 1988.

Angelo, Richard. "The Social Transformation of American Higher Education." In *The Transformation of Higher Learning 1860–1930,* edited by Konrad H. Jarausch, 261–92. Chicago: University of Chicago Press, 1983.

Applebee, Arthur N. *Tradition and Reform in the Teaching of English: A History.* Urbana: NCTE, 1974.

Association of American Universities. *Journal of Proceedings and Addresses of the Tenth Annual Conference.* Chicago: Association of American Universities, 1909.

Beadie, Nancy. "Academy Students in the Mid-Nineteenth Century: Social Geography, Demography, and the Culture of Academy Attendance." *History of Education Quarterly* 41 (2001), no. 2: 251–62.

Berlin, James A. *Rhetoric and Reality: Writing Instruction in American Colleges, 1900–1985.* Carbondale: Southern Illinois University Press, 1987.

———. *Writing Instruction in Nineteenth-Century American Colleges.* Carbondale: Southern Illinois University Press, 1984.

Bledstein, Burton J. *The Culture of Professionalism: The Middle Class and the Development of Higher Education in America.* New York: W. W. Norton, 1976.

Bonner, Thomas Neville. *Iconoclast: Abraham Flexner and a Life in Learning.* Baltimore: Johns Hopkins University Press, 2002.

Bowles, Frank, and Frank De Costa. *Between Two Worlds: A Profile of Negro Higher Education.* New York: McGraw Hill, 1971.

Brereton, John C., ed. *The Origins of Composition Studies.* Pittsburgh: University of Pittsburgh Press, 1995.

Briggs, Thomas H. "Formal English Grammar as a Discipline." *Teacher's College Record* 16, no. 4 (September 1913), 254–99. Google Books.

Broome, Edwin Cornelius. *A Historical and Critical Discussion of College Admission Requirements.* New York: Macmillan, 1903.

Brown, John Franklin. *American High School.* New York: Macmillan Company, 1915. Google Books.

Buchanan, Lindal. *Regendering Delivery: The Fifth Canon and Antebellum Women Rhetors.* Carbondale: Southern Illinois University Press, 2005.

Burke, Colin. "The Expansion of American Higher Education." In *The Transformation of Higher Learning 1860–1930,* edited by Konrad H. Jarausch, 108–30. Chicago: University of Chicago Press, 1983.

Bush, Bryan S. *Louisville and the Civil War: A History and Guide.* Charleston, SC: The History Press, 2008.

Bush, Jonathan. "Finding Connections, Seeking Reciprocity: Toward an Inclusive Community of Writing Teachers—Kindergarten to College and Beyond." *Pedagogy: Critical Approaches to Teaching Literature, Language, Composition, and Culture* 5, no. 2 (2005): 339–44.

Carr, Jean Ferguson, Stephen L. Carr, and Lucille M. Schultz. *Archives of Instruction: Nineteenth-Century Rhetorics, Readers, and Composition Books in the United States.* Carbondale: Southern Illinois University Press, 2005.

"Colored Troops Regiments from Kentucky, U.S. Civil War." Notable Kentucky African Americans Database. https://nkaa.uky.edu/nkaa/items/show/3129.

Conley, Thomas. *Rhetoric in the European Tradition.* Chicago: University of Chicago Press, 1990.

Connors, Robert J. *Composition-Rhetoric: Backgrounds, Theory, and Pedagogy.* Pittsburgh: University of Pittsburgh Press, 1997.

———. "Textbooks and the Evolution of the Discipline." *College Composition and Communication* 37, no. 2 (1986), 178–94.

Council of Writing Program Administrators. *WPA Outcomes Statement for First-Year Composition (3.0), Approved July 17, 2014.* http://wpacouncil.org/positions/outcomes.html.

Council of Writing Program Administrators, National Council of Teachers of English, and National Writing Project. *Framework for Success in Postsecondary Writing,* 2011. http://wpacouncil.org/files/framework-for-success-postsecondary-writing.pdf.

Cox, Dwayne D., and William J. Morison. *The University of Louisville.* Lexington: University Press of Kentucky, 1999.

Cremin, Lawrence A. *The Transformation of the School: Progressivism in American Education, 1876–1957.* New York: Knopf, 1961.

Crowley, Sharon. "Afterword: The Material of Rhetoric." In *Rhetorical Bodies,* edited by Jack Selzer and Sharon Crowley. Madison: University of Wisconsin Press, 1999.

———. *The Methodical Memory: Invention in Current-Traditional Rhetoric.* Carbondale: Southern Illinois University Press, 1990.

Davies, Margery W. *Woman's Place Is at the Typewriter.* Philadelphia: Temple University Press, 1982.

DeGenaro, William. "William Rainey Harper and the Ideology of Service at Junior Colleges." In *Local Histories: Reading the Archives of Composition,* edited by Patricia Donahue and Gretchen Flesher Moon, 181–98. Pittsburgh: University of Pittsburgh Press, 2007.

Denman, William. "Rhetoric, the 'Citizen-Orator,' and the Revitalization of Civic Discourse in American Life." In *Rhetorical Education in America,* edited by Cheryl Glenn, Margaret M. Lyday, and Wendy B. Sharer, 3–17. Tuscaloosa: University of Alabama Press, 2004.

Donahue, Patricia. "Disciplinary Histories: A Meditation on Beginnings." In *Local Histories: Reading the Archives of Composition*, edited by Patricia Donahue and Gretchen Flesher Moon, 220–36. Pittsburgh: University of Pittsburgh Press, 2007.

Donahue, Patricia, and Gretchen Flesher Moon, eds. *Local Histories: Reading the Archives of Composition.* Pittsburgh: University of Pittsburgh Press, 2007.

Doyle, Ruby. *Recalling the Record: A Documentary History of the African-American Experience within the Louisville Public School System of Kentucky* (1870–1975).Chapel Hill: Professional Press, 2005.

Draper, Andrew S. "The New York Secondary School System." Vol. 1 of *Report of the Commissioner of Education for the Year Ending June 30, 1905*, 143–54. Washington: Government Printing Office, 1907. Internet Archive. https://archive.org/details/reportcommissi005educgoog.

Elbow, Peter. "What Is Real College Writing? Let the Disagreement Never End." Review Essay. *WPA: Writing Program Administration* 34, no. 2 (2011): 153–61.

Eldred, Janet, and Peter Mortenson. *Imagining Rhetoric: Composing Women of the Early United States.* Pittsburgh: University of Pittsburgh Press, 2002.

Ellis, William E. *A History of Education in Kentucky.* Lexington: University Press of Kentucky, 2011.

Enoch, J. *Refiguring Rhetorical Education: Women Teaching African American, Native American, and Chicano/a Students, 1865–1911.* Carbondale: Southern Illinois University Press, 2008.

———. "A Woman's Place Is in the School: Rhetorics of Gendered Space in Nineteenth-Century America." *College English* 70, no. 3 (2008): 275–95.

Estrem, Heidi. "Making Pedagogy Our Business: Strengthening the Ties between English Education and Composition-Rhetoric." In *Academic Cultures: Professional Preparation and the Teaching Life*, edited by Sean P. Murphy, 221–34. New York: MLA, 2008.

Farnham, Christie Anne. *Education of the Southern Belle: Higher Education and Student Socialization in the Antebellum South.* New York: New York University Press, 1994.

Federal Writers' Project of the Work Projects Administration for the State of Kentucky. *A Centennial History of the University of Louisville.* Louisville: University of Louisville, 1939.

Fitzgerald, Kathryn. "A Rediscovered Tradition: European Pedagogy and Composition in Nineteenth-Century Midwestern Normal Schools." *College Composition and Communication* 53, no. 2 (2001): 224–50.

Fleming, David. *From Form to Meaning: Freshman Composition and the Long Sixties, 1957–1974*. Pittsburgh: University of Pittsburgh Press, 2011.

Garland, Sarah. *Divided We Fail: The Story of an African American Community That Ended the Era of Desegregation*. Boston: Beacon Press, 2014.

Gates, Henry Louis, Jr. *Stony the Road: Reconstruction, White Supremacy, and the Rise of Jim Crow*. New York: Penguin Press, 2019.

Geiger, Roger L. "The Era of Multipurpose Colleges in American Higher Education, 1850–1890." In *The American College in the Nineteenth Century*, edited by Roger Geiger, 127–52. Nashville: Vanderbilt University Press, 2000.

Gelber, Scott. "'City Blood Is No Better than Country Blood': The Populist Movement and Admissions Policies at Public Universities." *History of Education Quarterly* 51, no. 3 (2011): 273–95.

Gere, Anne Ruggles. "Kitchen Tables and Rented Rooms." *CCC* 45, no. 1 (1994), 75–92.

Gidney, R. D., and W. Millar. *Inventing Secondary Education: The Rise of the High School in Nineteenth-Century Ontario*. Montreal: McGill-Queen's University Press, 1990.

Gilyard, Keith. "Getting It Together: Notes toward a Shared Future for NCTE and CCCC." *College Composition and Communication* 62, no. 3 (2011): 539–49.

Glenn, Cheryl, Margaret M. Lyday, and Wendy B. Sharer. *Rhetorical Education in America*. Tuscaloosa: University of Alabama Press, 2004.

Gold, David. "Remapping Revisionist Historiography." *College Composition and Communication* 64, no. 1 (2012): 15–34.

———. *Rhetoric at the Margins: Revising the History of Writing Instruction at American Colleges, 1873–1947*. Carbondale: Southern Illinois University Press, 2008.

Gold, David, and Catherine L. Hobbs. *Educating the New Southern Woman: Speech, Writing and Race at the Public Women's Colleges, 1884–1945*. Carbondale: Southern Illinois University Press, 2014.

Gordon, Lynn. *Gender and Higher Education in the Progressive Era*. New Haven: Yale University Press, 1990.

Gough, Robert J. "High School Inspection by the University of Wisconsin, 1877–1931. *History of Education Quarterly* 50, no. 3 (2017), 263–97.

Graff, Harvey J. *The Literacy Myth: Cultural Integration and Social Structure in the Nineteenth Century*. New York: Routledge, 2017 [1979].

Graves, Karen. *Girls' Schooling during the Progressive Era: From Female Scholar to Domesticated Citizen*. New York: Garland Publishing, 1998.

Grivas, Theodore. "A History of the Los Angeles Young Men's Christian Association: The First Twenty Years," *California Historical Society* 44, March 1965, 211.

Gutowski, Thomas W. "Student Initiative and the Origins of the High School Extracurriculum: Chicago 1880–1915." *History of Education Quarterly* 28, no. 1 (1988), 49–72.

Hackensmith, Charles William. *Out of Time and Tide: The Evolution of Education in Kentucky*. Lexington: College of Education, University of Kentucky, 1970.

Hampel, Robert L. "The Long View: Blurring the Boundaries." *Kappan* 99, no. 3 (November 2017), 8–12.

Hayden, Wendy. "'Gifts' of the Archives: A Pedagogy for Undergraduate Research." *College Composition and Communication* 66, no. 3 (2015): 402–26.

Herbst, Jurgen. *And Sadly Teach: Teacher Education and Professionalization in American Culture*. Madison: University of Wisconsin Press, 1989.

———. "Diversification in American Higher Education." In *The Transformation of Higher Learning 1860–1930*, edited by Konrad H. Jarausch, 196–206. Chicago: University of Chicago Press, 1983.

Hewes, Dorothy W. *W. N. Hailmann: Defender of Froebel*. Grand Rapids, MI: The Froebel Foundation, 2001.

Hewett, Beth. "Samuel P. Newman's *A Practical System of Rhetoric:* An American Cousin of Scottish Rhetoric." In *Scottish Rhetoric and Its Influences*, edited by Lynee Lewis Gaillet, 179–92. New York: Routledge, 2008.

"History." Atherton High School. Jefferson County Public Schools, accessed March 15, 2015, http://schools.jefferson.kyschools.us/high/atherton/history.html.

Hobbs, Catherine L., and James A. Berlin. "A Century of Writing Instruction in School and College English." In *A Short History of Writing Instruction: From Ancient Greece to Modern America*, edited by James J. Murphy, 247–90. Mahwah, NJ: Lawrence Erlbaum Associates, Inc., 2001.

Hoogeveen, Jeff. "The Progressive Faculty/Student Discourse of 1969–1970 and the Emergence of Lincoln University's Writing Program." In *Local Histories: Reading the Archives of Composition*, edited by Patricia

Donahue and Gretchen Flesher Moon, 199–219. Pittsburgh: University of Pittsburgh Press, 2007.

Horner, Bruce, Tim Lockridge, and Cindy Selfe. *Translinguality, Transmodality, and Difference: Exploring Dispositions and Change in Language and Learning.* Digital monograph. Enculturation Intermezzo, 2015.

Horner, Bruce, Min Zhan Lu, Jacqueline Jones Royster, and John Trimbur. "Language Difference in Writing: Toward a Translingual Perspective." *College English* 73, no. 3 (2011): 303–21.

Horner, Bruce, Samantha NeCamp, and Christiane Donahue. "Toward a Multilingual Composition Scholarship: From English Only to a Translingual Norm." *CCC* 63, no. 2, 269–300.

"The Howard Family." Howard Steamboat Museum. http://www.steamboatmuseum.org/thehowardsaga/thehowardfamily.html, n.d. Accessed on June 1, 2014.

Hudson, J. Blaine. "The Establishment of Louisville Municipal College: A Case Study in Racial Conflict and Compromise." *Journal of Negro Education* 64, no. 2 (1995): 111–23.

———. "'Upon This Rock'—The Free African American Community of Antebellum Louisville, Kentucky." *Register of the Kentucky Historical Society* 109, no. 3–4 (2011): 295–326.

Hutcheson, Philo A. "Reconsidering the Community College." *History of Education Quarterly* 39, no. 3 (2017), 307–20.

Hutchins, Robert Maynard. *Higher Learning in America.* New Haven: Yale University Press, 1936.

Jarausch, Konrad H., ed. *The Transformation of Higher Learning 1860–1930.* Chicago: University of Chicago Press, 1983.

Jarratt, Susan C. "Classics and Counterpublics in Nineteenth-Century Historically Black Colleges." *College English* 72, no. 2 (2009): 134–59.

Johnson, Nan. *Nineteenth-Century Rhetoric in North America.* Carbondale: Southern Illinois University Press, 1991.

Johnston, J. Stoddard. *Memorial History of Louisville from Its First Settlement to the Year 1896.* Vol. 1. Chicago: American Biographical Publishing Co., 1896.

Jones, Joseph. "The Beginnings of AP and the Ends of First-Year College Writing." In *College Credit for Writing in High School: The 'Taking-Care-of' Business,* edited by Kristine Hansen and Christine Farris, 43–67. Urbana, IL: NCTE, 2010.

Jordan, Jay. "Material Translingual Ecologies." *College English* 77, no. 4 (2015): 360–78.

Katanski, Amelia V. *Learning to Write "Indian": The Boarding-School Experience and American Indian Literature*. Norman: University of Oklahoma Press, 2005.

Katz, Michael B. *The Irony of Early School Reform: Educational Innovation in Mid-Nineteenth Century Massachusetts*. Cambridge: Harvard University Press, 1968.

———. *Reconstructing American Education*. Cambridge: Harvard University Press, 1987.

Katz, Michael B., Edward Stevens Jr., and Maris A. Vinovskis. "The Origins of Public High Schools." *History of Education Quarterly* 27, no. 2 (1987): 241–58.

Keeling, Harold S. *History of Public Education in Louisville*. University of Louisville, dissertation, 1943.

Kerr, Clark. "Abraham Flexner's *Universities*." *Society* (May/June 1994): 40–47.

Kirsch, Gesa, and Jacqueline Jones Royster. *Feminist Rhetorical Practices: New Horizons for Rhetoric, Composition, and Literacy Studies*. Carbondale: Southern Illinois Press, 2014.

Kitzhaber, Albert. *Rhetoric in American Colleges, 1850–1900*. Dallas: Southern Methodist University Press, 1990.

Kleber, John. *Encyclopedia of Louisville*. Lexington: University Press of Kentucky, 2001.

Krug, Edward A. *Shaping of the American High School 1880–1920*. Madison: University of Wisconsin Press, 1969.

Labaree, David. *Making of an American High School: The Credentials Market and the Central High School of Philadelphia, 1838–1939*. New Haven: Yale University Press, 1992.

———. *The Trouble with Ed Schools*. New Haven: Yale University Press, 2004.

———. "2013 Dewey Lecture: College—What Is It Good For?" *Education and Culture* 30, no. 1 (2014): 3–15.

Lane, Richard. "A 'Forgotten' Location: A Rhetorical Curriculum in English Education." In *Rhetorical Education in America*, edited by Cheryl Glenn, Margaret M. Lyday, and Wendy B. Sharer, 87–106. Tuscaloosa: University of Alabama Press, 2004.

Lee, Jerry Won. "Beyond Translingual Writing." *College English* 79, no. 2 (2016): 174–95.

L'Eplattenier, Barbara. "An Argument for Archival Research Methods: Thinking beyond Methodology." *College English* 72, no. 1 (2009): 67–79.

Lepore, Jill. "Historians Who Love Too Much: Reflections on Microhistory and Biography." *Journal of American History* 88, no. 1 (2001):

129–44. Accessed August 1, 2016, http://www.jstor.org.libproxy.scu.edu/stable/2674921.

Leslie, W. Bruce. "The Curious Tale of Liberal Education, Professional Training and the American College, 1880–1910." *History of Education* 40, no. 1 (January 2011): 83–95.

———. *Gentlemen and Scholars: College and Community in the "Age of the University," 1865–1917.* College Park: Pennsylvania State University Press, 1992.

———. "Where Have All the Academies Gone?" *History of Education Quarterly* 41, no. 2 (Summer 2001): 262–70.

Lindblom, Kenneth, William Banks, and Risë Quay. "Mid-Nineteenth-Century Writing Instruction at Illinois State Normal University: Credentials, Correctness, and the Rise of the Teaching Class." In *Local Histories: Reading the Archives of Composition*, edited by Patricia Donahue and Gretchen Flesher Moon, 94–115. Pittsburgh: University of Pittsburgh Press, 2007.

Logan, Shirley Wilson. *Liberating Language: Sites of Rhetorical Education in Nineteenth-Century Black America.* Carbondale: Southern Illinois University Press, 2008.

———. "'To Get an Education and Teach My People': Rhetoric for Social Change." In *Rhetorical Education in America*, edited by Cheryl Glenn, Margaret M. Lyday, and Wendy B. Sharer, 36–52. Tuscaloosa: University of Alabama Press, 2004.

———. *"We Are Coming": The Persuasive Discourse of Nineteenth-Century Black Women.* Carbondale: Southern Illinois University Press, 1999.

Louisville Girls High School Alumnae Club collection finding aid, University of Louisville. https://nyx.uky.edu/fa/findingaid/?id=xt7vt43hxs9d.

Lueck, Amy J. "'Classbook Sense': Genre and Girls' School Yearbooks in the Early-Twentieth-Century American High School." *College English* 79, no. 4 (2017): 381–406.

———. "'A Maturity of Thought Very Rare in Young Girls': Women's Public Engagement in Nineteenth-Century Commencement Essays." *Rhetoric Review* 34, no. 2 (2015): 129–46.

Manolescu, Beth Innocenti. "Traditions of Rhetoric, Criticism and Argument in Kames's Elements of Criticism." *Rhetoric Review* 22, no. 3 (2003): 225–42.

Mastrangelo, Lisa. "Learning from the Past: Rhetoric, Composition, and Debate at Mount Holyoke College." *Rhetoric Review* 18, no. 1 (1999): 46–64.

———. *Writing a Progressive Past: Women Teaching and Writing in the Progressive Era.* Anderson, SC: Parlor Press, 2012.

Matsuda, Paul. "Process and Post-Process: A Discursive History." *Journal of Second Language Writing* 12, no. 1 (2003): 65–83.

Mattingly, Carol. *Secret Habits: Catholic Literacy Education for Women in the Early Nineteenth Century.* Carbondale: Southern Illinois University Press, 2016.

McAfee, Ward. *Race, Religion, and Reconstruction.* Albany: SUNY Press, 1998.

McComiskey, Bruce, ed. *Microhistories of Composition.* Boulder: Utah State University Press, 2016.

McMullen-Light, Mary. "In Our Own Backyard: What Makes a Community College–Secondary School Connection Work?" In *WAC Partnerships between Secondary and Postsecondary Institutions*, edited by Jacob S. Blumner and Pamela B. Childers, 87–112. Fort Collins, CO: WAC Clearinghouse, 2016.

Mendenhall, Annie. "Joseph V. Denney, the Land-Grant Mission, and Rhetorical Education at Ohio State: An Institutional History." *College English* 74, no. 2 (2011): 131–56.

Miller, Thomas P. "Lest We Go the Way of Classics: Toward a Rhetorical Future for English Departments." In *Rhetorical Education in America*, edited by Cheryl Glenn, Margaret M. Lyday, and Wendy B. Sharer, 18–35. Tuscaloosa: University of Alabama Press, 2004.

Moreland, Casie Rachelle. *White Resistance, White Complacency: The Absent-Presence of Race in the Development of Dual Enrollment Programs.* Arizona State University, dissertation, 2018.

"Mt. Oread Manifesto on Rhetorical Education 2013." *Rhetoric Society Quarterly* 44, no. 1 (2014): 1–5.

Myers, Whitney. "'Raise Your Right Arm/And Pull on Your Tongue!': Reading Silence(s) at the Albuquerque Indian School." In *In the Archives of Composition: Writing and Rhetoric in High Schools and Normal Schools*, edited by Lori Ostergaard and Henrietta Rix Wood, 42–60. Pittsburgh: University of Pittsburgh Press, 2015.

Nordquist, Brice. *Literacy and Mobility: Complexity, Uncertainty, and Agency at the Nexus of High School and College.* New York: Routledge, 2017.

Ogren, Christine A. *The American State Normal School: An Instrument of Great Good.* New York: Palgrave MacMillan, 2005.

Ostergaard, Lori. *Composition in the Illinois State Normal University and Illinois High Schools, 1892-1921.* Illinois State University, dissertation, 2007.

Ostergaard, Lori, and Henrietta Rix Wood, eds. *In the Archives of Composition: Writing and Rhetoric in High Schools and Normal Schools.* Pittsburgh: University of Pittsburgh Press, 2015.

Patton, June O. "The Black Community in Augusta and the Struggle for Ware High School, 1880–1899." In *New Perspectives on Black Educational History*, edited by Vincent P. Franklin and James D. Anderson, 45–59. Boston: G. K. Hall and Co., 1978.

Payne, Eva. "Dual Enrollment, The Good, the Bad, and the Potentially Ugly, Part III." Blog. January 24, 2016. National Council of Teachers of English. http://www2.ncte.org/blog/2016/01/dual-enrollment-the-good-the-bad-and-the-potentially-ugly/.

Reese, William J. *The Origins of the American High School.* New Haven and London: Yale University Press, 1995.

Ritter, Kelly. Foreword to *In the Archives of Composition: Writing and Rhetoric in High Schools and Normal Schools*, edited by Lori Ostergaard and Henrietta Rix Wood, xi–xvi. Pittsburgh: University of Pittsburgh Press, 2015.

———. *To Know Her Own History: Writing at the Woman's College 1943–1963.* Pittsburgh: University of Pittsburgh Press, 2012.

Robbins, Sarah. "The Future Good and Great of Our Land": Republican Mothers, Female Authors, and Domesticated Literacy in Antebellum New England." *The New England Quarterly* 75, no. 4 (December 2002): 562–91.

Roberts, Margaret Manning. *The Man Who Pioneered in Kindergartens: William N. Hailmann.* University of Southern California, thesis, 1933.

Rose, Mike. "The Language of Exclusion: Writing Instruction at the University." *College English* 47, no. 4 (April 1985): 341–59.

———. *The Mind at Work: Valuing the Intelligence of the American Worker.* New York: Penguin Books, 2005.

Royster, Jacqueline Jones. *Traces of a Stream: Literacy and Social Change among African American Women.* Pittsburgh: University of Pittsburgh Press, 2000.

Royster, Jacqueline Jones and Jean C. Williams. "History in the Spaces Left: African American Presence and Narratives of Composition Studies." *College Composition and Communication* 50, no. 4 (June 1999): 163–84.

Russell, David R. *Writing in the Academic Disciplines: A Curricular History.* Carbondale: Southern Illinois University Press, 1991/2002.

Salvatori, Mariolina. *Pedagogy: Disturbing History, 1819–1929.* Pittsburgh: University of Pittsburgh Press, 1996.

Schultz, Lucille M. "Elaborating Our History: A Look at Mid-19th Century First Books of Composition." *College Composition and Communication* 45, no. 1 (1994): 10–30.

———. "Pestalozzi's Mark on Nineteenth-Century Composition Instruction: Ideas Not in Words but in Things," *Rhetoric Review* 14, no. 1 (Autumn 1995): 23–43.

———. *The Young Composers: Composition's Beginnings in Nineteenth-Century Schools.* Carbondale: Southern Illinois University Press, 1999.

Shipka, Jody. "Transmodality in/and Processes of Making: Changing Dispositions and Practice." *College English* 78, no. 3 (2016), 250–57.

Sizer, Theodore R. "The Academies: An Interpretation." In *The Age of the Academies*, edited by Theodore R. Sizer, 1–48. New York: Teachers College, 1964.

———. *Secondary Schools at the Turn of the Century.* Westport, CT: Greenwood Press, 1964.

Skinnell, Ryan. *Conceding Composition: A Crooked History of Composition's Fortunes.* Boulder: Utah State University Press, 2016.

———. "Harvard, Again: Considering Articulation and Accreditation in Rhetoric and Composition." *Rhetoric Review* 33, no. 2 (2014): 95–112.

———. "Institutionalizing Normal: Rethinking Composition's Precedence in Normal Schools." *Composition Studies* 41, no. 1 (2013): 10–26.

Snyder, Thomas D., ed. *120 Years of American Education: A Statistical Portrait.* Washington, D.C: U.S. Dept. of Education, Office of Educational Research and Improvement, National Center for Education Statistics, 1993. https://nces.ed.gov/pubs93/93442.pdf.

Stanley, Jane. *The Rhetoric of Remediation: Negotiating Entitlement and Access to Higher Education.* Pittsburgh: University of Pittsburgh Press, 2010.

Strickland, Donna. *The Managerial Unconscious in the History of Composition Studies.* Carbondale: Southern Illinois University Press, 2011.

Stock, Patricia Lambert. *Composition's Roots in English Education.* Portsmouth, NH: Boynton/Cook Publishers, 2012.

Stout, John Elbert. "Development of High School Curricula in North Central States from 1860 to 1910." University of Chicago, dissertation, 1921. Hathi Trust. https://babel.hathitrust.org/cgi/pt?id=loc.ark:/13960/t57d3h610;view=1up;seq=10.

Sullivan, Patrick, and Howard Tinberg, eds. *What Is 'College-Level' Writing?* Urbana, IL: National Council of Teachers of English, 2011. https://wac.colostate.edu/books/collegelevel/.

Thelin, John. *A History of American Higher Education.* Baltimore: Johns Hopkins University Press, 2011.

Tinberg, Howard, and Jean Paul Nadeau. "What Happens When High School Students Write in a College Course? A Study of Dual Credit." *English Journal* 102, no. 5 (2013): 35–42.

Turner, James, and Paul Bernard. "The German Model and the Graduate School." In *The American College in the Nineteenth Century*, edited by Roger Geiger, 221–41. Nashville: Vanderbilt University Press, 2000.

Two Year College English Association. "TYCA Executive Committee Statement on Concurrent Enrollment," March 24, 2012. http://www.ncte.org/library/NCTEFiles/Groups/TYCA/Concurrent_Enrollment.pdf.

Tyack, David. *Turning Points in Educational History.* Waltham, MA: Blaisdell Publishing Company, 1967.

Ueda, Reed. *Avenues to Adulthood: The Origins of the High School and Social Mobility in an American Suburb.* New York: Cambridge University Press, 1987.

VanOverbeke, Marc A. *The Standardization of American Schooling: Linking Secondary and Higher Education, 1870–1910.* New York: Palgrave Macmillan, 2008.

Veblen, Thorstein. *Higher Learning in America: A Memorandum on the Conduct of Universities by Business Men.* New York: Hill and Wang, 1957. Original 1918.

Veysey, Laurence R. *The Emergence of the American University.* Chicago: University of Chicago Press, 1965.

Vinovskis, Maris A. "Have We Underestimated the Extent of Antebellum High School Attendance?" *History of Education Quarterly* 28, no. 4 (1988): 551–67.

———. *The Origins of Public High Schools: A Reexamination of the Beverly High School Controversy.* Madison: University of Wisconsin Press, 1985.

Walker, W. G. "The Development of the Free Public High School in Illinois during the Nineteenth Century." *History of Education Quarterly* 4, no. 4 (December 1964): 264–79.

Williams, Bronwyn. "Seeking New Worlds." *College Composition and Communication* 62, no. 1 (2010): 127–46.

Wood, Henrietta Rix. *Praising Girls: The Rhetoric of Young Women, 1895–1930.* Carbondale: Southern Illinois University Press, 2016.

———. "The Rhetorical Praxis of Central High School Students, 1894–1924." In *In the Archives of Composition: Writing and Rhetoric in High Schools and Normal Schools*, edited by Lori Ostergaard and Henrietta Rix Wood, 27–41. Pittsburgh: University of Pittsburgh Press, 2015.

Wright, Elizabethada A., and S. Michael Halloran. "From Rhetoric to Composition: The Teaching of Writing in America to 1900." In *A Short*

History of Writing Instruction: From Ancient Greece to Modern America, edited by James J. Murphy, 213–46. Mahwah, NJ: Lawrence Erlbaum Associates, Inc., 2001.

Yancey, Kathleen Blake. "Delivering College Composition: A Vocabulary for Discussion." In *Delivering College Composition: The Fifth Canon*, edited by Kathleen Blake Yancey, 1–16. Portsmouth: Boynton/Cook, 2006.

Yater, George. *Two Hundred Years at the Falls of the Ohio: A History of Louisville and Jefferson County*. Louisville: The Filson Club, 1987.

INDEX

Page locators in italics refer to figures.

abstraction, 124–25
academical departments, 105
academic-community divide, 85
academic hierarchy, 155, 159; changing definitions of, 1–2, 7–11, 29; Female High School in, 121; fixed definitions, 1, 3, 13–14; as future-directed, progressive system, 164, 174, 180; Male High School in, 158–59; unclear categorization of, 1–4; underexamination of, 9–10, 13, 18, 174, 177–78. *See also* high school–college divide
"academic procession," 4
academies, 2, 4, 28–31, 46, 75, 102, 155, 188n5, 195n1
accelerated learning, 210n3; Advanced Placement (AP), 6, 20, 172; dual-credit and concurrent enrollment programs, xiii–xiv, 20–21, 23, 171–74, 178, 180
access to education, 6, 74, 127, 179
Adams, Charles Francis, 102, 177
admission: college examinations and requirements, 108, 164–65; high school requirements, 39; to professional schools, 3, 103, 161
Advanced Course of Composition and Rhetoric (Quackenbos), 48–49, 59, 61, 91, 109–10, 113
African American community: legislative struggles, 132, 133–37; poverty linked to educational funds, 133–34; public school enrollment, 130–31; self-advocacy, 130
African American schools and students, 16–17, 104; classical or college preparatory education, 146; graduation rates, 129–30; job preparation concerns, 144–45; junior colleges/community colleges, 131; resistance to education of, 130, 133, 136; standardization and professionalization, 150–51; teaching certificate examinations, 147, 149–50. *See also* Central Colored High School
age of students, 4, 56, 65, 155, 163, 195n1
"A" Grade program, 131, 132, 137–42
Aids to English Composition (Parker), 90, 109, 110
alternative collegiate traditions, 22, 57–58, 72
American Missionary Association, 129
American Philological Association, 155
Analysis of English (Green), 59, 139
Anderson (author), 141
Anderson, E. A., 115, 117, 118, 147
Anderson, George W. (superintendent), 35, 41, 45, 46
Angelo, Richard, 7–8

Annual Report of Central Colored (1873–74), 136
anti-Catholicism, 37–38
archival research methods, xiv–xvi
articulation programs, 103–4
Atherton High School, 15, 160

baccalaureate curriculum, 7–8
bachelor's degrees, 2, 19, 43, 101; admission to professional schools without, 3, 32, 103, 161; conferred by Male High School, 15, 50, 114–15, 142
backformations, 14
Baltimore schools, 43
Beach, William F., 40–41
"before," concept of, 11
beginnings, 9–12, 24
Bell, John T. (student), 144
belles-lettres tradition (English literature), 83, 93, 202n20; abstraction of, 124–25; at Female High School, 123–24; at Male High School, 111–14, 117–18; rhetoric and composition displaced by, 113–14, 117–18
Berea College, 30, 129
Berlin, James A., 74, 78, 167
"Bill for the More General Diffusion of Knowledge" (Jefferson), 30, 33
Blackwell, Elizabeth, 66
Blair, Hugh, 49, 83
Board of Visitors of the Colored Schools, 135
Bonheur, Rosa, 66
Bonnell, John Mitchell, 113, 119
boundaries, disciplinary, 11–13, 182. *See also* disciplinary concerns in rhetoric and composition; high school–college divide
Bowles, Frank, 130
Boyd, James R., 121
Brereton, John, 165
Broome, Edwin Cornelius, 160
Brown v. Board of Education of Topeka, 206n17
Burke, Laura (student), 60–62
Bush, Bryan S., 95
Bush, Jonathan, 182, 183
Butler, R. L., 111
Butler, Thomas D., 67–68

Campbell, George, 49, 81, 83
Campbell, Thomas, 55
Carnegie Foundation for the Advancement of Teaching, 161
Carr, Jean Ferguson, 48, 141–42, 195n9
Carr, Stephen L., 48, 141–42, 195n9
Catholic and religious schools, 29, 37–38
Central Colored High School, xv, 16, 23, 128, 136–53, 204n41; "A" Grade program, 131–32, 137–42; civic rhetoric in, 133; commencement exercises, 143–46; curriculum, 139–46, *140*, 208n37; four-year course of study, 146–47, 149; hybrid identity, 132; as normal school, 133, 159; political economy course, 150–51; teacher training at, 36, 133, 204n46; teacher training controversy, 147–53. *See also* African American schools and students
Central Colored School (grades 1 through 8), 16, 132, 136–37, *140*, 142, 149, 207n26
Central High School (Baltimore), 43
Central High School (Philadelphia), 19, 43
Central High School (former Central Colored High School), dual-credit programs, 2000s, 172
Chase, George, 68–71, 76
Chicago, high school, 113
citizens, 127, 183
citizenship training, 24, 27, 75, 177
city colleges, 43, 113
Civil War years, 22, 37–38, 94–97, 129
Clark, Thomas, 94

classical curriculum, 10; African American schools and, 146; decline of, 2–3, 7–8, 45–46, 58, 76, 169; in high schools, 28–29, 45–47, 50, 58, 73–74, 146; hybrid with modern English curriculum, 28, 38, 46–47; women students and, 44, 58. *See also* curriculum
Cleveland (author), 109, 110
co-educational high schools, 36, 194n34
"College Entrance Examinations" (Flexner), 154
"college level," 172, 181
"college-level writing," xiv, 7, 20–21, 183; alternative pedagogies for, 22, 57–58, 72; what college-level writers do, 178–80. *See also* first-year writing
"college readiness," 20, 164–65, 180
colleges: city, 43, 113; community/ junior, 103, 131, 177–79; competition with high schools, 10–11, 39, 168–69; definitions of, 1–2, 172; graduation rates, 72; high school as critique of, 75; high school–college combinations, 103–4; high schools, comparison with, xii, 5, 41, 58, 72, 108–11, *110*; influence of high schools on, 5, 79–80, 167; land-grant, 75, 76, 130, 153; "multipurpose," 101–2; physical location of, 172–73; preparatory departments, 2–3; "senior college," 103–4; southern women's, 16, 176; undergraduate, 1, 15, 79, 102–3, 161, 190n23. *See also* first-year writing; high school–college divide; overlap between high schools and colleges
Collegiate Department of Louisville schools, 41
Colored Educational Convention (1867), 133–34
Colored High School. *See* Central Colored High School
Colored School Committee, 142
Colored Teacher's State Educational Association, 138–39
Columbia University Teacher's College, 164
commencement exercises, 22; Central Colored High School, 143–46; Female High School, 60–68, 123–24; in local newspapers, 88–89; Male High School, 51–54; public examinations, 51, 89–90; shared cultural experiences, 61, 64
Committee of Ten on the Teaching of Secondary English (NEA), 155
Committee of Twelve (American Philological Association), 155, 166
Committee on College-Entrance Requirements, 155
Committee on Colored Schools, 150
Committee on Examination and Control (Louisville), 34, 76, 90, 125
Common Core State Standards, 179
"common nature," appeals to, 66
common school system, 17, 22, 92–93, 132; literacy and numeracy skills taught, 1, 5, 27–28; teacher training and, 33–38; women's higher schooling and, 119–25
communication theories, 81
community colleges/junior colleges, 103, 131, 177–78
A Compendium of English Literature (Cleveland), 109
composition: across the public schools, 125–27; downgrading of, 165–69; in lower schools, 125–26; as term, 112. *See also* rhetoric and composition in high schools
Composition-Rhetoric (Connors), 141
"composition-rhetoric," 119, 141–42
Conceding Composition (Skinnell), 177
concurrent enrollment, 172–73, 175, 178, 180
Confederacy, Louisville and, 95
Conley, Thomas, 119

Connors, Robert, 49, 50, 91, 141, 166–67, 183
Coppee, 50, 91, 109, 110, 113, 117
courses: "correspondence courses," 210n26; Male High School, 50, 102–3, *116*; partial (two-year), 50, 114–15, 176; physical location of, 172–73; political economy, 150–51. *See also* curriculum
credentialing, education as, 174–75
"credit hour," 210n26
credits, transferable, 173, 180
Cremin, Lawrence, 163, 164, 170, 202n12
Crowley, Sharon, 7, 49, 78, 83, 91
current-traditional rhetoric, 78, 83, 84, 86, 90–91, 92; abstraction in, 123–24
curriculum, 2–3, 45; baccalaureate, 7–8; Central Colored High School, 139–46, *140*, 208n37; changeability of, 28–29; elective system, 58, 106, 118, 169, 210n26; Female High School, 15, 22, 68–70, 120–23, *122*, 146–47; hybrid, 28, 38, 46–47; split identity of, 46–47; university model, 22–23; vertical, 6, 174, 180–81. *See also* classical curriculum; courses; European pedagogies; liberal arts curriculum; modern English curriculum; practical curriculum
CWPA Outcomes Statement for First Year Writing, 179

Day Law (1908), 131, 206n17
declamation assignments, 47, 48, 50, 110, 113–14, 118
De Costa, Frank A., 130, 205n7
DeGenaro, William, 103
delayed revelation, in student writing, 62–63
deliberative rhetoric, in student writing, 63, 65
democratization of education, 5, 30, 34, 75, 84, 93, 127, 177
developmental theories, 78, 81, 162
Dewey, John, 19, 81, 164
difference: beginnings and, 11, 24; internal management of, 103, 114–15; production of, 8–9, 11, 168–69
disciplinary concerns in rhetoric and composition, xi–xiii, 4–5, 19–23, 47, 177; boundaries and beginnings, 11–13. *See also* rhetoric and composition in high schools
"Disunion" (Gibbons), 62–65
Donahue, Patricia, 8, 10
dual-credit and concurrent enrollment programs, xiii–xiv, 6, 20–21, 23, 171–74, 178, 180
DuPont Manual Training High School, xiv, 153, 155, 159, 187n2, 204n41; dual-credit programs, 2000s, 172

Ealy Normal School, 129, 135
Eastern Colored School, 138
eighteenth-century rhetoricians, 82
elective curriculum, 58, 106, 118, 169, 210n26
Elements of Criticism (Kame), 49, 109, 110, 113
Elements of English Composition (Boyd), 121
Elements of Rhetoric (Coppee), 50, 113, 117
Elements of Rhetoric (Whately), 49–50
Eliot, Charles, 46, 79, 155, 163
eloquence, shift away from, 123
Emancipation Proclamation, 95
"English," as term, 191n2
English A examination, 164–65, 169
English curriculum. *See* modern English curriculum
English literature. *See* belles-lettres tradition (English literature)
English Literature (Cleveland), 109, 110
English Synonyms (Graham), 109, 110, 121

entrance examinations, 38–39, 154–55, 165–67, 210n26
epideictic rhetoric, in student writing, 63
Estrem, Heidi, 182–83
European pedagogies, 28, 46, 77–79, 83, 162; in normal schools, 13, 79; university model traced to, 102
Everett, Edward, 55
"exceptional normal," 19, 171
exclusionary education, 28, 31, 75–76
expertise, as university domain, 8–9
extracurricular education, 64, 88

faculty, xvi; "loyalty oaths" required of, 94; medical, at University of Louisville, 32; pedagogical philosophies of, 22; specialization and, 114. *See also* teachers; *individual educators*
Farnham, Christie Anne, 16, 44, 176–77
Female High School, 21, 58–72; 1851 charter, 15; belles-lettres at, 123–24; challenges to male-centered rhetoric, 59; as "college," 34; colleges, comparison with, 58, 72; commencement ceremonies, reading at, 59–60; compositions by students, 59–68; curriculum, 15, 22, 68–70, 120–23, *122*, 146–47; *Esse quam videri* as motto of, 71, 76; former students hired at, 61–62; "Grammar Certificate," 124; hard study, practice of, 85–86; higher schooling at, 119–25; as "high school," 44; Latin study, 70–71; merger with Male High School, 1950, 172; new buildings, 95–96, 119–21, *120*; as normal school, 68–70, 159; opening of, 38; principalship controversy, 41–42; status of, 42–43; teacher training at, 15, 36, 69, 198n41, 204–5n46; textbooks, 59, 61. *See also* commencement exercises
Fifth Ward school (Louisville), 40
Filson Historical Society, xiv
first-year writing, 3, 7, 20, 166–69, 183, 212–13n18; course requirement as mark of high school failure, 180. *See also* "college-level writing"
Fitzgerald, Kathryn, 13–14, 78–79, 177
Flexner, Abraham, xvi, 23, 154, 209n12, 210n26; "A Freshman at Nineteen," 163; at Male High School, 162; Report on medical education, 18–19, 161; *Universities: American, English, German*, 168
"Footprints on the Sands of Time" (Thuston), 124–25
Fourteenth amendment, 136
Framework for Success in Post-Secondary Writing, 179–80, 181
Free Academy (New York), 36, 43
Freedmen's Bureau, 129
Free High School, 32
"A Freshman at Nineteen" (Flexner), 163
Froebel, Friedrich, 80
future-directed conception of education, 164, 174, 180

Geiger, Roger, 3, 101
general education, 1, 33, 113–15, 160–61, 168–69; definitions of, 28; shifts in, 22, 46, 104; suppression of, 113
General History (Anderson), 141
Gere, Anne Ruggles, 64
German model, 102, 114, 161, 168
Gheen, J. P., 96
Gibbons, Rachel H. (student), 62–65, 66
Gilyard, Keith, 182
girls/women, as students: barred from reading commencement essays, 60; classical curriculum and, 44, 58; health concerns about, 68, 119; higher schooling and, 119–25; overlap between women's institutions,

girls/women (*continued*)
71–72; private schools for, 29–30; southern women's colleges, 16, 176; as threat to sex-segregated labor market, 44; women's rights, student arguments for, 65–67. *See also* Female High School; normal schools; teachers; teacher training
Gold, David, 18
graduate schools, 161
graduation rates, 57, 72, 129–30, 152, 155, *156*, 191n26
Graham, 109, 110, 121
grammar: late nineteenth-century theories, 77–78, 82; New Education, 81–83; teaching of, in high school, 166–67
grammar departments, 34
grammar/lower schools, 29; African American, 132; composition increase, 125–27; gap with high schools, 112, 126
Grant, E. A., 51, 94, 96, 106–7, 111, 203n38; on "hard studies," 108
Graves, Karen, 44, 68
Great Flood of the Ohio River (1937), xiv
Green, 59, 139

Hailmann, Eudora, 80
Hailmann, William N., xvi, 18, 73, 80–84, 86–87, 92, 162, 199nn13,14, 200n29
Halloran, S. Michael, 118, 123
"hand-training," 153
Harney, William W., 40–41, 193n29
Harper, William Rainey, 103
Harris, William Torrey, 2
Hart, 141–42
Harvard College, 85, 163, 167
Harvard reports of the 1890s, 9, 20
Henderson, A. M., 138
"higher learning/schooling," xiii, xvi, 27–28, 128, 131–32, 171–72, 188n5
high school–college combinations, 103–4
high school–college divide, 1–14, 131, 132; dual-credit and concurrent enrollment programs, xiii–xiv, 20–21, 23, 171–74; instability of, xi–xiii, 1–4, 12, 147, 171–81; ongoing conversations about, xiii, 4, 20–21, 23; physical location of courses, 172–73; retheorizing, 170–72. *See also* academic hierarchy; overlap between high schools and colleges
high schools: admission requirements, 39; classical curriculum in, 28–29, 45–47, 50, 58, 73–74, 146; colleges, comparison with, xii, 5, 41, 58, 72, 108–11, *110*; competition with colleges, 10–11, 39, 168–69; critique of college, 75; definitions of, changing, 1–2, 7–11, 40–41; devaluation/suppression of, xiv, 6–10, 14, 107, 157–58, 167–68, 180; entrance examinations, 38–39; establishment of, 1–2, 38–44; gender-segregated, 42–43; as "higher learning," 27; influence on colleges, 5, 79–80, 167; invention of, 7–11; as multipurpose institutions, 102, 159; New Education in, 92–93; omission from historical studies, 4–5; as "people's college," 5, 31, 73; percentage of public school students enrolled, 111; rhetoric and composition in, 57. *See also* curriculum; high school–college divide; overlap between colleges and high school
Hillsdale College (Michigan), 59
historically black colleges and universities (HBCUs), 4, 129
histories: critical and imaginative engagement with, 170–71; high schools omitted from, 4–5; local, 5, 18, 21; microhistorical analysis, 19–21; revisionist, 14

A History of American Higher Education (Thelin), 14
A History of English Literature (Shaw), 117
Hobbs, 167
Holland, Robert A. (student), 55–58
Holyoke, Edward Augustus (E. A.), 42, 48, 59, 68–69, 84–87, 162
Horner, Bruce, 175, 178
Hosmer, Harriet, 66
Howard, Edmonds J., 62
Hudson, J. Blaine, 129, 131, 138

Illinois public schools, 30
imaginative reason, 162
individuality, as topic in student writing, 64–65
industrialization, 106
institutional morphology, xii–xiv, 22, 178
International Baccalaureate, 6
In the Archives of Composition (ed. Ostergaard and Wood), 5
invention, 81–82, 91

Jefferson, Thomas, 30, 33
Jefferson Seminary, 14, 31, 33, 191
job preparation, 46, 78, 92, 144–45
Johnson, Nan, 59, 78–79, 82
judgment, 81
junior colleges/community colleges, 103, 131, 177–78

Kame, 49, 109, 110
Katz, Michael, 8, 20
Kentucky, 94; legislation concerning African American education, 132, 133–37
Kentucky Association of Teachers, 85
Kentucky Colored Teacher's Association, 143
Kentucky Family Journal, 85
Kentucky State University, 129, 206n17
Kentucky University, College of Science, Literature, and Arts, 109–11
"kindergarten idea," 162
kindergarten movement, 79, 210n15
Kinne, William, 41–42
Kirsch, Gesa, 170
Kitzhaber, Albert, 77–78, 82
Krug, Edward, 103

labor market, sex-segregated, 44
Lancasterian, or monitorial, system of instruction, 35–36
land-grant colleges, 75, 76, 130, 153
language varieties, 175
Latin study, 28, 70–71, 146. *See also* classical curriculum
legislation: concerning African American education, 132, 133–37
L'Eplattenier, Barbara, xiv
Leslie, W. Bruce, 30, 102, 188n5
"Letters" (Burke), 60–62
leveling, educational, 7, 23, 210n26
liberal arts curriculum, 3, 15, 102–3, 201n3; at Central Colored High School, 145–46; controversies over, 32–33, 160–61
Lincoln School (Columbia University Teacher's College), 164
literacy and numeracy skills, 1, 5, 27
literacy crisis, manufactured, 114
literacy myth, 34
literacy-related fields, 183, 189n8
local focus, 37
local histories, 5, 18, 21
Local Histories: Reading the Archives of Composition (ed. Donahue and Moon), 10
location of classrooms, 172–73
Logan, Shirley Wilson, 146
Logic (Whately), 49, 110
logos, appeals to, 65
Louisville, Kentucky: city charter (1851), 33; Civil War years, 94–97; first free public schools, 29; higher

Louisville, Kentucky (*continued*) learning before high schools, 29–33; as hub of commerce and education, 17–18; public school growth in, 35–36

Louisville Charter (1870), 134–35

Louisville College, 31, 33

Louisville Collegiate Institute (Louisville College), 31

Louisville (Kentucky) high schools, xiii, 6, 10, 14–23; proposal to merge Male and Female High Schools, 111; racial, gendered, and programmatic segregation, 15–18

Louisville Medical Institute, 31

Louisville Municipal College, 130

Louisville Normal School, 15

lower schools. *See* grammar/lower schools

Lu, Min Zhan, 175

lyceum movement, 88

Male High School, 21, *39*; advanced studies, 104–5, 108–9; Athenaeum literary society, 96; bachelor's degrees conferred by, 15, 50, 114–15, 142; belles-lettres at, 111–14, 117–18; chartered as college, 50; Boys' High School name change, 158; as college, 43, 101, 104–5; collegiate curriculum, 47–58; controversy about degrees awarded, 115, 117; courses of study, 50, 102–3, *116*; diplomas bestowed, 41, 43, 115, 202n15; dual courses, high school and university, 114–15; dual-credit programs, 2000s, 172; elite curriculum, 47–48; master's degrees conferred by, 36, 190n23; modern English curriculum, 108–18, *110*, *116*; opening of, 38; partial (two-year) course of study, 50, 114–15, 176; polytechnic proposal, 105; postwar curricular transformations, 22; preparatory department, 112–18, *116*; principalship controversy, 39–41; property dispute, 158; specialization (vocational education) at, 105–7; student speeches, 51–58, 196n16; suppression of, 157–58; textbooks used at, 48–50, 90–91, 109–12; as too stringent, 111; University of Louisville and, 15, 142, 157–58; as "university of public schools," 104–7, 117; writing instruction changes after 1863, 107–19. *See also* commencement exercises

"managerial unconscious," 9

Mann, Horace, 27

Manolescu, Beth Innocenti, 109

manual education, 17, 92, 104, 152–53, 201–2n10. *See also* vocational education

A Manual of Composition and Rhetoric (Hart), 141–42

Manual of the Art of Prose Composition: For the Use of Colleges and Schools (Bonnell), 19

Manual Training High School (DuPont). *See* DuPont Manual Training High School

manual training high schools, 97, 104, 159

Manual Training School of Washington University (St. Louis), 159

market economy, 92

master narratives, 20

master's degrees, 36, 190n23

Mastrangelo, Lisa, 90

Matthews, J. D., 37

Maxwell, John Miller (J. M.), xvi, 128, 132–33, 138–39, 143, *148*, 206n17, 207n27; politics of, 150; teacher training controversy and, 147–53

McComiskey, Bruce, 19

McDonald, William N., 48

McMullen-Light, Mary, 177–78

medical education system, 18–19, 31–32, 161

memorization, 81, 91

Mendenhall, Annie, 76
"mental discipline" pedagogies, 28, 46, 59, 71, 81, 91, 159
meritocracy, 74, 173, 178
microhistorical analysis, 19–21
Miller, Thomas, 114
mobility framework, 175
modern English curriculum, 2–3, 10, 28, 101; high schools influence on colleges, 167; hybrid with classical curriculum, 28, 38, 46–47; natural sciences as part of, 76
Morrill Act of 1862, 106
Morris, Charles S. (student), 145–46
Morris, George W., 75, 95, 97, 119
Morris, William H., 105, 111–12
Mt. Oread Manifesto (2013), 183
Mulligan, 110
multipurpose institutions, xiii, 3, 38, 101–2, 155, 188n5

Nadeau, Jean Paul, 182
naming conventions, 16, 29, 38, 131, 156; "faculty" vs. "teachers," 42; principal controversy and, 40; women's colleges, 16
National Alliance of Concurrent Enrollment Partnerships (NACEP), 172
National Education Association, 155
national education system, 10, 75, 155–56, 160–61; committees, 156–57, 168; Progressive Era educational reform, 162–65; reform movements, 7, 23
"natural development," 81–84
New Education, 79–84, 125, 162; circulation of, 84–88; legacy of in high schools, 92–93; textbooks and, 90–91
"The New Education" (Eliot), 79
New England education reformers, 1, 27
Newman, Samuel, 50, 91
New Orleans Exhibition (1884), 143
New York, 36
New York Free Academy, 19
nineteenth-century instruction studies, 3–4
nineteenth-century (late) rhetorical theory, 77–78, 82
Nordquist, Brice, 172–73, 174, 175, 179
normal departments, 36, 193n23
normal schools, 3, 5; for African Americans, 131, 133; European pedagogies in, 13, 79; Female High School as, 68–70; pedagogy in, 8, 13–14
Normal Training School, 69
Northern educators, 37, 42

Oberlin College, 60, 128
object teaching, 79–80, 82; critiques of, 90–91, 199n23
observation, 79–83, 86
officializing processes, 12–13
Ogren, Christine, 3
Ohio State University, 76
oral examination questions, 89–90
Ostergaard, Lori, 4–5
Outlines of English Literature (Shaw), 121
overlap between high schools and colleges, xi–xii, 1–7, 59, 131, 159–60, 168–69; high school and college in same building, 113–18; women's institutions, 71–72. *See also* colleges; high school–college divide; high schools

Parker, 90–91, 109, 110
partial (two-year) courses of study, 50, 114–15, 176
Payne, Eva, 173
pedagogies, xii, 8; alternative, 22, 57–58, 72; European, 13, 77–79, 83, 102, 162; "mental discipline," 28, 46, 59, 81, 91, 159; "natural development," 81–84; object teaching, 79–80, 82, 90–91, 199n23; perception, conception, judgment, 81;

pedagogies (*continued*)
"practice without theory," 77–78; student-centered learning, 17, 19, 74, 79–80, 92, 125; "systematically unsystematical," 83, 91. *See also* New Education
"people's colleges," 5, 31, 73
Perry, William H., 138
personal themes, in student writing, 60–62
Pestalozzi, Johann Heinrich, 79, 90
Philbrick, John D., 120
Philosophy of Rhetoric (Campbell), 49
physical location of high schools and colleges, 172–73
placemaking, 174, 179
"The Pleasures of Hope" (Campbell), 55
Poetry and Prose by Marie Radcliffe Butler, 68
political philosophies, xii–xiv, 10, 21–24, 42–44, 193–94n29
postsecondary, concept of, 7–8
Practical and Critical Grammar (Butler), 139
practical curriculum, 10, 28, 46–47, 71, 73–93, 105; arguments, production of, 109; civic life, preparation for, 75, 167; composition in lower schools, 125–26; as remedial, 114; science and, 75–76, 78
A Practical System of Rhetoric (Newman), 50
practice, 10, 85–87, 92
Praising Girls (Wood), 5
Prentice, George D., 67, 68
preparatory departments, 2–3, 108, 112–18, *116*
preparatory schools, 163–64
principals, 22; controversies over, 23–24, 39–43
Pritchett, Henry, 160
private schools, 29–30
process, rhetorical, 81
professionalization, 111, 114, 150–51
professional schools, 160–61; admission without bachelor's degree, 3, 103, 161; classical curriculum and, 7–8
professions (law, medicine, and clergy), 10, 28
Progressive Era educational reform, 162–65
Progressive Exercises (Parker), 90
public schools: composition across, 125–27; expansion of, 35–36; funding, 30, 34–35, 134–35, 206n10; justification of, 30–31; normal departments, 36, 193n23. *See also individual schools*

Quackenbos, George Payne, 48–49, 59, 61, 91, 109–10, 113

racialized, gendered, and class-based privilege, 6, 74, 132, 153, 154
racism, 23; internalized, 145–46; Jim Crow South, 134; political economy course questioned, 150–51; in reports of Central Colored accomplishments, 143; resistance to education of African Americans, 130, 133, 136
Radcliffe, Marie B., 65–68
Reconstruction era, 127, 132, 149, 155
Reese, William, 2
regional distrust, 37
religious arguments, in student writing, 65
religious sectarianism, 37–38
republican ideals, 30–31
Republican Motherhood, 65
research university, 7, 102, 114
Rhetoric (Bonnell), 113
Rhetoric (Campbell), 49
Rhetoric (Whately), 49
rhetorical opportunities, 24, 44
rhetorical theory, 77–78, 81–82
rhetoric and composition in high schools: changes in after 1863, 107–19; "composition-rhetoric," 119,

141–42; displaced by belles lettres, 113–14, 117; as global proposition, 182; Harvard reports and, 9; at Male High School, 47–58, 109; as preparatory subject only, 117–18, 167–69; student themes, 9, 61, 89–90, 124, 133, 144; superficial/surface correctness, focus on, 50–51, 77–78, 83, 86, 90, 126; value of, 118. *See also* classical curriculum; "college level writing"; disciplinary concerns in rhetoric and composition; modern English curriculum; practical curriculum
Rhetoric and *Logic* (Coppee), 109
Ritter, Kelly, 5
Royster, Jacqueline Jones, 12–13, 131, 170, 175

Said, Edward, 10
Salvatori, Mariolina, 8
Sargent, Epes, 48
satire, in student writing, 63–64
Schultz, Lucille, 48, 49, 60, 64, 78–79, 90, 141, 195n9
science, 75–76, 78, 84
Science Hill Female Academy (Bardstown, Kentucky), 30
segregation, xiii, 16–18, 43–44, 131, 138, 148–49, 153, 206n17
seminaries, 2
"senior college," 103–4
sensory observation, 81
Seymour, Francis A. (student), 51–54, 196n16
Shaw, Thomas B., 117, 121
Simmons University, 129
Simpson, George F., 152
Skinnell, Ryan, 13–14, 177
Smith, Z. F., 134
southern women's colleges, 16, 44, 176
specialization, 1, 92, 101–8, 114–15, 118, 121, 160; manual training, 152–53, 159; "multipurpose college," 101–2; opposition to, 32–33, 106–7; vocational education, 105–7, 153
Spencer, Herbert, 84
Spenser, J. C., 41
standardization, 9, 92, 97, 132, 175, 179; African American schools and, 150–51
Standard Speaker (Sargent), 48
State Normal School (Kentucky), 37
State Teacher's Institute, 149
St. Louis, 36
Strickland, Donna, 9–10
Structure of the English Language (Mulligan), 110
student-centered learning, 17, 19, 74, 78–80, 83, 92, 125
students: age of, 4, 56, 65, 155, 163, 195n1; elite, 54, 55–56; embodiment of, 5; as future teachers, 17, 35; as "girls" and "boys," 17, 34; parents' occupations, 74; privileged, 54; school reform discourse used by, 53–54. *See also* African American schools and students; commencement exercises; girls/women, as students
student themes, 9, 61, 89–90, 124, 133, 144
superficial/surface correctness, 50–51, 77–78, 83, 86, 90, 126; English A examination, 165

taste, 123
teachers: African American, 139; devaluation of, 8, 12; as innovators and theorists, 18; need for, 35–37; salaries, 42–43, 69, 194n33. *See also* faculty
teacher training: common school system and, 33–38; exclusion of normal and high school models, 8; at Female High School, 15, 36, 69, 198n41, 204–5n46; gendering of, 22; "Grammar Certificate," 124; practical methods, 70; Training School, 121
technical universities, 153

textbooks, 22, 57, 195–96n9; abstract rhetoric, move away from, 77–78; combined college–high school audience, 141–42; European pedagogies in, 78–79; expository, 48–49; at Female High School, 59, 61; geography, 58–59; for lower schools, 125; at Male High School, 48–50, 90–91, 109–12; New Education and, 90–91; question-and-answer based, 50
Thelin, John, 14
theoretical impoverishment, 78
Thum, Mandeville, 48
Thuston, Sallie (student), 123–24
Tinberg, Howard, 182
Tingley, George H., Jr., 69, 70, 92
titles, institutional, 4, 6, 22, 29
tracking, 107
Training School, 121
translanguaging/translingual approach, 175–78, 211n11
Transylvania University, 37
Trimbur, John, 175
Two Year College Association (TYCA), 173

undergraduate college, 1, 15, 79, 102–3, 161, 190n23
Union Army, Louisville and, 94–97
United States Colored Troop Regiments, 94
universal education, 30, 75
universal principles, 81–83
universities: expert knowledge claimed by, 8–9; German model, 102, 114, 161, 168; research, 7, 102, 114
Universities: American, English, German (Flexner), 168
university model, 22–23; Male High School and, 102–7; as relative form, 102; specialization and vocational education, 105–7
University of Chicago, 103
University of Louisville, 14–15, 54, 191n6; African American branches of, 130, 131; liberal arts curriculum controversy, 32–33; Louisville College renamed as, 31; Male High School and, 15, 142, 157–58; medical and law focus, 31–32; retroactive degrees conferred, 142
University of Michigan, 103
"university of public schools," 104–7, 117

VanOverbeke, Marc, 7
vertical curriculum, 6, 174, 180–81
vocational education, 92, 105–7, 202n12; African American students and, 130–31; distinguished from manual training, 153, 159. *See also* manual education

Walker, W. G., 30
ward schools, 40–42, 88–89, 149–50
War of 1812, 62
Washington, Booker T., 152
Whately, Richard, 49, 110
Willard, Emma, 66
Williams, Bronwyn, 183
Williams, Jean, 12–13, 131
Woerner, Emma, 15, 160
women. *See* girls/women, as students
"Women and Dreams" (Radcliffe), 65–68
Wood, Henrietta Rix, 5
Woodward, Calvin M., 159
work in home, value of education to, 66–67
Wright, Elizabethada, 118, 123
"writing at the edges of school," 64
writing studies, 6, 21, 119

Yale Report of 1828, 46
Yancey, Kathleen Blake, 172
Yandell, Dr. (school board), 115, 117
Yankee Notions (economic magazine), 64

Amy J. Lueck is an assistant professor of English at Santa Clara University, where she teaches undergraduate writing and rhetoric courses with a focus on archival research, histories of rhetoric, and digital public memory. Her historical work has appeared in journals such as *College English*, *Rhetoric Review*, *Composition Studies*, and the *Atlantic Monthly*.

WRITING RESEARCH, PEDAGOGY, AND POLICY

The Writing Research, Pedagogy, and Policy series publishes cutting-edge empirical scholarship about writing, broadly conceived, with a particular focus on work that impacts pedagogy, practice, and policy at various levels and locations, such as elementary, secondary, postsecondary, national, and international. The series takes a particular interest in empirical research on writing centers, writing across the curriculum, multilingual writers, assessment, and writing center–library collaborations—all subjects related to the work of the Howe Center for Writing Excellence, which provides financial support. The focus of the series includes not only institutional research sites but also cross-institutional research sites.

This series draws on the definition of empirical research used by the Dartmouth Summer Seminar for Composition Research: "systematic or replicable inquiry in response to [one or more research questions] that generate interpretable data; inquiry that is grounded in previous research and designed to extend existing knowledge and, through scholarly publication or other public contributions, to be extended itself." Systematic research may include archival and ethnographic methods, among many others.

Please send all queries and submissions via email to

Elizabeth Wardle, Director
Howe Center for Writing Excellence
King Library 133
Miami University
Oxford, OH 45056
writingresearchseries@miamioh.edu